PENGUIN BOOKS

SEVEN AGES

David Owen was born in Plymouth in July 1938. He studied medicine at Sidney Sussex College, Cambridge, and St Thomas's Hospital, London. He was a Member of Parliament for Plymouth from 1966 until 1992, Minister for the Navy, Minister of Health and Foreign Secretary. He helped to found the SDP and became its leader in 1983. He resigned in August 1987 after opposing the merger with the Liberal Party, but resumed the leadership in March 1988 until mid-1990, when the party ceased to operate nationwide.

David Owen is the editor of *A Unified Health Service* (1968) and a contributor to *Social Services for All* (1968). He is also the author of *The Politics of Defence* (1972), *In Sickness and in Health – the Politics of Medicine* (1976), *Human Rights* (1978), *Face the Future* (1981), *A Future That will Work* (Penguin, 1984), *A United Kingdom* (Penguin, 1986) and *Our NHS* (1988). His autobiography, *Time to Declare*, was published by Penguin in 1991. His wife, Deborah, is a literary agent and they have two sons and a daughter. He now sits in the House of Lords.

D0809786

SEVEN AGES

Poetry for a Lifetime

Chosen by
DAVID OWEN

PENGUIN BOOKS

PENGUIN BOOKS

Published by the Penguin Group
Penguin Books Ltd, 27 Wrights Lane, London W8 5TZ, England
Penguin Books USA Inc., 375 Hudson Street, New York, New York 10014, USA
Penguin Books Australia Ltd, Ringwood, Victoria, Australia
Penguin Books Canada Ltd, 10 Alcorn Avenue, Toronto, Ontario, Canada M4V 3B2
Penguin Books (NZ) Ltd, 182–190 Wairau Road, Auckland 10, New Zealand

Penguin Books Ltd, Registered Offices: Harmondsworth, Middlesex, England

First published by Michael Joseph 1992
Published in Penguin Books 1995
1 3 5 7 9 10 8 6 4 2

The acknowledgements on pp. 411–13 constitute an extension of this copyright page

The moral right of the author has been asserted

Printed in England by Clays Ltd, St Ives plc

Contents

Introduction	*xvii*
Seven Ages – William Shakespeare	1

1: INFANT

A Time For Everything – Ecclesiastes	5
Baby Song – Thom Gunn	5
The Victory – Anne Stevenson	6
108. Surgeons – Emily Dickinson	6
Grief Fills the Room Up – William Shakespeare	7
Fancy – William Shakespeare	7
The Guppy – Ogden Nash	8
Gentle Jesus, Meek and Mild – Charles Wesley	8
The Grand Old Duke of York – Traditional	8
Doctor Foster – Traditional	9
The Old Woman – Traditional	9
Spring and Fall – Gerard Manley Hopkins	9
On My First Daughter – Ben Jonson	10
I Remember, I Remember – Thomas Hood	10
The Fairies – William Allingham	11
A Parental Ode – Thomas Hood	13
I Saw a Jolly Hunter – Charles Causley	14
The Quangle Wangle's Hat – Edward Lear	15
My Shadow – Robert Louis Stevenson	17
Little Willie – Anon.	17
The Owl and the Pussy Cat – Edward Lear	18
London Bells – Anon.	19
Jim – Hilaire Belloc	19
Hug O'War – Shel Silverstein	21
Tree House – Shel Silverstein	21

An Old Cornish Litany – Anon.   22
A Considered Reply to a Child – Jonathan Price   22
Solomon Grundy – Anon.   23
Buckingham Palace – A. A. Milne   23
Sneezles – A. A. Milne   24
The Walrus and the Carpenter – Lewis Carroll   26
Jellyfish – Ted Hughes   28
Crab – Ted Hughes   28
Where Go the Boats? – Robert Louis Stevenson   29
The Stern Parent – Harry Graham   30
Tender-Heartedness – Harry Graham   30
Walking Song – William E. Hickson   30
The Spider and the Fly – Mary Howitt   30
'You are Old, Father William' – Lewis Carroll   32
The Donkey – G. K. Chesterton   33
The Donkey – Stevie Smith   33
A Warning to Cat Owners – Sue Townsend   34
The End – A. A. Milne   34

2: SCHOOL

To Any Reader – Robert Louis Stevenson   39
Under Milk Wood – Dylan Thomas   39
The Collier – Vernon Watkins   43
On My Son – Ben Jonson   44
Widdicombe Fair – Traditional   45
Christmas in Africa – Jeni Couzyn   46
The Yarn of the *Nancy Bell* – W. S. Gilbert   49
The Common Cormorant – Anon.   52
Sick – Shel Silverstein   52
The First Lord's Song – W. S. Gilbert   53
The Pied Piper of Hamelin – Robert Browning   55
The Landlord's Tale – Henry Wadsworth Longfellow   60
The Barefoot Boy – John Greenleaf Whittier   63
Full Fathom Five – William Shakespeare   64
Rosa Mystica – Oscar Wilde   64
A Smuggler's Song – Rudyard Kipling   65
Walking Away – C. Day Lewis   66
Tarantella – Hilaire Belloc   67
Macavity: The Mystery Cat – T. S. Eliot   68

Boring – John Whitworth   70
Mothers who Don't Understand – Augusta Skye   71
If – Rudyard Kipling   72
Remember Now Thy Creator – Ecclesiastes   73
This Above All – William Shakespeare   74
Don't Quite Know – Roy Fuller   75

3: LOVER

The Arrow – W. B. Yeats   79
The Arrow and the Song – Henry Wadsworth Longfellow   79
The First Day – Christina Rossetti   79
So Let Us Love – Edmund Spenser   80
The Song of Torrismond – Thomas Lovell Beddoes   80
They Who are Near to Me – Rabindranath Tagore   81
My Delight and Thy Delight – Robert Bridges   81
Sonnet 43 – Elizabeth Barrett Browning   82
One Day I Wrote – Edmund Spenser   82
The Virginity – Rudyard Kipling   83
The Longest Journey – Percy Bysshe Shelley   84
To Phyllis – Edmund Waller   85
I Loved You Wednesday – Edna St Vincent Millay   85
Sonnet 138 – William Shakespeare   86
Lullaby – W. H. Auden   86
Your Face – Anon.   87
Non Sum Qualis Eram Bonae Sub Regno Cynarae – Ernest Dowson 88
Lovey-Dovey – Anon.   89
We Have Known Treasure – Anon.   89
Echo – Christina Rossetti   90
The Bargain – Sir Philip Sidney   90
Sonnet 116 – William Shakespeare   91
We Two Lay Sunk – Rabindranath Tagore   92
To—— – Percy Bysshe Shelley   92
Delusions I Did Cherish – Rabindranath Tagore   93
Return – C. P. Cavafy   93
Lust – Rupert Brooke   93
Renouncement – Alice Meynell   94
Sonnet 18 – William Shakespeare   94
Never Give All the Heart – W. B. Yeats   95
When I Was One-and-Twenty – A. E. Housman   95

I Think I am in Love – Wendy Cope | 96
Let's Do It, Let's Fall In Love – Cole Porter | 96
Annus Mirabilis – Philip Larkin | 98
La Figlia Che Piange – T. S. Eliot | 99
A Thunderstorm In Town – Thomas Hardy | 100
A Touch of Impatience – Fleur Adcock | 100
Upon the Nipples of Julia's Breast – Robert Herrick | 101
Busts and Bosoms Have I Known – Anon. | 102
To His Coy Mistress – Andrew Marvell | 102
Invocation – Percy Bysshe Shelley | 103
My Love Is Like to Ice – Edmund Spenser | 105
Sonnet 129 – William Shakespeare | 105
You Suck My Soul – Anna Akhmatova | 106
The Ballad of the Oysterman – Oliver Wendell Holmes | 106
Gray – C. P. Cavafy | 108
Counting the Beats – Robert Graves | 108
Lochinvar – Sir Walter Scott | 109
My Love is Like a Red, Red Rose – Robert Burns | 110
The Clod and the Pebble – William Blake | 111
Poem – Boris Pasternak | 111
Where Are You, My Prince? – Irina Ratushinskaya | 112
If I Could Tell You – W. H. Auden | 112
A Farewell – May Sarton | 113
Lasca – Frank Desprez | 114
Where Be You Going, You Devon Maid? – John Keats | 117
The Night has a Thousand Eyes – Francis William Bourdillon | 117
A Reflection – Thomas Hood | 118
The Foggy, Foggy Dew – Anon. | 118
Too Dear, Too Vague – W. H. Auden | 119
La Belle Dame Sans Merci – John Keats | 120
The Speech of Silence – Ella Wheeler Wilcox | 122
To One That Asked Me Why I Loved J. G. – Ephelia | 123
Thou Shalt Dwell in Silence – Rabindranath Tagore | 123
A Man's Requirements – Elizabeth Barrett Browning | 124
Lemon Haired Ladies – Dory Previn | 126
Angels and Devils the Following Day – Dory Previn | 128
Lines from Endymion – John Keats | 129
i like my body when it is with your – e. e. cummings | 130
Poor but Honest – Anon. | 130

A Drinking Song – W. B. Yeats   131
A Man That Looks on Glass – George Herbert   132
Frankie and Johnny – American Folk Song, Anon.   132
Social Note – Dorothy Parker   134
One Perfect Rose – Dorothy Parker   134
Celia Celia – Adrian Mitchell   134
I Loved You – Alexander Pushkin   135
The Hill – Rupert Brooke   135
Looking at Each Other – Muriel Rukeyser   135
New Year's Eve – D. H. Lawrence   136
Green – D. H. Lawrence   137
To My Valentine – Ogden Nash   137
Administration – Philip Larkin   138
In Praise of Cocoa, Cupid's Nightcap – Stanley J. Sharples   138
A Last Confession – W. B. Yeats   139
After Love – Maxine Kumin   139
Unfortunate Coincidence – Dorothy Parker   140
There Was a Young Lady – Arthur Buller   140
Polly Perkins – Anon.   141
Song – Oliver Goldsmith   142
A Subaltern's Love-song – John Betjeman   142
Trilogy for X – Louis MacNeice   144
My Young Man's a Cornishman – Charles Causley   145
Rose Aylmer – W. S. Landor   146
Now That I am Forever With Child – Audre Lorde   146
Safe Period – Carol Rumens   147
Smokers for Celibacy – Fleur Adcock   147
A Code of Morals – Rudyard Kipling   149
A Lover's Quarrel – Ella Wheeler Wilcox   150
Daybreak – Stephen Spender   152
Twelve Songs, IX – W. H. Auden   152
The Mermaid – W. B. Yeats   153
Episode – Zbigniew Herbert   153
Bloody Men – Wendy Cope   154
The House – Alexander Blok   154
Poem for Blok – Marina Tsvetayeva   155
Love – Miroslav Holub   156
Naked – Pablo Neruda   157
The Saddest Lines – Pablo Neruda   157

Marriage – Philip Larkin   158
A Dedication to My Wife – T. S. Eliot   158
Song by the Subconscious Self – A. Lang   158

4: SOLDIER

Make Bright the Arrows – Jeremiah   161
Make Bright the Arrows – Edna St Vincent Millay   161
The Destruction of Sennacherib – Lord Byron   161
Prologue, *King Henry V* – William Shakespeare   162
Once to Every Man and Nation – James Russell Lowell   163
Rendezvous – Alan Seeger   164
Elegy in a Country Churchyard – G. K. Chesterton   165
Luck – Dennis McHarrie   165
An Irish Airman Foresees His Death – W. B. Yeats   166
A Dead Statesman – Rudyard Kipling   167
When Statesmen Gravely Say – W. H. Auden   167
A Ballad of Glyn Dŵr's Rising – A. G. Prys-Jones   167
Horatius – Thomas Babington Macaulay   168
Scots, Wha Hae – Robert Burns   178
Before Harfleur – William Shakespeare   179
Before Agincourt – William Shakespeare   180
Say not the Struggle Nought Availeth – Arthur Hugh Clough 181
Lepanto – G. K. Chesterton   182
Drake's Drum – Sir Henry Newbolt   183
Valiant-for-Truth's Song – John Bunyan   184
The Gift Outright – Robert Frost   184
The Star-Spangled Banner – Francis Scott Key   185
A March in the Ranks Hard-Prest – Walt Whitman   186
Address at Gettysburg – Abraham Lincoln   187
The Martyr – Herman Melville   188
O Captain! My Captain! – Walt Whitman   189
Let America Be America Again – Langston Hughes   190
The Song of the Western Men – Robert S. Hawker   193
The Charge of the Light Brigade – Alfred, Lord Tennyson   194
The Burial of Sir John Moore After Corunna – Charles Wolfe 195
Drummer Hodge – Thomas Hardy   197
The Wearing of the Green – Anon.   197
Ulster, 1912 – Rudyard Kipling   198
Whatever You Say, Say Nothing – Seamus Heaney   200

The Soldier – Rupert Brooke   203
Letter from the Front – Wilfred Owen   203
The Dead-Beat – Wilfred Owen   203
Pre-Existence – Frances Cornford   204
In Flanders Fields – John McCrea   205
Magpies in Picardy – T. P. Cameron Wilson   205
Perhaps – Vera Brittain   207
Insensibility – Wilfred Owen   207
Lamplight – May Wedderburn Cannan   209
Anthem for Doomed Youth – Wilfred Owen   210
Dulce Et Decorum Est – Wilfred Owen   211
Pluck – Eva Dobell   212
Clearing Station – Wilhelm Klemm   212
The Kite – Alexander Blok   214
Greater Love – Wilfred Owen   214
Grass – Carl Sandburg   215
The Fabulists – Rudyard Kipling   215
The Cenotaph– Charlotte Mew   217
Afterwards – Margaret Postgate Cole   218
In Memory of W. B. Yeats – W. H. Auden   218
Their Finest Hour – Winston Churchill   219
Long, Dark Months – Winston Churchill   220
To the French People – Winston Churchill   220
At a War Grave – John Jarmain   220
El Alamein – John Jarmain   221
Chief Petty Officer – Charles Causley   222
Save the Tot – Anon.   223
The Flying Bum: 1944 – William Plomer   224
Punishment Enough – Norman Cameron   226
Handbag – Ruth Fainlight   227
Salvage Song – Elsie Cawser   227
The Dying Airman – Anon.   227
The Englishman's Home – Harry Graham   228
The Dead in Europe – Robert Lowell   228
Royal Naval Air Station – Roy Fuller   229
Written with a Pencil in a Sealed Wagon – Dan Pagis   229
Dover Beach – Matthew Arnold   230
Drink, Britannia – Thomas Lovell Beddoes   231
England – Rudyard Kipling   231

The White Cliffs – Alice Duer Miller 231
Think of Europe – Roger Woddis 232
The Secret People – G. K. Chesterton 233
No Man is an Island – John Donne 235

5: WISDOM

The Price of Wisdom – Job 239
The Quality of Mercy – William Shakespeare 240
Whatsoever Things Are True – St Paul 241
What is Good – John Boyle O'Reilly 241
Four Things – Henry Van Dyke 242
Leaves of Grass – Walt Whitman 242
New Eyes Each Year – Philip Larkin 242
Addendum to the Ten Commandments – Anon. 243
Once I was Young – A. C. S. Gimson 243
A Student – Geoffrey Chaucer 244
Solitude – Alexander Pope 244
The Greatest of These – St Paul 245
Abou Ben Adhem – James Leigh Hunt 247
The Lord is Full of Mercy – Yehuda Amichai 247
The Cave Man's Prayer 247
The Agnostic's Creed – Walter Malone 249
On Woman – W. B. Yeats 250
The Female of the Species – Rudyard Kipling 251
Trial and Error – Phyllis McGinley 254
The Song of Hiawatha – Henry Wadsworth Longfellow 254
My Heart Leaps Up – William Wordsworth 257
Song of the Open Road – Ogden Nash 257
Auguries of Innocence – William Blake 258
Monarch of All I Survey – Alexander Selkirk 261
Of All the Souls That Stand Create – Emily Dickinson 263
The Listeners – Walter de la Mare 263
Dream-Pedlary – Thomas Lovell Beddoes 264
The Hound of Heaven – Francis Thompson 266
The Nightmare – W. S. Gilbert 268
Solitude – Ella Wheeler Wilcox 270
Leap Before You Look – W. H. Auden 271
The Tyger – William Blake 271
Bagpipe Music – Louis MacNeice 272

Jazz Fantasia – Carl Sandburg   274
A Bookshop Idyll – Kingsley Amis   274
Chorus of Spirits – Percy Bysshe Shelley   275
It's the First of January – Irina Ratushinskaya   276
No, I'm Not Afraid – Irina Ratushinskaya   278
The Ballad of Reading Gaol – Oscar Wilde   279
Oh Who is that Young Sinner – A. E. Housman   283
18 June 1961 – Dag Hammarskjold   284
Ode – Arthur William Edgar O'Shaughnessy   284
Kubla Khan – Samuel Taylor Coleridge   285
A Truthful Song – Rudyard Kipling   287
A Man's a Man for A' That – Robert Burns   289
The Song of the Shirt – Thomas Hood   290
Vagabond – John Masefield   293
The Bleed'n' Sparrer – Anon.   293
Leisure – W. H. Davies   294
The Man With the Hoe – John Vance Cheney   295
Song – Helen Hay Whitney   297
The Village Blacksmith – Henry Wadsworth Longfellow   297
Psalm 146 – The Bible   299
Impromptu on Charles II – John Wilmot   299
The Vicar of Bray – Anon.   300
The Touch – James Graham   301
The Road Not Taken – Robert Frost   301
Is this a Dagger? – William Shakespeare   302
To Be, or Not To Be – William Shakespeare   302
The King of Brentford – William Makepeace Thackeray   304
London, 1802 – William Wordsworth   305
The Lost Leader – Robert Browning   305
This England – William Shakespeare   306
Home-Thoughts, from Abroad – Robert Browning   307
The Old Stone Cross – W. B. Yeats   308
The British Journalist – Humbert Wolfe   308
England Expects – Ogden Nash   309
The Old Vicarage, Grantchester – Rupert Brooke   310

6: SIXTH AGE

The View – Philip Larkin   315
Peekaboo, I Almost See You – Ogden Nash   315

Politics – W. B. Yeats — 316
Late-Flowering Lust – John Betjeman — 317
He Loved Three Things – Anna Akhmatova — 318
Sad Steps – Philip Larkin — 318
Talking in Bed – Philip Larkin — 319
Samson Agonistes – Ogden Nash — 319
'Twas at the Pictures, Child, We Met – A. P. Herbert — 319
Young Men – Anon. — 322
Mary's Lamb – Anon. — 322
The Thin People – Sylvia Plath — 323
Peas – Anon. — 324
Burns Grace at Kirkcudbright – Anon. — 325
Plymouth – Philip Larkin — 325
Sea-Fever – John Masefield — 326
76. Exultation – Emily Dickinson — 326
The Mountaineers – Dannie Abse — 327
We Have Been Here Before – Morris Bishop — 328
The Great Carbuncle – Sylvia Plath — 328
The Brook – Alfred, Lord Tennyson — 329
Night Mail – W. H. Auden — 331
The Urals for the First Time – Boris Pasternak — 333
Sunday Morning, King's Cambridge – John Betjeman — 334
Upon Westminster Bridge – William Wordsworth — 334
Gehazi – Rudyard Kipling — 335
Note on Intellectuals – W. H. Auden — 336
Lines to a Don – Hilaire Belloc — 336
Satire upon the Heads – Thomas Gray — 338
Why are the Clergy . . .? – Stevie Smith — 339
Pseudo-Hymn – Samuel Wilberforce — 340
Mystery – William Blake — 340
A Priest in the Sabbath Dawn – Peter Didsbury — 340
The Suburban Classes – Stevie Smith — 341
Hymn and Prayer for Civil Servants – Anon. — 342
Limerick – M. E. Hare — 342
I Had a Duck-Billed Platypus – Patrick Barrington — 343
Oedipus – Victor Gray — 344
The City – John Betjeman — 344
Not Waving but Drowning – Stevie Smith — 345
Snow Joke – Simon Armitage — 345

This Be the Verse – Philip Larkin   346
Wishes of an Elderly Man – Walter Raleigh   346
Report on Experience – Edmund Blunden   347
Resolutions – Jonathan Swift   347
A Song – John Wilmot   348
John Anderson, My Jo – Robert Burns   349
Bill and Joe – Oliver Wendell Holmes   350
The Bridge – Henry Wadsworth Longfellow   352
Upper Lambourne – John Betjeman   354
Uphill – Christina Rossetti   355
Song – Christina Rossetti   355
Days of 1903 – C. P. Cavafy   356
Candles – C. P. Cavafy   356
I Remember – Stevie Smith   357
Turn the Key Deftly – Edwin Brock   357
Body, Remember . . . C. P. Cavafy   358
What the Bones Know – Carolyn Kizer   358
The Way Through the Woods – Rudyard Kipling   359
Roads Go Ever On – J. R. R. Tolkien   360

7: LAST SCENE

The Rubá 'iyat of Omar Khayyám – Edward Fitzgerald   363
Demogorgon – Percy Bysshe Shelley   364
Tomorrow – William Shakespeare   365
Ceremony After a Fire Raid – Dylan Thomas   365
Come Away – Pamela Gillilan   366
When You Died – Pamela Gillilan   367
Time – Edna St Vincent Millay   369
In Death Divided – Thomas Hardy   369
On Prince Frederick – Anon.   370
The *Mary Gloster* – Rudyard Kipling   371
Cheltenham Waters – Anon.   379
Because I Liked You Better – A. E. Housman   379
Indian Prayer – Traditional, Anon.   380
Code Poem for the French Resistance – Leo Marks   380
The Last Word – Matthew Arnold   380
Do Not Go Gentle Into That Good Night – Dylan Thomas   381
And Death Shall Have No Dominion – Dylan Thomas   382
Recessional – Rudyard Kipling   383

Evolution – John Banister Tabb 384
On a Tired Housewife – Anon. 384
Old Men – Ogden Nash 384
Invictus – W. E. Henley 385
Friends, Romans, Countrymen – William Shakespeare 385
In Praise of Famous Men – Ecclesiasticus 386
To George Washington – James Russell Lowell 387
Sonnet XVI – John Milton 388
Fame is a Food that Dead Men Eat – Austin Dobson 389
For the Fallen – Laurence Binyon 389
'Ostler Joe – George R. Sims 390
On an Old Song – William Edward Hartpole Lecky 394
Adonais – Percy Bysshe Shelley 395
A Hymn to God the Father – John Donne 397
It is Time to be Old – Ralph Waldo Emerson 398
Final Apology – W. B. Yeats 398
Requiem – Robert Louis Stevenson 399
In Memory – Anon. 399
Cherry Stones – Anon. 399
Felix Randal – Gerard Manley Hopkins 400
Sleeping at Last – Christina Rossetti 400
Meanwhile – Amos Oz 401
When You are Old – W. B. Yeats 401
Fire and Ice – Robert Frost 402
Ghosts, Fire, Water – James Kirkup 403
The Hollow Men – T. S. Eliot 404
501. This World is not Conclusion – Emily Dickinson 407
Death, Be Not Proud – John Donne 408
Psalm 23 – The Bible 408
Fear No More – William Shakespeare 409

Acknowledgements 411
Index of authors 415
Index of titles 419
Index of first lines 424

Introduction

This anthology is a 'Tuzzy-Muzzy', the old English description for
a nosegay or bunch of flowers. I have picked these poems like
flowers for the music of their language, the memories they evoke
or for the way they complement each other, adding to the beauty
of the whole.

The first collection of poetry I knew was *Other Men's Flowers*,
compiled by Field Marshal Viscount Wavell. It is still the one I
turn to most. His anthology was bought by my mother in 1944
when it first came out and while he was Viceroy of India. She used
to read its poems aloud to us by the fireside even before I could
read them myself and it was there that my love of poetry began.
Now in its nineteenth edition, I know I cannot match Wavell's
selection but there have been many beautiful poems written since
he died. Also his choice had some surprising omissions – he admitted
even then that it was a little old-fashioned – there being nothing
from W. H. Auden or T. S. Eliot – Wavell recognised some of
Eliot's poems had obvious dignity and beauty, but others seemed to
him deliberately ugly as well as cryptic.

Poetry for me is the music of the spoken word. Yet it goes deeper
than that; as Voltaire said, it 'is the music of the soul'. Like many
people, I find it easier to express my emotions by writing poetry.
Much has been written about the coldness of the English. As a Celt, I
have less difficulty with being overtly emotional, and this is generally
so for the Welsh and the Irish. Yet the English do have a deeply

passionate side to their nature, albeit often hidden, which finds expression in a rich poetic heritage. Poetry sometimes holds the key to loosening the legendary stiff upper lip of the English.

Some poems are sung and, when read, many songs sound like poetry. All that poetry requires is the memory of the words. One does not need a book, or spectacles or an instrument. Poems can be enjoyed while sailing a boat, climbing a mountain or lounging in a deckchair. If a poem is not recited aloud, I find it is best savoured by mouthing the words quietly to oneself. The King James Bible and Shakespearean plays offer good examples of prose melding into poetry and out again, as do some political speeches like the Gettysburg Address by Abraham Lincoln and those by Winston Churchill, which I have included in this anthology. There are songs too from lyricists as diverse as W. S. Gilbert, Dory Previn, Cole Porter and H. F. Lyte, author of 'Abide with Me'.

Wavell quotes Montaigne: 'I have gathered a posie of other men's flowers and nothing but the thread that binds them is my own.' For this anthology of poems, mainly from the English-speaking world, I have used the structure of Shakespeare's Seven Ages of Man to bind it together. I have added only the minimum of notes, leaving the poems and my selection to speak for themselves. If anyone wants to know more about the whys and wherefores they will find most of the answers in my autobiography, *Time to Declare*. Suffice to say that the Sixth Age is me at fifty-four. The choice throughout is deeply personal and meant to be read by the fireside, lying in bed or anywhere else where one can relax and escape the pressures of life. Not all the poems are comfortable, sometimes the language is florid, as in 'Clearing Station' (page 212), and the violence and sexuality of 'Smokers for Celibacy' (page 147), for example, may offend.

I know that some will miss favourite poems. My plea in mitigation is that there are many poems I too like that have had to be left out but I wanted to keep a balance between familiar and unknown, old and modern and also to include a number of poems by the same poet.

I am grateful to all those copyright holders who have reduced the fee on their poems because they know that the royalties of this book are going to the Hospital for Sick Children at Great Ormond Street, London, which helped save my eldest son's life.

Seven Ages
from *As You Like It*, Act II, Scene vii

All the world's a stage,
And all the men and women merely players:
They have their exits and their entrances;
And one man in his time plays many parts,
His acts being seven ages. At first the infant,
Mewling and puking in the nurse's arms.
Then the whining school-boy, with his satchel
And shining morning face, creeping like snail
Unwillingly to school. And then the lover,
Sighing like furnace, with a woeful ballad
Made to his mistress' eyebrow. Then a soldier,
Full of strange oaths, and bearded like the pard,
Jealous in honour, sudden and quick in quarrel,
Seeking the bubble reputation
Even in the cannon's mouth. And then the justice,
In fair round belly with good capon lined,
With eyes severe and beard of formal cut,
Full of wise saws and modern instances;
And so he plays his part. The sixth age shifts
Into the lean and slipper'd pantaloon,
With spectacles on nose and pouch on side,
His youthful hose, well saved, a world too wide
For his shrunk shank; and his big manly voice,
Turning again toward childish treble, pipes
And whistles in his sound. Last scene of all,
That ends this strange eventful history,
Is second childishness, and mere oblivion,
Sans teeth, sans eyes, sans taste, sans everything.

WILLIAM SHAKESPEARE 1564–1616

INFANT

And one man in his time plays many parts,
His acts being seven ages. At first the infant,
Mewling and puking in the nurse's arms.

A Time for Everything

To every thing there is a season,
And a time to every purpose under the heaven:
A time to be born, and a time to die;
A time to plant, and a time to pluck up that which is planted;
A time to kill, and a time to heal;
A time to break down, and a time to build up;
A time to weep, and a time to laugh;
A time to mourn, and a time to dance;
A time to cast away stones, and a time to gather stones together;
A time to embrace, and a time to refrain from embracing;
A time to get, and a time to lose;
A time to keep, and a time to cast away;
A time to rend, and a time to sew;
A time to keep silence, and a time to speak;
A time to love, and a time to hate;
A time of war, and a time of peace.

ECCLESIASTES, CHAPTER 3, VERSES 1–8

Baby Song

From the private ease of Mother's womb
I fall into the lighted room.

Why don't they simply put me back
Where it is warm and wet and black?

But one thing follows on another.
Things were different inside Mother.

Padded and jolly I would ride
The perfect comfort of her inside.

They tuck me in a rustling bed
—I lie there, raging, small, and red.

I may sleep soon, I may forget,
But I won't forget that I regret.

A rain of blood poured round her womb,
But all time roars outside this room.

THOM GUNN 1929–

The Victory

I thought you were my victory
though you cut me like a knife
when I brought you out of my body
into your life.

Tiny antagonist, gory,
blue as a bruise. The stains
of your cloud of glory
bled from my veins.

How can you dare, blind thing,
blank insect eyes?
You barb the air. You sting
with bladed cries.

Snail! Scary knot of desires!
Hungry snarl! Small son.
Why do I have to love you?
How have you won?

ANNE STEVENSON 1933–

108. *Surgeons*

Surgeons must be very careful
When they take the knife!
Underneath their fine incisions
Stirs the Culprit—*Life*!

EMILY DICKINSON

Grief Fills the Room Up
from *King John*, Act III, Scene iv

Grief fills the room up of my absent child,
Lies in his bed, walks up and down with me,
Puts on his pretty looks, repeats his words,
Remembers me of all his gracious parts,
Stuffs out his vacant garments with his form;
Then have I reason to be fond of grief.
Fare you well; had you such a loss as I,
I could give better comfort than you do,
I will not keep this form upon my head,
When there is such disorder in my wit.
O Lord! my boy, my Arthur, my fair son!
My life, my joy, my food, my all the world!
My widow-comfort, and my sorrows' cure!

WILLIAM SHAKESPEARE

Fancy
from *The Merchant of Venice*, Act III, Scene ii

Tell me where is Fancy bred,
Or in the heart, or in the head?
How begot, how nourishèd?
Reply, reply.

It is engendered in the eyes;
With gazing fed; and Fancy dies
In the cradle where it lies.
Let us all ring Fancy's knell.
I'll begin it: – Ding, dong, bell.
– Ding, dong, bell.

WILLIAM SHAKESPEARE

The Guppy

Whales have calves,
Cats have kittens,
Bears have cubs,
Bats have bittens.
Swans have cygnets,
Seals have puppies,
But guppies just have little guppies.

OGDEN NASH 1902–71

from *Gentle Jesus, Meek and Mild*

Gentle Jesus, meek and mild,
Look upon a little child;
Pity my simplicity,
Suffer me to come to thee.

CHARLES WESLEY 1707–88

The Grand Old Duke of York

O, the grand old Duke of York,
  He had ten thousand men;
He marched them up to the top of the hill
  And he marched them down again!
When they were up, they were up,
  And when they were down, they were down,
And when they were only half way up,
  They were neither up nor down.

ANON.

Doctor Foster

Doctor Foster went to Glo'ster
    In a shower of rain;
He stepped in a puddle, right up to his middle,
    And never went there again.

ANON.

The Old Woman

There was an old woman
    Lived under a hill,
And if she's not gone
    She lives there still.

ANON.

Spring and Fall
to a young child

Márgarét, áre you gríeving
Over Goldengrove unleaving?
Léaves, líke the things of man, you
With your fresh thoughts care for, can you?
Áh! ás the heart grows older
It will come to such sights colder
By and by, nor spare a sigh
Though worlds of wanwood leafmeal lie,
And yet you *will* weep and know why.
Now no matter, child, the name:
Sórrow's spríngs áre the same.
Nor mouth had, no nor mind, expressed
What heart heard of, ghost guessed:
It ís the blight man was born for,
It is Margaret you mourn for.

GERARD MANLEY HOPKINS 1844–89

On My First Daughter

Here lies to each her parents' ruth
Mary, the daughter of their youth:
Yet, all Heaven's gifts being Heaven's due,
It makes the father less to rue.
At six months' end she parted hence
With safety of her innocence;
Whose soul Heaven's Queen (whose name she bears)
In comfort of her mother's tears,
Hath placed amongst her virgin-train;
Where, while that severed doth remain,
This grave partakes the fleshly birth,
Which cover lightly, gentle earth.

BEN JONSON 1573?–1637

I Remember, I Remember

I remember, I remember,
  The house where I was born,
The little window where the sun
  Came peeping in at morn;
He never came a wink too soon,
  Nor brought too long a day,
But now, I often wish the night
  Had borne my breath away.

I remember, I remember,
  The roses, red and white;
The violets, and the lily-cups,
  Those flowers made of light!
The lilacs where the robin built,
  And where my brother set
The laburnum on his birthday –
  The tree is living yet!

I remember, I remember,
  Where I was used to swing;
And thought the air must rush as fresh

To swallows on the wing:
My spirit flew in feathers then,
   That is so heavy now,
And summer pools could hardly cool
   The fever on my brow!

I remember, I remember,
   The fir trees dark and high;
I used to think their slender tops
   Were close against the sky:
It was a childish ignorance,
   But now 'tis little joy
To know I'm farther off from Heav'n
   Than when I was a boy.
                THOMAS HOOD 1799–1845

The Fairies

Up the airy mountain,
   Down the rushy glen,
We daren't go a-hunting
   For fear of little men;
Wee folk, good folk,
   Trooping all together;
Green jacket, red cap,
   And white owl's feather!

Down along the rocky shore
   Some make their home,
They live on crispy pancakes
   Of yellow tide-foam;
Some in the reeds
   Of the black mountain-lake,
With frogs for their watch-dogs,
   All night awake.

High on the hill-top
   The old King sits;
He is now so old and grey

He's nigh lost his wits.
With a bridge of white mist
   Columbkill he crosses,
On his stately journeys
   From Slieveleague to Rosses;
Or going up with music
   On cold starry nights,
To sup with the Queen
   Of the gay Northern Lights.

They stole little Bridget
   For seven years long;
When she came down again
   Her friends were all gone.
They took her lightly back,
   Between the night and morrow;
They thought that she was fast asleep,
   But she was dead with sorrow.
They have kept her ever since
   Deep within the lake,
On a bed of flag-leaves,
   Watching till she wake.

By the craggy hill-side,
   Through the mosses bare,
They have planted thorn-trees
   For pleasure here and there.
Is any man so daring
   As to dig them up in spite,
He shall find their sharpest thorns
   In his bed at night.

Up the airy mountain,
   Down the rushy glen,
We daren't go a-hunting
   For fear of little men;
Wee folk, good folk,
   Trooping all together;
Green jacket, red cap,
   And white owl's feather!

WILLIAM ALLINGHAM 1824–89

A Parental Ode to my Son, aged Three Years and Five Months

Thou happy, happy elf!
(But stop, – first let me kiss away that tear) –
Thou tiny image of myself!
(My love, he's poking peas into his ear!)
Thou merry, laughing sprite!
With spirits feather-light,
Untouched by sorrow, and unsoiled by sin –
(Good heavens! the child is swallowing a pin!)

Thou little tricksy Puck!
With antic toys so funnily bestuck,
Light as the singing bird that wings the air –
(The door! the door! he'll tumble down the stair!)
Thou darling of thy sire!
(Why, Jane, he'll set his pinafore a-fire!)
Thou imp of mirth and joy!
In Love's dear chain so strong and bright a link,
Thou idol of thy parents – (Drat the boy!
There goes my ink!)

Thou cherub – but of earth;
Fit playfellow for Fays, by moonlight pale,
In harmless sport and mirth,
(That dog will bite him if he pulls its tail!)
Thou human humming-bee extracting honey
From ev'ry blossom in the world that blows,
Singing in Youth's Elysium ever sunny,
(Another tumble! – that's his precious nose!)
Thy father's pride and hope!
(He'll break the mirror with that skipping-rope!)
With pure heart newly stamped from Nature's mint –
(Where did he learn that squint?)

Thou young domestic dove!
(He'll have that jug off, with another shove!)
Dear nurseling of the hymeneal nest!
(Are those torn clothes his best!)
Little epitome of man!

13

(He'll climb upon the table, that's his plan!)
Touched with the beauteous tints of dawning life –
      (He's got a knife!)

      Thou enviable being!
No storms, no clouds, in thy blue sky foreseeing,
      Play on, play on,
      My elfin John!
Toss the light ball – bestride the stick –
(I knew so many cakes would make him sick!)
With fancies buoyant as the thistle down,
Prompting the face grotesque, and antic brisk,
      With many a lamb-like frisk,
(He's got the scissors, snipping at your gown!)

      Thou pretty opening rose!
(Go to your mother, child, and wipe your nose!)
Balmy, and breathing music like the South,
(He really brings my heart into my mouth!)
Fresh as the morn, and brilliant as its star, –
(I wish that window had an iron bar!)
Bold as the hawk, yet gentle as the dove, –
      (I tell you what, my love,
I cannot write, unless he's sent above!)

THOMAS HOOD

I Saw a Jolly Hunter

from *Figgie Hobbin*

I saw a jolly hunter
    With a jolly gun
Walking in the country
    In the jolly sun.

In the jolly meadow
    Sat a jolly hare.
Saw the jolly hunter.
    Took jolly care.

Hunter jolly eager –
    Sight of jolly prey.
Forgot gun pointing
    Wrong jolly way.

Jolly hunter jolly head
    Over heels gone.
Jolly old safety-catch
    Not jolly on.

Bang went the jolly gun.
    Hunter jolly dead.
Jolly hare got clean away.
    Jolly good, I said.

CHARLES CAUSLEY 1917–

The Quangle Wangle's Hat

On the top of the Crumpetty Tree
    The Quangle Wangle sat,
But his face you could not see,
    On account of his Beaver Hat.
For his Hat was a hundred and two feet wide,
With ribbons and bibbons on every side
And bells, and buttons, and loops, and lace,
So that nobody ever could see the face
        Of the Quangle Wangle Quee.

The Quangle Wangle said
    To himself on the Crumpetty Tree, –
'Jam; and jelly; and bread;
    Are the best food for me!
But the longer I live on this Crumpetty Tree
The plainer than ever it seems to me
That very few people come this way
And that life on the whole is far from gay!'
        Said the Quangle Wangle Quee.

15

But there came to the Crumpetty Tree,
    Mr and Mrs Canary;
And they said, – 'Did you ever see
    Any spot so charmingly airy?
May we build a nest on your lovely Hat?
Mr Quangle Wangle, grant us that!
O please let us come and build a nest
Of whatever material suits you best,
        Mr Quangle Wangle Quee!'

And besides, to the Crumpetty Tree
    Came the Stork, the Duck, and the Owl;
    The Snail, and the Bumble-Bee,
    The Frog, and the Fimble Fowl;
(The Fimble Fowl, with a Corkscrew leg;)
And all of them said, – 'We humbly beg,
We may build our homes on your lovely Hat, –
Mr Quangle Wangle, grant us that!
        Mr Quangle Wangle Quee!'

And the Golden Grouse came there,
    And the Pobble who has no toes, –
And the small Olympian bear, –
    And the Dong with a luminous Nose.
And the Blue Baboon, who played the Flute, –
And the Orient Calf from the Land of Tute, –
And the Attery Squash, and the Bisky Bat, –
All came and built on the lovely Hat
        Of the Quangle Wangle Quee.

And the Quangle Wangle said
    To himself on the Crumpetty Tree, –
'When all these creatures move
    What a wonderful noise there'll be!'
And at night by the light of the Mulberry moon
They danced to the Flute of the Blue Baboon,
On the broad green leaves of the Crumpetty Tree,
And all were as happy as happy could be,
        With the Quangle Wangle Quee.
                    EDWARD LEAR 1812–88

My Shadow

I have a little shadow that goes in and out with me,
And what can be the use of him is more than I can see.
He is very, very like me from the heels up to the head;
And I see him jump before me, when I jump into my bed.

The funniest thing about him is the way he likes to grow –
Not at all like proper children, which is always very slow;
For he sometimes shoots up taller like an india-rubber ball,
And he sometimes gets so little that there's none of him at all.

He hasn't got a notion of how children ought to play,
And can only make a fool of me in every sort of way.
He stays so close beside me, he's a coward you can see;
I'd think shame to stick to nursie as that shadow sticks to me!

One morning, very early, before the sun was up,
I rose and found the shining dew on every buttercup;
But my lazy little shadow, like an arrant sleepy-head,
Had stayed at home behind me and was fast asleep in bed.

ROBERT LOUIS STEVENSON 1850–89

Little Willie

Little Willie from his mirror
Licked the mercury right off,
Thinking, in his childish error,
It would cure the whooping cough.

At the funeral his mother
Brightly said to Mrs. Brown:
' 'Twas a chilly day for Willie
When the mercury went down!'

ANON.

The Owl and the Pussy Cat

The Owl and the Pussy-Cat went to sea
   In a beautiful pea-green boat.
They took some honey, and plenty of money
   Wrapped up in a five-pound note.
The Owl looked up to the stars above,
   And sang to a small guitar,
'O lovely Pussy! O Pussy, my love,
What a beautiful Pussy you are,
        You are,
        You are!
What a beautiful Pussy you are!'

Pussy said to the Owl, 'You elegant fowl!
   How charmingly sweet you sing!
O let us be married! too long we have tarried:
   But what shall we do for a ring?'
They sailed away, for a year and a day,
   To the land where the Bong-Tree grows,
And there in a wood a Piggy-wig stood,
With a ring at the end of his nose,
        His nose,
        His nose!
With a ring at the end of his nose.

'Dear Pig, are you willing to sell for one shilling
   Your ring?' Said the Piggy, 'I will.'
So they took it away, and were married next day
   By the Turkey who lives on the hill.
They dined on mince, and slices of quince,
   Which they ate with a runcible spoon;
And hand in hand, on the edge of the sand
   They danced by the light of the moon,
        The moon,
        The moon,
   They danced by the light of the moon.

EDWARD LEAR

London Bells

Two sticks and an apple,
Ring the bells at Whitechapel.

Old Father Bald Pate,
Ring the bells Aldgate.

Maids in white aprons,
Ring the bells at St. Catherine's.

Oranges and lemons,
Ring the bells at St. Clement's.

When will you pay me?
Ring the bells at the Old Bailey.

When I am rich,
Rings the bells at Fleetditch.

When will that be?
Ring the bells at Stepney.

When I am old,
Ring the great bell at Paul's.
ANON. (*Early 18th century.*)

Jim
Who ran away from his Nurse, and was eaten by a Lion.

There was a Boy whose name was Jim;
His Friends were very good to him.
They gave him Tea, and Cakes, and Jam,
And slices of delicious Ham,
And Chocolate with pink inside,
And little tricycles to ride,
And read him stories through and through,
And even took him to the Zoo –
But there it was the dreadful Fate
Befell him, which I now relate.

You know – at least you *ought* to know,
For I have often told you so –
That Children never are allowed
To leave their Nurses in a Crowd;
Now this was Jim's especial foible,
He ran away when he was able,
And on this inauspicious day
He slipped his hand and ran away!
He hadn't gone a yard when –
      Bang!
With open Jaws, a Lion sprang,
And hungrily began to eat
The Boy: beginning at his feet.

Now just imagine how it feels
When first your toes and then your heels,
And then by gradual degrees,
Your shins and ankles, calves and knees,
Are slowly eaten, bit by bit.
No wonder Jim detested it!
No wonder that he shouted 'Hi!'
The Honest Keeper heard his cry,
Though very fat, he almost ran
To help the little gentleman.
'Ponto!' he ordered as he came
(For Ponto was the Lion's name),
'Ponto!' he cried, with angry Frown.
'Let go, Sir! Down, Sir! Put it down!'

The Lion made a sudden stop,
He let the Dainty Morsel drop,
And slunk reluctant to his Cage,
Snarling with Disappointed Rage.
But when he bent him over Jim,
The Honest Keeper's Eyes were dim.
The Lion having reached his Head,
The Miserable Boy was dead!

When Nurse informed his Parents, they
Were more Concerned than I can say: –

His Mother, as She dried her eyes,
Said, 'Well – it gives me no surprise,
He would not do as he was told!'
His Father, who was self-controlled,
Bade all the children round attend
To James's miserable end,
And always keep a-hold of Nurse
For fear of finding something worse.

HILAIRE BELLOC 1870–1953

Hug O' War

I will not play at tug o' war.
I'd rather play at hug o' war,
Where everyone hugs
Instead of tugs,
Where everyone giggles
And rolls on the rug,
Where everyone kisses,
And everyone grins,
And everyone cuddles,
And everyone wins.

SHEL SILVERSTEIN 1932–

Tree House

A tree house, a free house,
A secret you and me house,
A high up in the leafy branches
Cozy as can be house.

A street house, a neat house,
Be sure and wipe your feet house
Is not my kind of house at all –
Let's go live in a tree house.

SHEL SILVERSTEIN

from *An Old Cornish Litany*

From Ghoulies and Ghosties,
And long-leggity Beasties,
And all Things that go bump in the Night,
Good Lord deliver us.

ANON.

A Considered Reply to a Child

'I love you,' you said between two mouthfuls of pudding.
But not funny; I didn't want to laugh at all.
Rolling three years' experience in a ball,
You nudged it friendlily across the table.

A stranger, almost, I was flattered – no kidding.
It's not every day I hear a thing like that;
And when I do my answer's never pat.
I'm about nine times your age, ten times less able

To say – what you said; incapable of unloading
Plonk at someone's feet, like a box of bricks,
A declaration. When I try, it sticks
Like fish-bones in my throat; my eyes tingle.

What's called 'passion', you'll learn, may become
    'overriding'.
But not in me it doesn't: I'm that smart,
I can give everything and keep my heart.
Kisses are kisses. No need for souls to mingle.

Bed's bed, what's more, and you'd say it's meant for
    sleeping;
And, believe me, you'd be absolutely right.
With luck you'll never lie awake all night,
Someone beside you (rather like 'crying') weeping.

JONATHAN PRICE 1931–85

Solomon Grundy

Solomon Grundy,
Born on a Monday,
Christened on Tuesday,
Married on Wednesday,
Took ill on Thursday,

Worse on Friday,
Died on Saturday,
Buried on Sunday.
This is the end
Of Solomon Grundy

ANON.

Buckingham Palace

They're changing guard at Buckingham Palace –
Christopher Robin went down with Alice.
Alice is marrying one of the guard.
'A soldier's life is terrible hard,'
                    Says Alice.

They're changing guard at Buckingham Palace –
Christopher Robin went down with Alice.
We saw a guard in a sentry-box.
'One of the sergeants looks after their socks,'
                    Says Alice.

They're changing guard at Buckingham Palace –
Christopher Robin went down with Alice.
We looked for the King, but he never came.
'Well, God take care of him, all the same,'
                    Says Alice.

They're changing guard at Buckingham Palace –
Christopher Robin went down with Alice.
They've great big parties inside the grounds.
'I wouldn't be King for a hundred pounds,'
                    Says Alice.

They're changing guard at Buckingham Palace –
Christopher Robin went down with Alice.
A face looked out, but it wasn't the King's.
'He's much too busy a-signing things,'
                    Says Alice.

They're changing guard at Buckingham Palace –
Christopher Robin went down with Alice.
'Do you think the King knows all about *me*?'
'Sure to, dear, but it's time for tea,'
                    Says Alice.
                    A. A. MILNE 1882–1956

Sneezles

Christopher Robin
Had wheezles
And sneezles,
They bundled him
Into
His bed.
They gave him what goes
With a cold in the nose,
And some more for a cold
In the head.
They wondered
If wheezles
Could turn
Into measles,
If sneezles
Would turn
Into mumps;
They examined his chest
For a rash,
And the rest
Of his body for swelling and lumps.
They sent for some doctors
In sneezles
And wheezles

To tell them what ought
To be done.
All sorts and conditions
Of famous physicians
Came hurrying round
At a run.
They all made a note
Of the state of his throat,
They asked if he suffered from thirst;
They asked if the sneezles
Came *after* the wheezles,
Or if the first sneezle
Came first.
They said, 'If you teazle
A sneezle
Or wheezle,
A measle
May easily grow.
But humour or pleazle
The wheezle
Or sneezle,
The measle
Will certainly go.'
They expounded the reazles
For sneezles
And wheezles,
The manner of measles
When new.
They said 'If he freezles
In draughts and in breezles,
Then PHTHEEZLES
May even ensue.'

Christopher Robin
Got up in the morning,
The sneezles had vanished away.
And the look in his eye
Seemed to say to the sky,
'Now, how to amuse them to-day?'
                                      A. A. MILNE

The Walrus and the Carpenter

The sun was shining on the sea,
   Shining with all his might:
He did his very best to make
   The billows smooth and bright –
And this was odd, because it was
   The middle of the night.

The moon was shining sulkily,
   Because she thought the sun
Had got no business to be there
   After the day was done –
'It's very rude of him,' she said,
   'To come and spoil the fun!'

The sea was wet as wet could be,
   The sands were dry as dry.
You could not see a cloud, because.
   No cloud was in the sky:
No birds were flying overhead –
   There were no birds to fly.

The Walrus and the Carpenter
   Were walking close at hand:
They wept like anything to see
   Such quantities of sand:
'If this were only cleared away,'
   They said, 'it *would* be grand!'

'If seven maids with seven mops
   Swept it for half a year,
Do you suppose,' the Walrus said,
   'That they could get it clear?'
'I doubt it,' said the Carpenter,
   And shed a bitter tear.

'O Oysters, come and walk with us!'
   The Walrus did beseech.
'A pleasant walk, a pleasant talk,
   Along the briny beach:

We cannot do with more than four,
  To give a hand to each.'

The eldest Oyster looked at him,
  But not a word he said:
The eldest Oyster winked his eye,
  And shook his heavy head –
Meaning to say he did not choose
  To leave the oyster-bed.

But four young Oysters hurried up,
  All eager for the treat:
Their coats were brushed, their faces washed,
  Their shoes were clean and neat –
And this was odd, because, you know,
  They hadn't any feet.

Four other Oysters followed them,
  And yet another four;
And thick and fast they came at last,
  And more, and more, and more –
All hopping through the frothy waves,
  And scrambling to the shore.

The Walrus and the Carpenter
  Walked on a mile or so,
And then they rested on a rock
  Conveniently low:
And all the little Oysters stood
  And waited in a row.

'The time has come,' the Walrus said,
  'To talk of many things:
Of shoes – and ships – and sealing wax –
  Of cabbages – and kings –
And why the sea is boiling hot –
  And whether pigs have wings.'

'But wait a bit,' the Oysters cried,
  'Before we have our chat;
For some of us are out of breath,

And all of us are fat!'
'No hurry!' said the Carpenter.
They thanked him much for that.

'A loaf of bread,' the Walrus said,
 'Is what we chiefly need:
Pepper and vinegar besides
 Are very good indeed –
Now, if you're ready, Oysters dear,
 We can begin to feed.'

LEWIS CARROLL 1832–98

Jellyfish

When my chandelier
Waltzes pulsing near
Let the swimmer fear.

Beached and bare
I'm less of a scare.
But I don't care.

Though I look like a slob
It's a delicate job
Being just a blob.

TED HUGHES 1930–

Crab

In the low tide pools
I pack myself like
A handy pocket
Chest of tools.

But as the tide fills
Dancing I go

Under lifted veils
Tiptoe, tiptoe.

And with pliers and pincers
Repair and remake
The daintier dancers
The breakers break.

TED HUGHES

Where Go the Boats?

Dark brown is the river,
  Golden is the sand.
It flows along for ever,
  With trees on either hand.

Green leaves a-floating,
  Castles of the foam,
Boats of mine a-boating –
  Where will all come home?

On goes the river
  And out past the mill,
Away down the valley,
  Away down the hill.

Away down the river,
  A hundred miles or more,
Other little children
  Shall bring my boats ashore.

ROBERT LOUIS STEVENSON

from *Ruthless Rhymes*
The Stern Parent

Father heard his Children scream,
So he threw them in the stream,
Saying, as he drowned the third,
'Children should be seen, *not* heard!'

Tender-Heartedness

Billy, in one of his nice new sashes,
Fell in the fire and was burnt to ashes;
Now, although the room grows chilly,
I haven't the heart to poke poor Billy.

HARRY GRAHAM 1874–1936

Walking Song

We waited for an omnibus,
In which there was no room for us,
But Right foot first, then Left, his brother,
Tried which could overtake the other;
And that's the way,
With nought to pay,
To do without an omnibus,
In which there is no room for us.

WILLIAM E. HICKSON 1803–70

The Spider and the Fly

'Will you walk into my parlour?' said the Spider to the Fly,
''Tis the prettiest little parlour that ever you did spy;
The way into my parlour is up a winding stair,
And I have many curious things to show when you are there.'

'Oh no, no,' said the little Fly, 'to ask me is in vain,
For who goes up your winding stair can ne'er come down again.'

'I'm sure you must be weary, dear, with soaring up so high;
Will you rest upon my little bed?' said the Spider to the Fly.
'There are pretty curtains drawn around, the sheets are fine and thin;
And if you like to rest awhile, I'll snugly tuck you in!'
'Oh no, no,' said the little Fly, 'for I've often heard it said,
They never, never wake again, who sleep upon your bed!'

Said the cunning Spider to the Fly, 'Dear friend, what can I do,
To prove the warm affection I've always felt for you?
I have within my pantry good store of all that's nice;
I'm sure you're very welcome – will you please to take a slice?'
'Oh no, no,' said the little Fly, 'kind sir, that cannot be,
I've heard what's in your pantry, and I do not wish to see.'

'Sweet creature,' said the Spider, 'you're witty and you're wise;
How handsome are your gauzy wings, how brilliant are your eyes!
I have a little looking-glass upon my parlour shelf,
If you'll step in a moment, dear, you shall behold yourself.'
'I thank you, gentle sir,' she said, 'for what you're pleased to say,
And bidding you good morning now, I'll call another day.'

The Spider turned him round about, and went into his den,
For well he knew the silly Fly would soon come back again;
So he wove a subtle web, in a little corner sly,
And set his table ready, to dine upon the Fly.
Then he came out to his door again, and merrily did sing:
'Come hither, hither, pretty Fly, with the pearl and silver wing;
Your robes are green and purple – there's a crest upon your head;
Your eyes are like the diamond bright, but mine are dull as lead.'

Alas, alas! how very soon this silly little Fly,
Hearing his wily, flattering words, came slowly flitting by;
With buzzing wings she hung aloft, then near and nearer drew,
Thinking only of her brilliant eyes, and green and purple hue;
Thinking only of her crested head – poor foolish thing! At last,
Up jumped the cunning Spider, and fiercely held her fast.
He dragged her up his winding stair, into his dismal den,
Within his little parlour – but she ne'er came out again!

MARY HOWITT 1799–1888

'You are Old, Father William'

'You are old, Father William,' the young man said,
  'And your hair has become very white;
And yet you incessantly stand on your head –
  Do you think, at your age, it is right?'

'In my youth,' Father William replied to his son,
  'I feared it might injure the brain;
But, now that I'm perfectly sure I have none,
  Why, I do it again and again.'

'You are old,' said the youth, 'as I mentioned before,
  And have grown most uncommonly fat;
Yet you turned a back-somersault in at the door –
  Pray, what is the reason of that?'

'In my youth,' said the sage, as he shook his grey locks,
  'I kept all my limbs very supple
By the use of this ointment – one shilling the box –
  Allow me to sell you a couple?'

'You are old,' said the youth, 'and your jaws are too weak
  For anything tougher than suet;
Yet you finished the goose, with the bones and the beak –
  Pray, how did you manage to do it?'

'In my youth,' said his father, 'I took to the law,
  And argued each case with my wife;
And the muscular strength, which it gave to my jaw,
  Has lasted the rest of my life.'

'You are old,' said the youth, 'one would hardly suppose
  That your eye was as steady as ever;
Yet you balance an eel on the end of your nose –
  What made you so awfully clever?'

'I have answered three questions, and that is enough,'
  Said his father. 'Don't give yourself airs!
Do you think I can listen all day to such stuff?
  Be off, or I'll kick you down-stairs!'

LEWIS CARROLL

The Donkey

When fishes flew and forests walked
    And figs grew upon thorn,
Some moment when the moon was blood
    Then surely I was born;

With monstrous head and sickening cry
    And ears like errant wings,
The devil's walking parody
    On all four-footed things.

The tattered outlaw of the earth,
    Of ancient crooked will;
Starve, scourge, deride me: I am dumb,
    I keep my secret still.

Fools! For I also had my hour;
    One far fierce hour and sweet:
There was a shout about my ears,
    And palms before my feet.

G. K. CHESTERTON 1874–1936

The Donkey

It was such a pretty little donkey
It had such pretty ears
And it used to gallop round the field so briskly
Though well down in years.

It was a retired donkey,
After a life-time of working
Between the shafts of regular employment
It was now free to go merrymaking.

Oh in its eyes was such a gleam
As is usually associated with youth
But it was not a youthful gleam really,
But full of mature truth.

And of the hilarity that goes with age,
As if to tell us sardonically
No hedged track lay before this donkey longer
But the sweet prairies of anarchy.

STEVIE SMITH 1902—71

A Warning to Cat Owners

Cats don't have a Highway Code,
They like the freedom of the road.
Our cat, called Zoe, soft and nice,
Ignored the signs and paid the price.
She tried to bear the rush hour traffic,
We fetched a shoe box from the attic.
We dug a grave behind the shed,
And there we laid poor Zoe's head.
We sang a song and gathered flowers,
We cried until the early hours.
But cats don't have a Highway Code,
They like the freedom of the road.

SUE TOWNSEND

The End

When I was One,
I had just begun.

When I was Two,
I was nearly new.

When I was Three,
I was hardly Me.

When I was Four,
I was not much more.

When I was Five,
I was just alive.

But now I am Six, I'm as clever as clever.
So I think I'll be six now for ever and ever.

A. A. MILNE

SCHOOL

Then the whining school-boy, with his satchel,
And shining morning face, creeping like snail
Unwillingly to school.

To Any Reader

As from the house your mother sees
You playing round the garden trees,
So you may see, if you will look
Through the windows of this book,
Another child, far, far away,
And in another garden, play.
But do not think you can at all,
By knocking on the window, call
That child to hear you. He intent
Is all on his play-business bent.
He does not hear; he will not look,
Nor yet be lured out of this book.
For, long ago, the truth to say,
He has grown up and gone away,
And it is but a child of air
That lingers in the garden there.

ROBERT LOUIS STEVENSON

Under Milk Wood

(*Silence*)

FIRST VOICE (*Very softly*)

To begin at the beginning:

It is spring, moonless night in the small town, starless and
bible-black, the cobblestreets silent and the hunched, courters'-
and-rabbits' wood limping invisible down to the sloeblack,
slow, black, crowblack, fishingboat-bobbing sea. The houses
are blind as moles (though moles see fine to-night in the snout-
ing, velvet dingles) or blind as Captain Cat there in the muffled
middle by the pump and the town clock, the shops in mourn-
ing, the Welfare Hall in widows' weeds. And all the people of
the lulled and dumbfound town are sleeping now.

Hush, the babies are sleeping, the farmers, the fishers, the
tradesmen and pensioners, cobblers, school-teacher, postman
and publican, the undertaker and the fancy woman, drunkard,
dressmaker, preacher, policeman, the webfoot cocklewomen

and the tidy wives. Young girls lie bedded soft or glide in their dreams, with rings and trousseaux, bridesmaided by glow-worms down the aisles of the organplaying wood. The boys are dreaming wicked or of the bucking ranches of the night and the jollyrodgered sea. And the anthracite statues of the horses sleep in the fields, and the cows in the byres, and the dogs in the wetnosed yards; and the cats nap in the slant corners or lope sly, streaking and needling, on the one cloud of the roofs.

You can hear the dew falling, and the hushed town breathing. Only *your* eyes are unclosed to see the black and folded town fast, and slow, asleep. And you alone can hear the invisible starfall, the darkest-before-dawn minutely dewgrazed stir of the black, dab-filled sea where the *Arethusa*, the *Curlew* and the *Skylark, Zanzibar, Rhiannon*, the *Rover*, the *Cormorant*, and the *Star of Wales* tilt and ride.

Listen. It is night moving in the streets, the processional salt slow musical wind in Coronation Street and Cockle Row, it is the grass growing on Llaregyb Hill, dewfall, starfall, the sleep of birds in Milk Wood.

Listen. It is night in the chill, squat chapel, hymning in bonnet and brooch and bombazine black, butterfly choker and bootlace bow, coughing like nannygoats, sucking mintoes, forty-winking hallelujah; night in the four-ale, quiet as a domino; in Ocky Milkman's lofts like a mouse with gloves; in Dai Bread's bakery flying like black flour. It is to-night in Donkey Street, trotting silent, with seaweed on its hooves, along the cockled cobbles, past curtained fernpot, text and trinket, harmonium, holy dresser, watercolours done by hand, china dog and rosy tin teacaddy. It is night neddying among the snuggeries of babies.

Look. It is night, dumbly, royally winding through the Coronation cherry trees; going through the graveyard of Bethesda with winds gloved and folded, and dew doffed; tumbling by the Sailors Arms.

Time passes. Listen. Time passes.

Come closer now.

Only you can hear the houses sleeping in the streets in the slow deep salt and silent black, bandaged night. Only you can see, in the blinded bedrooms, the combs and petticoats over the chairs, the jugs and basins, the glasses of teeth, Thou Shalt Not on the wall, and the yellowing dickybird-watching pictures of the dead. Only you can hear and see, behind the eyes of the sleepers, the movements and countries and mazes and colours and dismays and rainbows and tunes and wishes and flight and fall and despairs and big seas of their dreams.

From where you are, you can hear their dreams.

Captain Cat, the retired blind seacaptain, asleep in his bunk in the seashelled, ship-in-bottled, shipshape best cabin of Schooner House dreams of

SECOND VOICE

never such seas as any that swamped the decks of his S.S. *Kidwelly* bellying over the bedclothes and jellyfish-slippery sucking him down salt deep into the Davy dark where the fish come biting out and nibble him down to his wishbone, and the long drowned nuzzle up to him.

FIRST DROWNED

Remember me, Captain?

CAPTAIN CAT

You're Dancing Williams!

FIRST DROWNED

I lost my step in Nantucket.

Who pulls the townhall bellrope but blind Captain Cat? One by one, the sleepers are rung out of sleep this one morning as every morning. And soon you shall see the chimneys' slow upflying snow as Captain Cat, in sailor's cap and seaboots, announces to-day with his loud get-out-of-bed bell.

SECOND VOICE

The Reverend Eli Jenkins, in Bethesda House, gropes out of bed into his preacher's black, combs back his bard's white hair, forgets to wash, pads barefoot downstairs, opens the front door, stands in the doorway and, looking out at the day and up at the eternal hill, and hearing the sea break and the gab of birds, remembers his own verses and tells them softly to empty Coronation Street that is rising and raising its blinds.

Dear Gwalia! I know there are
Towns lovelier than ours,
And fairer hills and loftier far,
And groves more full of flowers,

And boskier woods more blithe with spring
And bright with birds' adorning,
And sweeter bards than I to sing
Their praise this beauteous morning.

By Cader Idris, tempest-torn,
Or Moel yr Wyddfa's glory,
Carnedd Llewelyn beauty born,
Plinlimmon old in story,

By mountains where King Arthur dreams,
By Penmaenmawr defiant,
Llaregyb Hill a molehill seems,
A pygmy to a giant.

By Sawdde, Senny, Dovey, Dee,
Edw, Eden, Aled, all,
Taff and Towy broad and free,
Llyfnant with its waterfall,

Claerwen, Cleddau, Dulais, Daw,
Ely, Gwili, Ogwr, Nedd,
Small is our River Dewi, Lord,
A baby on a rushy bed.

By Carreg Cennen, King of time,
Our Heron Head is only
A bit of stone with seaweed spread
Where gulls come to be lonely.

A tiny dingle is Milk Wood
By Golden Grove 'neath Grongar,
But let me choose and oh! I should
Love all my life and longer

To stroll among our trees and stray
In Goosegog Lane, on Donkey Down,
And hear the Dewi sing all day,
And never, never leave the town.

DYLAN THOMAS 1914–53

The Collier

When I was born on Amman hill
A dark bird crossed the sun.
Sharp on the floor the shadow fell;
I was the youngest son.

And when I went to the County School
I worked in a shaft of light.
In the wood of the desk I cut my name:
Dai for Dynamite.

The tall black hills my brothers stood;
Their lessons all were done.
From the door of the school when I ran out
They frowned to watch me run.

The slow grey bells they rung a chime
Surly with grief or age.
Clever or clumsy, lad or lout,
All would look for a wage.

I learnt the valley flowers' names
And the rough bark knew my knees.
I brought home trout from the river
And spotted eggs from the trees.

A coloured coat I was given to wear
Where the lights of the rough land shone.
Still jealous of my favour
The tall black hills looked on.

They dipped my coat in the blood of a kid
And they cast me down a pit,
And although I crossed with strangers
There was no way up from it.

Soon as I went from the County School
I worked in a shaft. Said Jim,
'You will get your chain of gold, my lad,
But not for a likely time.'

And one said, 'Jack was not raised up
When the wind blew out the light
Though he interpreted their dreams
And guessed their fears by night.'

And Tom, he shivered his leper's lamp
For the stain that round him grew;
And I heard mouths pray in the after–damp
When the picks would not break through.

They changed words there in darkness
And still through my head they run,
And white on my limbs is the linen sheet
And gold on my neck the sun.

VERNON WATKINS 1906–67

On My Son

Farewell, thou child of my right hand, and joy;
   My sin was too much hope of thee, loved boy.
Seven years thou wert lent to me, and I thee pay,
   Exacted by thy fate, on the just day.
O, could I lose all father now! For why
   Will man lament the state he should envy?
To have so soon 'scaped world's and flesh's rage,
   And, if no other misery, yet age?
Rest in soft peace, and, asked, say here doth lie
   Ben Jonson, his best piece of poetry.
For whose sake, henceforth, all his vows be such
   As what he loves may never like too much.

BEN JONSON

Widdicombe Fair

'Tom Pearse, Tom Pearse, lend me your gray mare,
    All along, down along, out along, lee.
For I want for to go to Widdicombe Fair,
    Wi' Bill Brewer, Jan Stewer, Peter Gurney, Peter Davy,
    Dan'l Whiddon, Harry Hawk,
Old Uncle Tom Cobleigh and all.'
    Old Uncle Tom Cobleigh and all.

'And when shall I see again my gray mare?' –
    All along, down along, out along, lee.
'By Friday soon, or Saturday noon,
    Wi' Bill Brewer, Jan Stewer, Peter Gurney, Peter Davy,
    Dan'l Whiddon, Harry Hawk,
Old Uncle Tom Cobleigh and all.'
    Old Uncle Tom Cobleigh and all.

Then Friday came and Saturday noon,
    All along, down along, out along, lee.
But Tom Pearse's old mare hath not trotted home,
    Wi' Bill Brewer, Jan Stewer, Peter Gurney, Peter Davy,
    Dan'l Whiddon, Harry Hawk,
Old Uncle Tom Cobleigh and all.
    Old Uncle Tom Cobleigh and all.

So Tom Pearse he got up to the top o' the hill,
    All along, down along, out along, lee.
And he sees his old mare down a-making her will,
    Wi' Bill Brewer, Jan Stewer, Peter Gurney, Peter Davy,
    Dan'l Whiddon, Harry Hawk,
Old Uncle Tom Cobleigh and all.
    Old Uncle Tom Cobleigh and all.

So Tom Pearse's old mare her took sick and her died,
    All along, down along, out along, lee.
And Tom he sat down on a stone, and he cried
    Wi' Bill Brewer, Jan Stewer, Peter Gurney, Peter Davy,
    Dan'l Whiddon, Harry Hawk,
Old Uncle Tom Cobleigh and all.
    Old Uncle Tom Cobleigh and all.

But this isn't the end o' this shocking affair,
    All along, down along, out along, lee.
Nor, though they be dead, of the horrid career
    Of Bill Brewer, Jan Stewer, Peter Gurney, Peter Davy,
    Dan'l Whiddon, Harry Hawk,
Old Uncle Tom Cobleigh and all.
    Old Uncle Tom Cobleigh and all.

When the wind whistles cold on the moor of a night,
    All along, down along, out along, lee.
Tom Pearse's old mare doth appear, gashly white,
    Wi' Bill Brewer, Jan Stewer, Peter Gurney, Peter Davy,
    Dan'l Whiddon, Harry Hawk,
Old Uncle Tom Cobleigh and all.
    Old Uncle Tom Cobleigh and all.

And all the long night he heard skirling and groans,
    All along, down along, out along, lee.
From Tom Pearse's old mare in her rattling bones,
    And from Bill Brewer, Jan Stewer, Peter Gurney, Peter
        Davy,
    Dan'l Whiddon, Harry Hawk,
Old Uncle Tom Cobleigh and all.
    OLD UNCLE TOM COBLEIGH AND ALL.

TRADITIONAL: ENGLISH

Christmas in Africa

One autumn afternoon when I was nine
feeding the chickens near the grapevine, brooding
in sunshine, my mother asked me to choose

a christmas present that year.
Anything I said, but a doll. Whatever you choose
but not a doll

my faith in her to know
better than I could myself what gift would please me.
.And so at the height of summer

46

we made our pilgrimage
to the earth's greenest riches and the ample ocean.
And christmas eve

was three white daughters
three bright angels singing silent night as my mother
lit the candles

the tree blooming
sea breathing, the beloved son in his cradle sleeping.
Over the hills and skies

on his sleigh the father
the awaited one, made his visitation. Weeks of dreaming
and wondering now

in a box in my hand.
Shoebox size. Not waterwings then or a time machine no
something the size

of a pair of shoes.
Not a pony then or a river canoe. Not a new dress no.
I pulled at the bright bowed ribbons

and little christmas angels
with trembling hands. Underneath the monkey-apple branch
dressed up in baubles and tinsel

and blobs of cotton wool
the sea soaring, stars and the fairy at the treetop
shining

his hand on my shoulder
my mother's eyes on my face two burning suns
piercing my mind and in the box

a doll.
A stupid pretty empty thing. Pink smiling girl. The world
rocked about my head

my face fell into a net
from that moment. My heart in me played possum
and never recovered.

I said I liked the wretched thing
joy broke over my face like a mirror cracking. I said it
so loud, so often

I almost believed it. All that christmas
a shameful secret bound me and the doll and my mother
irrevocably together

When I knew she was watching
I would grab for the doll in the night, or take it
tenderly with me to the beach

wrapped in a small towel.
At last on the last night of the journey home
staying at a hotel

my mother woke me early
to go out and find the maid. In my pyjamas, half asleep
I staggered out into the dawn

heat rising like mist
from the ground, birds making an uproar, snakes
not yet awake

a sense of something
about to happen under the heavy damp rustle
of the trees.

My feet left footprints
in the dew. When I returned I was clutching that precious
corpse to my chest

like one of the bereaved.
*Now I know, said my mother, that although you didn't
want a doll, you really do love her.*

I was believed!
Something fell from my face with a clatter –
my punishment was over

and in that moment
fell from my mother's face a particular smile, a kind of
dear and tender curling of the eyes

fell. Two gripped faces
side by side on the floor, smiled at each other
before we grabbed them back

and fitted them with a hollow rattle
to our love. And I laid the doll down in a suitcase
and slammed the lid on its face

and never looked at it again.
And in a sense my mother did the same, and in a sense
my punishment and hers

had always been, and just begun.

JENI COUZYN 1942–

The Yarn of the Nancy Bell

'Twas on the shores that round our coast
    From Deal to Ramsgate span,
That I found alone on a piece of stone
    An elderly naval man.

His hair was weedy, his beard was long,
    And weedy and long was he,
And I heard this wight on the shore recite,
    In a singular minor key:

'Oh, I am a cook and a captain bold,
    And the mate of the Nancy brig,
And a bo'sun tight, and a midshipmite,
    And the crew of the captain's gig.'

49

And he shook his fists and he tore his hair,
    Till I really felt afraid,
For I couldn't help thinking the man had been drinking,
    And so I simply said:

'Oh, elderly man, it's little I know
    Of the duties of men of the sea,
And I'll eat my hand if I understand
    How you can possibly be

'At once a cook, and a captain bold,
    And the mate of the *Nancy* brig,
And a bo'sun tight, and a midshipmite,
    And the crew of the captain's gig.'

Then he gave a hitch to his trousers, which
    Is a trick all seamen larn,
And having got rid of a thumping quid,
    He spun this painful yarn:

''Twas in the good ship *Nancy Bell*
    That we sailed to the Indian Sea,
And there on a reef we come to grief,
    Which has often occurred to me.

'And pretty nigh all the crew was drowned
    (There was seventy-seven o' soul),
And only ten of the *Nancy's* men
    Said "here" to the muster-roll.

'There was me and the cook and the captain bold,
    And the mate of the *Nancy* brig,
And the bo'sun tight, and a midshipmite,
    And the crew of the captain's gig.

'For a month we'd neither wittles nor drink,
    Till a-hungry we did feel,
So we drawed a lot, and accordin' shot
    The captain for our meal.

'The next lot fell to the *Nancy's* mate,
    And a delicate dish he made;
Then our appetite with the midshipmite
    We seven survivors stayed.

'And then we murdered the bos'un tight,
    And he much resembled pig;
Then we wittled free, did the cook and me,
    On the crew of the captain's gig.

'Then only the cook and me was left,
    And the delicate question, "Which
Of us two goes to the kettle?" arose,
    And we argued it out as sich.

'For I loved that cook as a brother, I did,
    And the cook he worshipped me;
But we'd both be blowed if we'd either be stowed
    In the other chap's hold, you see.

'"I'll be eat if you dines off me," says Tom.
    "Yes, that," says I, "you'll be, –
I'm boiled if I die, my friend," quoth I.
    And "Exactly so," quoth he.

'Says he, "Dear James, to murder me
    Were a foolish thing to do,
For don't you see that you can't cook *me*,
    While I can – and will – cook *you*!"

'So he boils the water, and takes the salt
    And the pepper in portions true
(Which he never forgot), and some chopped shallot,
    And some sage and parsley too.

'"Come here," says he, with a proper pride,
    Which his smiling features tell,
"'Twill soothing be if I let you see
    How extremely nice you'll smell."

'And he stirred it round and round and round,
    And he sniffed at the foaming froth;
When I ups with his heels, and smothers his squeals
    In the scum of the boiling broth.

'And I eat that cook in a week or less,
    And – as I eating be
The last of his chops, why, I almost drops,
    For a vessel in sight I see.

       ★   ★   ★

'And I never larf, and I never smile,
    And I never lark or play,
But sit and croak, and a single joke
    I have, – which is to say:

'Oh, I am a cook and a captain bold,
    And the mate of the *Nancy* brig,
And a bos'un tight, and a midshipmite, ·
    And the crew of the captain's gig.'

W. S. GILBERT 1836–1911

The Common Cormorant

The common cormorant or shag
Lays eggs inside a paper bag.
The reason you will see, no doubt,
It is to keep the lightning out,
But what these unobservant birds
Have never noticed is that herds
Of wandering bears may come with buns
And steal the bags to hold the crumbs.

ANON.

Sick

'I cannot go to school today,'
Said little Peggy Ann McKay.

'I have the measles and the mumps,
A gash, a rash and purple bumps.
My mouth is wet, my throat is dry,
I'm going blind in my right eye.
My tonsils are as big as rocks,
I've counted sixteen chicken pox
And there's one more – that's seventeen,
And don't you think my face looks green?
My leg is cut, my eyes are blue –
It might be instamatic flu.
I cough and sneeze and gasp and choke,
I'm sure that my left leg is broke –

My hip hurts when I move my chin,
My belly button's caving in,
My back is wrenched, my ankle's sprained,
My 'pendix pains each time it rains.
My nose is cold, my toes are numb,
I have a sliver in my thumb.
My neck is stiff, my spine is weak,
I hardly whisper when I speak.
My tongue is filling up my mouth,
I think my hair is falling out.
My elbow's bent, my spine ain't straight,
My temperature is one-o-eight.
My brain is shrunk, I cannot hear,
There is a hole inside my ear.
I have a hangnail, and my heart is – what?
What's that? What's that you say?
You say today is . . . Saturday?
G'bye, I'm going out to play!'

SHEL SILVERSTEIN

The First Lord's Song
(*HMS* Pinafore)

When I was a lad I served a term
As office boy to an Attorney's firm,
I cleaned the windows and I swept the floor,

	And I polished up the handle of the big front door.
Chorus:	He polished up the handle of the big front door.
Solo:	I polished up that handle so carefullee
	That now I am the ruler of the Queen's Navee!
Chorus:	He polished up that handle so carefullee
	That now he is the ruler of the Queen's Navee!

Solo:	As office boy I made such a mark
	That they gave me the post of a junior clerk.
	I served all the writs with a smile so bland,
	And I copied all the letters in a big round hand.
Chorus:	He copied all the letters in a big round hand.
Solo:	I copied all the letters in a hand so free
	That now I am the ruler of the Queen's Navee!
Chorus:	He copied all the letters in a hand so free
	That now he is the ruler of the Queen's Navee!

Solo:	In serving writs I made such a name
	That an articled clerk I soon became;
	I wore clean collars and a brand new suit
	For the pass examination at the Institute.
Chorus:	For the pass examination at the Institute.
Solo:	That pass examination did so well for me
	That now I am the ruler of the Queen's Navee!
Chorus:	That pass examination did so well for he
	That now he is the ruler of the Queen's Navee!

Solo:	Of legal knowledge I acquired such a grip
	That they took me into the partnership.
	And that junior partnership I ween
	Was the only ship that I ever had seen.
Chorus:	Was the only ship that he ever had seen.
Solo:	But that kind of ship so suited me
	That now I am the ruler of the Queen's Navee!
Chorus:	But that kind of ship so suited he
	That now he is the ruler of the Queen's Navee!

Solo:	I grew so rich that I was sent
	By a pocket borough into Parliament.
	I always voted at my party's call
	And I never thought of thinking for myself at all.
Chorus:	He never thought of thinking for himself at all.

Solo:	I thought so little, they rewarded me
	By making me the ruler of the Queen's Navee!
Chorus:	He thought so little they rewarded he
	By making him the ruler of the Queen's Navee!

Solo:	Now landsmen all, whoever you may be,
	If you want to rise to the top of the tree,
	If your soul isn't fettered to an office stool,
	Be careful to be guided by this golden rule:
Chorus:	Be careful to be guided by this golden rule:
Solo:	Stick close to your desks and never go to sea
	And you all may be rulers of the Queen's Navee!
Chorus:	Stick close to your desks and never go to sea
	And you all may be rulers of the Queen's Navee!

W. S. GILBERT

from *The Pied Piper of Hamelin*

Hamelin Town's in Brunswick,
By famous Hanover city;
   The river Weser, deep and wide,
   Washes its wall on the southern side;
   A pleasanter spot you never spied;
But, when begins my ditty,
   Almost five hundred years ago,
   To see the townsfolk suffer so
   From vermin, was a pity.

   Rats!
They fought the dogs, and killed the cats,
   And bit the babies in the cradles,
And ate the cheeses out of the vats,
   And licked the soup from the cooks' own ladles,
Split open the kegs of salted sprats,
Made nests inside men's Sunday hats,
And even spoiled the women's chats,
   By drowning their speaking
   With shrieking and squeaking
In fifty different sharps and flats.

At last the people in a body
   To the Town Hall came flocking:
''Tis clear,' cried they, 'our Mayor's a noddy;
   And as for our Corporation – shocking
To think we buy gowns lined with ermine
For dolts that can't or won't determine
What's best to rid us of our vermin!
You hope, because you're old and obese,
To find in the furry civic robe ease?
Rouse up, Sirs! Give your brains a racking
To find the remedy we're lacking,
Or, sure as fate, we'll send you packing!'
At this the Mayor and Corporation
Quaked with a mighty consternation.

★ ★ ★

He advanced to the council table:
And, 'Please your honours,' said he, 'I'm able,
By means of a secret charm to draw
All creatures living beneath the sun,
That creep or swim or fly or run,
After me so as you never saw!
And I chiefly use my charm
On creatures that do people harm,
The mole and toad and newt and viper;
And people call me the Pied Piper.'
(And here they noticed round his neck
A scarf of red and yellow stripe,
To match with his coat of the self-same cheque;
And at the scarf's end hung a pipe;
And his fingers, they noticed, were ever straying
As if impatient to be playing
Upon this pipe, as low it dangled
Over his vesture so old-fangled.)
'Yet,' said he, 'poor piper as I am,
In Tartary I freed the Cham,
Last June, from his huge swarms of gnats;
I eased in Asia the Nizam
Of a monstrous brood of vampyre-bats:
And as for what your brain bewilders,
If I can rid your town of rats

56

Will you give me a thousand guilders?'
'One? fifty thousand!' – was the exclamation
Of the astonished Mayor and Corporation.

Into the streets the Piper stept,
    Smiling first a little smile,
As if he knew what magic slept
    In his quiet pipe the while;
Then, like a musical adept,
To blow the pipe his lips he wrinkled,
And green and blue his sharp eyes twinkled
Like a candle-flame where salt is sprinkled;
And ere three shrill notes the pipe uttered,
You heard as if an army muttered;
And the muttering grew to a grumbling;
And the grumbling grew to a mighty rumbling;
And out of the houses the rats came tumbling.
Great rats, small rats, lean rats, brawny rats,
Brown rats, black rats, grey rats, tawny rats,
Grave old plodders, gay young friskers,
    Fathers, mothers, uncles, cousins,
Cocking tails and pricking whiskers,
    Families by tens and dozens,
Brothers, sisters, husbands, wives –
Followed the Piper for their lives.
From street to street he piped advancing,
And step by step they followed dancing,
Until they came to the river Weser
Wherein all plunged and perished!

★ ★ ★

You should have heard the Hamelin people
Ringing the bells till they rocked the steeple.
'Go,' cried the Mayor, 'and get long poles!
Poke out the nests and block up the holes!
Consult with carpenters and builders,
And leave in our town not even a trace
Of the rats!' – when suddenly, up the face
Of the Piper perked in the market-place,
With a, 'First, if you please, my thousand guilders!'

A thousand guilders! The Mayor looked blue;
So did the Corporation too.

★　★　★

To pay this sum to a wandering fellow
With a gipsy coat of red and yellow!
'Beside', quoth the Mayor with a knowing wink,
'Our business was done at the river's brink;
We saw with our eyes the vermin sink,
And what's dead can't come to life, I think.
So, friend, we're not the folks to shrink
From the duty of giving you something for drink,
And a matter of money to put in your poke;
But as for the guilders, what we spoke
Of them, as you very well know, was in joke.
Beside, our losses have made us thrifty.
A thousand guilders! come, take fifty!'

The piper's face fell, and he cried,
'No trifling! I can't wait, beside!'

★　★　★

Once more he stept into the street;
    And to his lips again
Laid his long pipe of smooth straight cane;
    And ere he blew three notes (such sweet
Soft notes as yet musicians' cunning
    Never gave the enraptured air)
There was a rustling, that seemed like a bustling
Of merry crowds justling at pitching and hustling,
Small feet were pattering, wooden shoes clattering,
Little hands clapping and little tongues chattering,
And, like fowls in a farm-yard when barley is scattering,

Out came the children running.
All the little boys and girls,
With rosy cheeks and flaxen curls,
And sparkling eyes and teeth like pearls,
Tripping and skipping, ran merrily after
The wonderful music with shouting and laughter.

58

The Mayor was dumb, and the Council stood
As if they were changed into blocks of wood,
Unable to move a step, or cry
To the children merrily skipping by –
And could only follow with the eye
That joyous crowd at the Piper's back.

* * *

When, lo, as they reached the mountain's side,
A wondrous portal opened wide,
As if a cavern was suddenly hollowed;
And the Piper advanced and the children followed,
And when all were in to the very last,
The door in the mountain-side shut fast.
Did I say, all? No! One was lame,
And could not dance the whole of the way;
And in after years, if you would blame
His sadness, he was used to say, –
'It's dull in our town since my playmates left!
I can't forget that I'm bereft
Of all the pleasant sights they see,
Which the Piper also promised me.
For he led us, he said, to a joyous land,
Joining the town and just at hand,
Where waters gushed and fruit-trees grew,
And flowers put forth a fairer hue,
And everything was strange and new;
The sparrows were brighter than peacocks here,
And their dogs outran our fallow deer,
And honey-bees had lost their stings,
And horses were born with eagles' wings:
And just as I became assured,
My lame foot would be speedily cured,
The music stopped and I stood still,
And found myself outside the Hill,
Left alone against my will,
To go now limping as before,
And never hear of that country more!'

ROBERT BROWNING 1812–89

The Landlord's Tale
Paul Revere's Ride

Listen, my children, and you shall hear
Of the midnight ride of Paul Revere,
On the eighteenth of April, in Seventy-five;
Hardly a man is now alive
Who remembers that famous day and year.

He said to his friend, 'If the British march
By land or sea from the town to-night,
Hang a lantern aloft in the belfry-arch
Of the North Church tower as a signal light, –
One, if by land, and two, if by sea;
And I on the opposite shore will be,
Ready to ride and spread the alarm
Through every Middlesex village and farm,
For the country-folk to be up and to arm.'
Then he said, 'Good night!' and with muffled oar
Silently rowed to the Charlestown shore,
Just as the moon rose over the bay,
Where swinging wide at her moorings lay
The *Somerset*, British man-of-war;
A phantom-ship, with each mast and spar
Across the moon like a prison-bar,
And a huge black hulk, that was magnified
By its own reflection in the tide.

Meanwhile, his friend, through alley and street,
Wanders and watches with eager ears,
Till in the silence around him he hears
The muster of men at the barrack-door,
The sound of arms, and the tramp of feet,
And the measured tread of the grenadiers,
Marching down to their boats on the shore.

Then he climbed to the tower of the Old North Church,
Up the wooden stairs, with stealthy tread,
To the belfry-chamber overhead,
And started the pigeons from their perch
On the sombre rafters, that round him made

Masses and moving shapes of shade, –
Up the trembling ladder, steep and tall,
To the highest window in the wall,
Where he paused to listen and look down
A moment on the roofs of the town,
And the moonlight flowing over all.

Beneath, in the churchyard, lay the dead,
In their night-encampment on the hill,
Wrapped in silence so deep and still
That he could hear, like a sentinel's tread,
The watchful night-wind, as it went,
Creeping along from tent to tent,
And seeming to whisper, 'All is well!'
A moment only he feels the spell
Of the place and the hour, and the secret dread
Of the lonely belfry and the dead;
For suddenly all his thoughts are bent
On a shadowy something far away,
Where the river widens to meet the bay, –
A line of black that bends and floats
On the rising tide, like a bridge of boats.

Meanwhile, impatient to mount and ride,
Booted and spurred, with a heavy stride
On the opposite shore walked Paul Revere.
Now he patted his horse's side,
Now gazed at the landscape far and near,
Then, impetuous, stamped the earth,
And turned and tightened his saddle-girth;
But mostly he watched with eager search
The belfry tower of the Old North Church,
As it rose above the graves on the hill,
Lonely and spectral, and sombre and still.
And lo! as he looks, on the belfry's height
A glimmer, and then a gleam of light!
He springs to the saddle, the bridle he turns,
But lingers and gazes, till full on his sight
A second lamp in the belfry burns!
A hurry of hoofs in a village street,
A shape in the moonlight, a bulk in the dark,

And beneath, from the pebbles, in passing, a spark
Struck out by a steed flying fearless and fleet;
That was all! And yet, through the gloom and the light,
The fate of a nation was riding that night;
And the spark struck out by that steed in his flight
Kindled the land into flame with its heat.

He has left the village and mounted the steep,
And beneath him, tranquil and broad and deep,
Is the Mystic, meeting the ocean tides;
And under the alders, that skirt its edge,
Now soft on the sand, now loud on the ledge,
Is heard the tramp of his steed as he rides.

It was twelve by the village clock,
When he crossed the bridge into Medford town.
He heard the crowing of the cock,
And the barking of the farmer's dog,
And felt the damp of the river fog,
That rises after the sun goes down.

It was one by the village clock,
When he galloped into Lexington.
He saw the gilded weathercock
Swim in the moonlight as he passed,
And the meeting-house windows, blank and bare,
Gaze at him with a spectral glare.
As if they already stood aghast
At the bloody work they would look upon.

It was two by the village clock,
When he came to the bridge in Concord town.
He heard the bleating of the flock,
And the twitter of birds among the trees,
And felt the breath of the morning breeze
Blowing over the meadows brown.
And one was safe and asleep in his bed
Who at the bridge would be first to fall,
Who that day would be lying dead,
Pierced by a British musket-ball.

You know the rest. In the books you have read,
How the British Regulars fired and fled, –
How the farmers gave them ball for ball,
From behind each fence and farmyard wall,
Chasing the red-coats down the lane,
Then crossing the field to emerge again
Under the trees at the turn of the road,
And only pausing to fire and load.

So through the night rode Paul Revere;
And so through the night went his cry of alarm
To every Middlesex village and farm, –
A cry of defiance and not of fear,
A voice in the darkness, a knock at the door,
And a word that shall echo for evermore!
For, borne on the night-wind of the Past,
Through all our history, to the last,
In the hour of darkness and peril and need
The people will waken and listen to hear
The hurrying hoof-beats of that steed,
And the midnight message of Paul Revere

HENRY WADSWORTH LONGFELLOW 1807–82

from *The Barefoot Boy*

Oh for boyhood's painless play,
Sleep that wakes in laughing day,
Health that mocks the doctor's rules,
Knowledge never learned of schools,
Of the wild bee's morning chase,
Of the wild-flower's time and place,
Flight of fowl and habitude
Of the tenants of the wood;
How the tortoise bears his shell,
How the woodchuck digs his cell,
And the ground-mole sinks his well;
How the robin feeds her young,
How the oriole's nest is hung;
Where the whitest lilies blow,

Where the freshest berries grow,
Where the ground-nut trails its vine,
Where the wood-grape's clusters shine;
Of the black wasp's cunning way,
Mason of his walls of clay,
And the architectural plans
Of gray hornet artisans!
For, eschewing books and tasks,
Nature answers all he asks;
Hand in hand with her he walks,
Face to face with her he talks,
Part and parcel of her joy, –
Blessings on the barefoot boy!

JOHN GREENLEAF WHITTIER 1807–92

Full Fathom Five

from *The Tempest*, Act I, Scene ii

Full fathom five thy father lies,
    Of his bones are coral made:
Those are pearls that were his eyes,
    Nothing of him that doth fade,
But doth suffer a sea-change
Into something rich, and strange:
Sea-nymphs hourly ring his knell –
    Hark! now I hear them,
      Ding-dong bell.

WILLIAM SHAKESPEARE

Rosa Mystica
REQUIESCAT

Tread lightly, she is near
    Under the snow,
Speak gently, she can hear
    The daisies grow.

All her bright golden hair
    Tarnished with rust,
She that was young and fair
    Fallen to dust.

Lily-like, white as snow,
    She hardly knew
She was a woman, so
    Sweetly she grew.

Coffin-board, heavy stone,
    Lie on her breast,
I vex my heart alone,
    She is at rest.

Peace, Peace, she cannot hear
    Lyre or sonnet,
All my life's buried here,
    Heap earth upon it.
        OSCAR WILDE 1854–1900
(A poem written on the death of his sister.)

A Smuggler's Song

If you wake at midnight, and hear a horse's feet,
Don't go drawing back the blind, or looking in the
    street,
Them that ask no questions isn't told a lie.
Watch the wall, my darling, while the Gentlemen go by!
    Five and twenty ponies,
    Trotting through the dark –
    Brandy for the Parson,
    'Baccy for the Clerk;
    Laces for a lady, letters for a spy,
And watch the wall, my darling, while the Gentlemen go by!

Running round the woodlump if you chance to find
Little barrels, roped and tarred, all full of brandy-wine,
Don't you shout to come and look, nor use 'em for your play.
Put the brishwood back again – and they'll be gone next day!

If you see the stable-door setting open wide;
If you see a tired horse lying down inside;
If your mother mends a coat cut about and tore;
If the lining's wet and warm – don't you ask no more!

If you meet King George's men, dressed in blue and red,
You be careful what you say, and mindful what is said.
If they call you 'pretty maid,' and chuck you 'neath the
      chin,
Don't you tell where no one is, nor yet where no one's
      been!

Knocks and footsteps round the house – whistles after
      dark –
You've no call for running out till the house-dogs bark.
Trusty's here, and *Pincher's* here, and see how dumb they
      lie –
They don't fret to follow when the Gentlemen go by!

If you do as you've been told, 'likely there's a chance,
You'll be give a dainty doll, all the way from France,
With a cap of Valenciennes, and a velvet hood –
A present from the Gentlemen, along o' being good!
            Five and twenty ponies,
            Trotting through the dark –
            Brandy for the Parson,
            'Baccy for the Clerk.
Them that asks no questions isn't told a lie –
Watch the wall, my darling, while the Gentlemen go by!
                              RUDYARD KIPLING 1865–1936

Walking Away

It is eighteen years ago, almost to the day –
A sunny day with the leaves just turning,
The touch-lines new-ruled – since I watched you play
Your first game of football, then, like a satellite
Wrenched from its orbit, go drifting away

Behind a scatter of boys. I can see
You walking away from me towards the school
With the pathos of a half-fledged thing set free
Into the wilderness, the gait of one ·
Who finds no path where the path should be.

That hesitant figure, eddying away
Like a winged seed loosened from its parent stem,
Has something I never quite grasp to convey
About nature's give-and-take – the small, the scorching
Ordeals which fire one's irresolute clay.

I have had worse partings, but none that so
Gnaws at my mind still. Perhaps it is roughly
Saying what God alone could perfectly show –
How selfhood begins with a walking away,
And love is proved in the letting go.

C. DAY LEWIS 1904–72

Tarantella

Do you remember an Inn,
Miranda?
Do you remember an Inn?
And the tedding and the spreading
Of the straw for a bedding,
And the fleas that tease in the High Pyrenees,
And the wine that tasted of the tar?
And the cheers and the jeers of the young muleteers
(Under the vine of the dark verandah)?
Do you remember an Inn, Miranda,
Do you remember an Inn?
And the cheers and the jeers of the young muleteers
Who hadn't got a penny,
And who weren't paying any,
And the hammer at the doors and the Din?
And the Hip! Hop! Hap!
Of the clap

Of the hands to the twirl and the swirl
Of the girl gone chancing,
Glancing,
Dancing,
Backing and advancing,
Snapping of a clapper to the spin
Out and in –
And the Ting, Tong, Tang of the Guitar!
Do you remember an Inn,
Miranda?
Do you remember an Inn?

Never more;
Miranda,
Never more.
Only the high peaks hoar:
And Aragon a torrent at the door.
No sound
In the walls of the Halls where falls
The tread
Of the feet of the dead to the ground
No sound:
But the boom
Of the far Waterfall like Doom.

HILAIRE BELLOC

Macavity: The Mystery Cat

Macavity's a Mystery Cat: he's called the Hidden Paw –
For he's the master criminal who can defy the Law.
He's the bafflement of Scotland Yard, the Flying Squad's despair:
For when they reach the scene of crime – *Macavity's not there!*

Macavity, Macavity, there's no one like Macavity,
He's broken every human law, he breaks the law of gravity.
His powers of levitation would make a fakir stare,
And when you reach the scene of crime – *Macavity's not there!*
You may seek him in the basement, you may look up in the air –
But I tell you once and once again, *Macavity's not there!*

Macavity's a ginger cat, he's very tall and thin;
You would know him if you saw him, for his eyes are sunken in.
His brow is deeply lined with thought, his head is highly domed;
His coat is dusty from neglect, his whiskers are uncombed.
He sways his head from side to side, with movements like a snake;
And when you think he's half asleep, he's always wide awake.

Macavity, Macavity, there's no one like Macavity,
For he's a fiend in feline shape, a monster of depravity.
You may meet him in a by-street, you may see him in the
    square –
But when a crime's discovered, then *Macavity's not there!*

He's outwardly respectable. (They say he cheats at cards.)
And his footprints are not found in any file of Scotland Yard's.
And when the larder's looted, or the jewel-case is rifled,
Or when the milk is missing, or another Peke's been stifled,
Or the greenhouse glass is broken, and the trellis past repair –
Ay, there's the wonder of the thing! *Macavity's not there!*

And when the Foreign Office find a Treaty's gone astray,
Or the Admiralty lose some plans and drawings by the way,
There may be a scrap of paper in the hall or on the stair –
But it's useless to investigate – *Macavity's not there!*
And when the loss has been disclosed, the Secret Service say:
'It *must* have been Macavity!' – but he's a mile away.
You'll be sure to find him resting, or a-licking of his thumbs,
Or engaged in doing complicated long division sums.

Macavity, Macavity, there's no one like Macavity,
There never was a Cat of such deceitfulness and suavity.
He always has an alibi, and one or two to spare:
At whatever time the deed took place – MACAVITY WASN'T
    THERE!
And they say that all the Cats whose wicked deeds are widely
    known
(I might mention Mungojerrie, I might mention Griddlebone)
Are nothing more than agents for the Cat who all the time
Just controls their operations: the Napoleon of Crime!

                                        T. S. ELIOT 1888–1965

Boring

I'm dead bored,
  bored to the bone.
Nobody likes me,
  I'm all alone.
I'll just go crawl
  under a stone.

Hate my family,
  got no friends,
I'll sit here till
  the universe ends
Or I starve to death –
  it all depends.

Then I'll be dead,
  dead and rotten,
Less than a blot when
  it's been well blotten,
Less than a teddy bear
  that's been forgotten.

Then I'll go to Heaven which
  is more than can be said
For certain persons
  when they're dead.
They'll go you-know-
  where instead.

Then they'll be sorry,
  Then they'll be glum,
Sitting on a stove till
  Kingdom Come.
Then they can all go
  kiss my . . .

Hmm, that's a sort of swearing;
   people shouldn't swear.
I won't go to Heaven but
   I don't care,
   I don't care,
   I don't care.
I'll sit here and swear
   so there.

Except that it's boring . . .
            JOHN WHITWORTH

Mothers who Don't Understand

'Why can't you tidy your room?' they cry,
Millions of mothers who fret round the land,
'It's a horrible mess, I've never seen worse,'
– Mothers who don't understand.

They don't understand how cosy it is
To have piles of books on the floor,
And knickers and socks making friends with the vest
Under the bed, where *they* like it best,
And notices pinned to the door.

They don't understand why Kylie and Craig
Are smiling all over the walls,
And toffees and Chewys and dozens of Smarties
Are scattered about reminding of parties,
And jeans are rolled into balls.

They don't understand why a good bed should be
All scrumpled and friendly and gritty,
Why the bears and the paints and the toys are much less
Easy to find if there *isn't* a mess –
To tidy would be a great pity.

They don't understand the point of a desk
Is to balance the muddle quite high:
To leave the drawers open, grow mould on the drink,
Is very much easier, some people think,
Than explaining to mothers just why.

'PLEASE can you tidy your room?' they wail,
Millions of mothers who fret round the land:
'What will you do when there's no one to nag you?'
– Mothers who don't understand.

AUGUSTA SKYE

If—

If you can keep your head when all about you
    Are losing theirs and blaming it on you,
If you can trust yourself when all men doubt you,
    But make allowance for their doubting too;
If you can wait and not be tired by waiting,
    Or being lied about, don't deal in lies,
Or being hated don't give way to hating,
    And yet don't look too good, nor talk too wise:

If you can dream – and not make dreams your master;
    If you can think – and not make thoughts your aim;
If you can meet with Triumph and Disaster
    And treat those two impostors just the same;
If you can bear to hear the truth you've spoken
    Twisted by knaves to make a trap for fools,
Or watch the things you gave your life to, broken,
    And stoop and build 'em up with worn-out tools;

If you can make one heap of all your winnings
    And risk it on one turn of pitch-and-toss,
And lose, and start again at your beginnings
    And never breathe a word about your loss;
If you can force your heart and nerve and sinew
    To serve your turn long after they are gone,
And so hold on when there is nothing in you
    Except the Will which says to them: 'Hold on!'

If you can talk with crowds and keep your virtue,
    Or walk with Kings – nor lose the common touch,
If neither foes nor loving friends can hurt you,
    If all men count with you, but none too much;
If you can fill the unforgiving minute
    With sixty seconds' worth of distance run,
Yours is the Earth and everything that's in it,
    And – which is more – you'll be a Man, my son!

RUDYARD KIPLING

Remember Now Thy Creator

Remember now thy Creator in the days of thy youth,
While the evil days come not,
Nor the years draw nigh, when thou shalt say,
'I have no pleasure in them';
While the sun, or the light,
Or the moon, or the stars, be not darkened,
Nor the clouds return after the rain:
In the day when the keepers of the house shall tremble,
And the strong men shall bow themselves,
And the grinders cease because they are few,
And those that look out of the windows be darkened,
And the doors shall be shut in the streets;
When the sound of the grinding is low,
And he shall rise up at the voice of the bird,
And all the daughters of music shall be brought low;
Also when they shall be afraid of that which is high,
And fears shall be in the way;
And the almond tree shall flourish,
And the grasshopper shall be a burden,
And desire shall fail:
Because man goeth to his long home,
And the mourners go about the streets:
Or ever the silver cord be loosed,
Or the golden bowl be broken,
Or the pitcher be broken at the fountain,
Or the wheel broken at the cistern;

Then shall the dust return to the earth as it was,
And the spirit shall return unto God who gave it.
Vanity of vanities, saith the preacher;
All is vanity.

ECCLESIASTES, CHAPTER 12, VERSES 1–8

This Above All

from *Hamlet*, Act I, Scene iii

And these few precepts in thy memory
See thou character. Give thy thoughts no tongue,
Nor any unproportioned thought his act.
Be thou familiar, but by no means vulgar.
Those friends thou hast, and their adoption tried,
Grapple them to thy soul with hoops of steel,
But do not dull thy palm with entertainment
Of each new-hatched unfledged comrade. Beware
Of entrance to a quarrel; but being in,
Bear't, that the opposed may beware of thee.
Give every man thy ear, but few thy voice:
Take each man's censure, but reserve thy judgement.
Costly thy habit as thy purse can buy,
But not expressed in fancy; rich, not gaudy:
For the apparel oft proclaims the man;
And they in France of the best rank and station
Are of a most select and generous chief in that.
Neither a borrower nor a lender be:
For loan oft loses both itself and friend,
And borrowing dulls the edge of husbandry.
This above all: to thine own self be true,
And it must follow, as the night the day,
Thou canst not then be false to any man.

WILLIAM SHAKESPEARE

Don't Quite Know

Why do I feel excited
When chance decides for us
We are to sit together
In an ordinary school bus?
    Don't quite know.

You pick me for your team (or
More likely I'm the one
Left over for your picking) –
Why is that such great fun?
    Don't quite know.

In the game or on the journey
My bare knee touches yours.
If only for a moment
I see strange opening doors.
    Why that is so
    I don't quite know.

                    ROY FULLER 1912–

LOVER

And then the lover,
Sighing like furnace, with a woeful ballad
Made to his mistress' eyebrow.

The Arrow

I thought of your beauty, and this arrow,
Made out of a wild thought, is in my marrow.
There's no man may look upon her, no man,
As when newly grown to be a woman,
Tall and noble but with face and bosom
Delicate in colour as apple blossom.
This beauty's kinder, yet for a reason
I could weep that the old is out of season.

W. B. YEATS 1865–1939

(Written after he had met Maud Gonne for the first time.)

The Arrow and the Song

I shot an arrow into the air,
It fell to earth, I knew not where;
For, so swiftly it flew, the sight
Could not follow it in its flight.

I breathed a song into the air,
It fell to earth, I knew not where;
For who has sight so keen and strong,
That it can follow the flight of song?

Long, long afterward, in an oak
I found the arrow, still unbroke;
And the song, from beginning to end,
I found again in the heart of a friend.

HENRY WADSWORTH LONGFELLOW

The First Day

I wish I could remember the first day,
First hour, first moment of your meeting me;
If bright or dim the season, it might be
Summer or winter for aught I can say.
So unrecorded did it slip away,

So blind was I to see and to foresee,
So dull to mark the budding of my tree
That would not blossom yet for many a May.

If only I could recollect it! Such
A day of days! I let it come and go
As traceless as a thaw of bygone snow.
It seemed to mean so little, meant so much!
If only now I could recall that touch,
First touch of hand in hand! – Did one but know!

CHRISTINA ROSSETTI 1830–94

So Let Us Love

So let us love, dear Love, like as we ought,
Love is the lesson that the Lord us taught.

EDMUND SPENSER 1552–99

from *The Song of Torrismond*

How many times do I love thee, dear?
Tell me how many thoughts there be
In the atmosphere
Of a new-fall'n year,
Whose white and sable hours appear
The latest flake of Eternity:
So many times do I love thee, dear.

How many times do I love again?
Tell me how many beads there are
In a silver chain
Of evening rain,
Unravell'd from the tumbling main,
And threading the eye of a yellow star.
So many times I love thee again.

THOMAS LOVELL BEDDOES 1803–49

They Who are Near to Me

They who are near to me do not know that
      you are nearer to me than they are.
They who speak to me do not know that my heart
      is full with your unspoken words.
They who crowd in my path do not know that
      I am walking alone with you.
They who love me do not know that their love
      brings you to my heart.

RABINDRANATH TAGORE 1861–1941

My Delight and Thy Delight

My delight and thy delight
Walking, like two angels white,
In the gardens of the night:

My desire and thy desire
Twining to a tongue of fire,
Leaping live, and laughing higher:

Thro' the everlasting strife
In the mystery of life.

Love, from whom the world begun,
Hath the secret of the sun.

Love can tell, and love alone,
Whence the million stars were strewn,
Why each atom knows its own,
How, in spite of woe and death,
Gay is life, and sweet is breath:

This he taught us, this we knew,
Happy in his science true,
Hand in hand as we stood
'Neath the shadows of the wood,

Heart to heart as we lay
In the dawning of the day.
ROBERT BRIDGES 1844–1930

Sonnet 43

from *Sonnets from the Portuguese*

How do I love thee? Let me count the ways.
I love thee to the depth and breadth and height
My soul can reach, when feeling out of sight
For the ends of Being and ideal Grace.
I love thee to the level of every day's
Most quiet need, by sun and candle-light.
I love thee freely, as men strive for Right;
I love thee purely, as they turn from Praise.
I love thee with the passion put to use
In my old griefs, and with my childhood's faith.
I love thee with a love I seemed to lose
With my lost saints, – I love thee with the breath,
Smiles, tears, of all my life! – and, if God choose,
I shall but love thee better after death.
ELIZABETH BARRETT BROWNING 1806–61

One Day I Wrote

One day I wrote her name upon the strand,
  But came the waves and washèd it away:
Again I wrote it with a second hand,
  But came the tide, and made my pains his prey.
'Vain man,' said she, 'thou do'st in vain assay,
  A mortal thing so to immortalize,
For I myself shall like to this decay,
  And eek my name be wipèd out likewise.'
'Not so,' quoth I, 'let baser things devise
  To die in dust, but you shall live by fame:
My verse your virtues rare shall eternize,

And in the heavens write your glorious name,
　　Where, whenas death shall all the world subdue,
　　Our love shall live, and later life renew.'

EDMUND SPENSER

The Virginity

Try as he will, no man breaks wholly loose
　　From his first love, no matter who she be.
Oh, was there ever sailor free to choose,
　　That didn't settle somewhere near the sea?

Myself, it don't excite me nor amuse
　　To watch a pack o' shipping on the sea;
But I can understand my neighbour's views
　　From certain things which have occurred to me.

Men must keep touch with things they used to use
　　To earn their living, even when they are free;
And so come back upon the least excuse –
　　Same as the sailor settled near the sea.

He knows he's never going on no cruise –
　　He knows he's done and finished with the sea;
And yet he likes to feel she's there to use –
　　If he should ask her – as she used to be.

Even though she cost him all he had to lose,
　　Even though she made him sick to hear or see,
Still, what she left of him will mostly choose
　　Her skirts to sit by. How comes such to be?

Parsons in pulpits, tax-payers in pews,
　　Kings on your thrones, you know as well as me,
We've only one virginity to lose,
　　And where we lost it there our hearts will be!

RUDYARD KIPLING

The Longest Journey

from *Epipsychidion*

I never was attached to that great sect,
Whose doctrine is, that each one should select
Out of the crowd a mistress or a friend,
And all the rest, though fair and wise, commend
To cold oblivion, though it is in the code
Of modern morals, and the beaten road
Which those poor slaves with weary footsteps tread,
Who travel to their home among the dead
By the broad highway of the world, and so
With one chained friend, perhaps a jealous foe,
The dreariest and the longest journey go.

True Love in this differs from gold and clay,
That to divide is not to take away.
Love is like understanding, that grows bright,
Gazing on many truths; 'tis like thy light,
Imagination! which from earth and sky,
And from the depths of human fantasy,
As from a thousand prisms and mirrors, fills
The Universe with glorious beams, and kills
Error, the worm, with many a sun-like arrow
Of its reverberated lightning. Narrow
The heart that loves, the brain that contemplates,
The life that wears, the spirit that creates
One object, and one form, and builds thereby
A sepulchre for its eternity.

Mind from its object differs most in this:
Evil from good; misery from happiness;
The baser from the nobler; the impure
And frail, from what is clear and must endure.
If you divide suffering and dross, you may
Diminish till it is consumed away;
If you divide pleasure and love and thought,
Each part exceeds the whole; and we know not
How much, while any yet remains unshared,
Of pleasure may be gained, of sorrow spared:
This truth is that deep well, whence sages draw

The unenvied light of hope; the eternal law
By which those live, to whom this world of life
Is as a garden ravaged and whose strife
Tills for the promise of a later birth
The wilderness of this Elysian earth.

PERCY BYSSHE SHELLEY 1792–1822

To Phyllis

Phyllis! why should we delay
Pleasures shorter than the day?
Could we (which we never can!)
Stretch our lives beyond their span,
Beauty like a shadow flies,
And our youth before us dies.
Or, would youth and beauty stay,
Love hath wings, and will away.
Love hath swifter wings than Time:
Change in love to Heaven does climb.
Gods, that never change their state,
Vary oft their love and hate.

Phyllis! to this truth we owe
All the love betwixt us two:
Let not you and I inquire
What has been our past desire;
On what shepherd you have smiled,
Or what nymphs I have beguiled.
Leave it to the planets, too,
What we shall hereafter do.
For the joys we now may prove,
Take advice of present love.

EDMUND WALLER 1606–87

I Loved You Wednesday

And why you come complaining
   Is more than I can see.
I loved you Wednesday – yes – but what
   Is that to me?
EDNA ST VINCENT MILLAY 1892–1950

Sonnet 138

When my love swears that she is made of truth,
I do believe her, though I know she lies,
That she might think me some untutored youth,
Unlearnèd in the world's false subtleties.
Thus vainly thinking that she thinks me young,
Although she knows my days are past the best,
Simply I credit her false-speaking tongue:
On both sides thus is simple truth suppressed.
But wherefore says she not she is unjust?
And wherefore say not I that I am old?
O, love's best habit is in seeming trust,
And age in love loves not to have years told.
   Therefore I lie with her and she with me,
   And in our faults by lies we flattered be.

WILLIAM SHAKESPEARE

Lullaby

Lay your sleeping head, my love,
Human on my faithless arm;
Time and fevers burn away
Individual beauty from
Thoughtful children, and the grave
Proves the child ephemeral:
But in my arms till break of day
Let the living creature lie,
Mortal, guilty, but to me
The entirely beautiful.

Soul and body have no bounds:
To lovers as they lie upon
Her tolerant enchanted slope
In their ordinary swoon,
Grave the vision Venus sends
Of supernatural sympathy,
Universal love and hope;
While an abstract insight wakes
Among the glaciers and the rocks
The hermit's carnal ecstasy.

Certainty, fidelity
On the stroke of midnight pass
Like vibrations of a bell
And fashionable madmen raise
Their pedantic boring cry:
Every farthing of the cost,
All the dreaded cards foretell,
Shall be paid, but from this night
Not a whisper, not a thought,
Not a kiss nor look be lost.

Beauty, midnight, vision dies:
Let the winds of dawn that blow
Softly round your dreaming head
Such a day of welcome show
Eye and knocking heart may bless,
Find our mortal world enough:
Noons of dryness find you fed
By the involuntary powers,
Nights of insult let you pass
Watched by every human love.

W. H. AUDEN 1907–73

87

Your Face

Your face	Your tongue	Your wit
So fair	So sweet	So sharp
First bent	Then drew	So hit
Mine eye	Mine ear	My heart
Mine eye	Mine ear	My heart
To like	To learn	To love
Your face	Your tongue	Your wit
Doth tend	Doth teach	Doth move

ANON.

(Form of verse popular in the 17th century. It can be read in almost any direction.)

Non Sum Qualis Eram Bonae Sub Regno Cynarae

Last night, ah, yesternight, betwixt her lips and mine
There fell thy shadow, Cynara! thy breath was shed
Upon my soul between the kisses and the wine;
And I was desolate and sick of an old passion,
    Yea, I was desolate and bowed my head:
I have been faithful to thee, Cynara! in my fashion.

All night upon mine heart I felt her warm heart beat,
Night-long within mine arms in love and sleep she lay;
Surely the kisses of her bought red mouth were sweet;
But I was desolate and sick of an old passion,
    When I awoke and found the dawn was gray:
I have been faithful to thee, Cynara! in my fashion.

I have forgot much, Cynara! gone with the wind,
Flung roses, roses riotously with the throng,
Dancing, to put thy pale, lost lilies out of mind;
But I was desolate and sick of an old passion,
    Yea, all the time, because the dance was long:
I have been faithful to thee, Cynara! in my fashion.

I cried for madder music and for stronger wine,
But when the feast is finished and the lamps expire,
Then falls thy shadow, Cynara! the night is thine;
And I am desolate and sick of an old passion,
    Yea hungry for the lips of my desire:
I have been faithful to thee, Cynara! in my fashion.

ERNEST DOWSON 1867–1900

Lovey-Dovey

The dove is a symbol of love pure and true;
But say! Have you heard the things they do?
Coo!

ANON.

We Have Known Treasure

We have known treasure fairer than a dream
Upon the hills of youth. And it shall stay
Jewelled in the distance, untarnished and supreme,
For the dark tentacles of life's decay shall never shadow it
Nor over throw its years like hours grown golden in the sun,
Its years lived full in the gathered light,
An amethyst across the sea of night.

For dawn and dusk we knew and caught our breath
With the exquisite maginings of Spring,
Lived deep, talked lightly of this stranger death,
And love grown wistful with remembering
A half familiar tune we used to sing, these were ours,
Love's touch upon our hands, music and flowers
Though in the faithless years they have no part
These are the endless things, the real of heart.

ANON.

Echo

Come to me in the silence of the night;
   Come in the sparkling silence of a dream;
Come with soft rounded cheeks and eyes as bright
    As sunlight on a stream;
      Come back in tears,
O memory, hope, love of finished years.

O dream how sweet, too sweet, too bitter sweet,
   Whose wakening should have been in Paradise,
Where souls brimfull of love abide and meet;
    Where thirsting longing eyes
      Watch the slow door
That opening, letting in, lets out no more.

Yet come to me in dreams, that I may live
   My very life again though cold in death:
Come back to me in dreams, that I may give
    Pulse for pulse, breath for breath:
      Speak low, lean low,
As long ago, my love, how long ago.

CHRISTINA ROSSETTI

The Bargain

My true love hath my heart, and I have his,
   By just exchange, one for the other given.

I hold his dear, and mine he cannot miss,
    There never was a better bargain driven.
His heart in me keeps me and him in one,
    My heart in him his thoughts and senses
    guides;
He loves my heart, for once it was his own,
    I cherish his, because in me it bides.
His heart his wound received from my sight,
    My heart was wounded with his wounded
    heart;
For as from me on him his hurt did light,
    So still methought in me his hurt did smart.
        Both equal hurt, in this change sought our
        bliss:
        My true love hath my heart and I have his.

SIR PHILIP SIDNEY 1554–86

Sonnet 116

Let me not to the marriage of true minds
Admit impediments; love is not love
Which alters when it alteration finds,
Or bends with the remover to remove.
O, no, it is an ever-fixèd mark
That looks on tempests and is never shaken;
It is the star to every wand'ring bark,
Whose worth's unknown, although his height be
    taken.
Love's not Time's fool, though rosy lips and
    cheeks,
Within his bending sickle's compass come;
Love alters not with his brief hours and weeks,
But bears it out even to the edge of doom.
    If this be error and upon me proved,
    I never writ, nor no man ever loved.

WILLIAM SHAKESPEARE

We Two Lay Sunk

We two lay sunk in the dusk of dreams;
the time of awakening has come
waiting for the last word from you.
Turn your face to me
and with a tear dimmed glance
make the sorrow of parting
ever beautiful.

The morning will appear with its early star
on the far distant sky of loneliness.
The pain of this farewell night has been captured in my vina
    strings,
the lost glory of my love will remain woven in my visions.
Open with your hands the door towards final separation.

RABINDRANATH TAGORE

To —

One word is too often profaned
    For me to profane it,
One feeling too falsely disdained
    For thee to disdain it;
One hope is too like despair
    For prudence to smother,
And pity from thee more dear
    Than that from another.

I can give not what men call love,
    But wilt thou accept not
The worship the heart lifts above
    And the Heavens reject not, —
The desire of the moth for the star,
    Of the night for the morrow,
The devotion to something afar
    From the sphere of our sorrow?

PERCY BYSSHE SHELLEY

Delusions I Did Cherish

Delusions I did cherish
but now I am rid of them.
Tracing the track of false hopes
I trod upon thorns
to know that they are not flowers.

I shall never trifle with love,
never play with heart.
I shall find my refuge in you
on the shore of the troubled sea.

RABINDRANATH TAGORE

Return

Return often and take me,
beloved sensation, return and take me –
when the memory of the body awakens,
and old desire again runs through the blood;
when the lips and the skin remember,
and the hands feel as if they touch again.

Return often and take me at night,
when the lips and the skin remember . . .

C. P. CAVAFY 1863–1933
(Translated by Rae Dalven.)

Lust

How should I know? The enormous wheels of will
    Drove me cold-eyed on tired and sleepless feet.
Night was void arms and you a phantom still,
    And day your far light swaying down the street.
As never fool for love, I starved for you;
    My throat was dry and my eyes hot to see.
Your mouth so lying was most heaven in view,

And your remembered smell most agony.
Love wakens love! I felt your hot wrist shiver,
And suddenly the mad victory I planned
    Flashed real, in your burning bending head. . . .
My conqueror's blood was cool as a deep river
    In shadow; and my heart beneath your hand
    Quieter than a dead man on a bed.

RUPERT BROOKE 1887–1915

Renouncement

I must not think of thee; and, tired yet strong,
I shun the thought that lurks in all delight –
    The thought of thee – and in the blue heaven's height,
And in the sweetest passage of a song.
Oh, just beyond the fairest thoughts that throng
    This breast, the thought of thee waits hidden yet bright;
But it must never, never come in sight;
I must stop short of thee the whole day long.

But when sleep comes to close each difficult day,
    When night gives pause to the long watch I keep,
And all my bonds, I needs must loose apart,
Must doff my will as raiment laid away, –
    With the first dream that comes with the first sleep
I run, I run, I am gathered to thy heart.

ALICE MEYNELL 1847–1922

Sonnet 18

Shall I compare thee to a summer's day?
Thou art more lovely and more temperate.
Rough winds do shake the darling buds of May,
And summer's lease hath all too short a date.
Sometime too hot the eye of heaven shines,
And often is his gold complexion dimmed;
And every fair from fair sometime declines,

By chance, or nature's changing course,
    untrimmed;
But thy eternal summer shall not fade,
Nor lose possession of that fair thou ow'st,
Nor shall Death brag thou wand'rest in his shade,
When in eternal lines to time thou grow'st.
  So long as men can breathe or eyes can see,
  So long lives this, and this gives life to thee.

WILLIAM SHAKESPEARE

Never Give All the Heart

Never give all the heart, for love
Will hardly seem worth thinking of
To passionate women if it seem
Certain, and they never dream
That it fades out from kiss to kiss;
For everything that's lovely is
But a brief, dreamy, kind delight.
O never give the heart outright,

For they, for all smooth lips can say,
Have given their hearts up to the play.
And who could play it well enough
If deaf and dumb and blind with love?
He that made this knows all the cost,
For he gave all his heart and lost.

W. B. YEATS

When I Was One-and-Twenty

When I was one-and-twenty
   I heard a wise man say,
'Give crowns and pounds and guineas
   But not your heart away;
Give pearls away and rubies
   But keep your fancy free.'

95

But I was one-and-twenty,
    No use to talk to me.

When I was one-and-twenty
    I heard him say again,
'The heart out of the bosom
    Was never given in vain;
'Tis paid with sighs a plenty
    And sold for endless rue.'
And I am two-and-twenty,
    And oh, 'tis true, 'tis true.
A. E. HOUSMAN 1859–1936

Another Unfortunate Choice

I think I am in love with A. E. Housman,
Which puts me in a worse-than-usual fix.
No woman ever stood a chance with Housman
And he's been dead since 1936.
WENDY COPE 1946–

Let's Do It, Let's Fall In Love

    When the little Bluebird,
    Who has never said a word,
    Starts to sing, 'Spring, spring';
    When the little Bluebell,
    At the bottom of the dell,
    Starts to ring: 'Ding, ding';
    When the little blue clerk,

Sitting sadly in the park,
Starts a tune to the moon up above,
It is nature, that's all,
Simply telling us to fall in love.

And that's why Chinks do it, Japs do it,
Up in Lapland, little Laps do it,
    Let's do it, let's fall in love.
In Spain the best upper sets do it,
Lithuanians and Letts do it,

The Dutch in old Amsterdam do it,
    Not to mention the Finns,
Folks in Siam do it —
    Think of Siamese twins.
Some Argentines, without means, do it,
People say, in Boston, even beans do it,

The nightingales, in the dark, do it,
Larks, karazy for a lark, do it,
    Let's do it, let's fall in love.
Canaries caged in the house do it,
When they're out of season, grouse do it,

The most sedate barnyard fowls do it,
    When a chantecleer cries;
High-brow'd old owls do it —
    They're supposed to be wise.
Penguins in flocks on the rocks do it,
Even little cuckoos in the clocks do it,

Romantic sponges, they say, do it,
Oysters down in Oyster Bay do it,
    Let's do it, let's fall in love.
Cold Cape Cod clams, 'gainst their wish, do it,
Even lazy jellyfish do it,

The most refined schools of cod do it,
    Though it shocks them, I fear,
Sturgeons, thank God, do it —
    Have some caviare, dear!

In shallow shoals Dover soles do it,
Goldfish in the privacy of bowls do it,

The dragonflies in their eaves do it,
Sentimental-scented leaves do it,
    Let's do it, let's fall in love,
    Mosquitoes (Heaven forbid) do it,
    So does every katydid do it,

The most refined lady bugs do it,
    When a gentleman calls,
Moths in your rugs do it –
    What's the use of moth-balls?
Locusts in trees do it, bees do it,
Even super-educated fleas do it,

The chimpanzees in the Zoos do it,
Some courageous kangaroos do it,
    Let's do it, let's fall in love.
And, sure, giraffes from the sky do it,
Heavens! Hippopotami do it!

Old sloths who hang down from twigs do it
    Though the effort is great.
Sweet guinea-pigs do it –
    Buy a couple and wait!
We know that bears in their pits do it,
Even Pekineses at the Ritz do it,
    Let's do it, let's fall in love!

                    COLE PORTER 1893–1964

Annus Mirabilis

Sexual intercourse began
In nineteen sixty-three
(Which was rather late for me) –
Between the end of the *Chatterley* ban
And the Beatles' first LP.

Up till then there'd only been
A sort of bargaining,
A wrangle for a ring,
A shame that started at sixteen
And spread to everything.

Then all at once the quarrel sank:
Everyone felt the same,
And every life became
A brilliant breaking of the bank,
A quite unlosable game.

So life was never better than
In nineteen sixty-three
(Though just too late for me) –
Between the end of the *Chatterley* ban
And the Beatles' first LP.

PHILIP LARKIN 1922–85

La Figlia Che Piange
O quam te memorem virgo . . .

Stand on the highest pavement of the stair –
Lean on a garden urn –
Weave, weave the sunlight in your hair –
Clasp your flowers to you with a pained surprise –
Fling them to the ground and turn
With a fugitive resentment in your eyes:
But weave, weave the sunlight in your hair.

So I would have had him leave,
So I would have had her stand and grieve,
So he would have left
As the soul leaves the body torn and bruised,
As the mind deserts the body it has used.
I should find
Some way incomparably light and deft,

Some way we both should understand,
Simple and faithless as a smile and shake of the hand.

She turned away, but with the autumn weather
Compelled my imagination many days,
Many days and many hours:
Her hair over her arms and her arms full of flowers.
And I wonder how they should have been together!
I should have lost a gesture and a pose.
Sometimes these cogitations still amaze
The troubled midnight and the moon's repose.

T. S. ELIOT

A Thunderstorm In Town

She wore a new 'terra-cotta' dress,
And we stayed, because of the pelting storm,
Within the hansom's dry recess,
Though the horse had stopped; yea, motionless
    We sat on, snug and warm.

Then the downpour ceased, to my sharp sad pain
And the glass that had screened our forms before
Flew up, and out she sprang to her door:
I should have kissed her if the rain
    Had lasted a minute more.

THOMAS HARDY 1840–1928

A Touch of Impatience

I was patient at the start,
full of diplomatic art;
you were young: I played my part
    with delicate good taste;
asking nothing but your heart
    I kept our courtship chaste.

Now you've reached a riper stage;
now the fire begins to rage;
now my virgin's come of age,
    with breasts new-grown and waiting –
wasted if we don't engage
    in something less frustrating.

Since we've coupled mind with mind
let's be physically entwined:
wrestling's a delight, you'll find,
    if you'll relax your guard.
Sweetest flower of all, be kind:
    let's play with no holds barred!

Grapes are luscious things to squeeze;
sucking honey's nice for bees.
What's my meaning? Darling, please
    accept a full translation:
not in language; what you'll see's
    a graphic demonstration.

FLEUR ADCOCK 1934–

Upon the Nipples of Julia's Breast

Have ye beheld (with much delight)
A red rose peeping through a white?
Or else a cherry (double grac'd)
Within a lily? Centre plac'd?
Or ever mark'd the pretty beam,
A strawberry shows, half drown'd in cream?
Or seen rich rubies blushing through
A pure smooth pearl, and orient too?
So like to this, nay all the rest,
Is each neat niplet of her breast.

ROBERT HERRICK 1591–1674

Busts and Bosoms Have I Known

Busts and bosoms have I known
Of various shapes and sizes
From grievous disappointments
To jubilant surprises.

ANON.

To His Coy Mistress

Had we but world enough, and time,
This coyness, lady, were no crime.
We would sit down, and think which way
To walk, and pass our long love's day.
Thou by the Indian Ganges' side
Should'st rubies find: I by the tide
Of Humber would complain. I would
Love you ten years before the Flood,
And you should, if you please, refuse
Till the conversion of the Jews.
My vegetable love should grow
Vaster than empires, and more slow.
An hundred years should go to praise
Thine eyes, and on thy forehead gaze:
Two hundred to adore each breast;
But thirty thousand to the rest;
An age at least to every part,
And the last age should show your heart.
For, lady, you deserve this state,
Nor would I love at lower rate.
    But at my back I always hear
Time's wingèd chariot hurrying near:
And yonder all before us lie
Deserts of vast eternity.
Thy beauty shall no more be found;
Nor, in thy marble vault, shall sound
My echoing song: then worms shall try
That long-preserved virginity,

And your quaint honour turn to dust,
And into ashes all my lust.
The grave's a fine and private place,
But none, I think, do there embrace.
   Now, therefore while the youthful hue
Sits on thy skin like morning dew,
And while thy willing soul transpires
At every pore with instant fires,
Now let us sport us while we may;
And now, like amorous birds of prey,
Rather at once our Time devour,
Than languish in his slow-chapt power.
Let us roll all our strength and all
Our sweetness up into one ball,
And tear our pleasures with rough strife
Thorough the iron gates of life.
Thus, though we cannot make our Sun
Stand still, yet we will make him run.

ANDREW MARVELL 1621–78

Invocation

Rarely, rarely, comest thou,
   Spirit of Delight!
Wherefore hast thou left me now
   Many a day and night?
Many a weary night and day
'Tis since thou art fled away.

How shall ever one like me
   Win thee back again?
With the joyous and the free
   Thou wilt scoff at pain.
Spirit false! thou hast forgot
All but those who need thee not.

As a lizard with the shade
   Of a trembling leaf,
Thou with sorrow art dismay'd;

Even the sighs of grief
Reproach thee, that thou art not near,
And reproach thou wilt not hear.

Let me set my mournful ditty
    To a merry measure –
Thou wilt never come for pity,
    Thou wilt come for pleasure; –
Pity then will cut away
Those cruel wings, and thou wilt stay.

I love all that thou lovest,
    Spirit of Delight!
The fresh Earth in new leaves drest
    And the starry night;
Autumn evening, and the morn
When the golden mists are born.

I love snow and all the forms
    Of the radiant frost;
I love waves, and winds, and storms,
    Everything almost
Which is Nature's, and may be
Untainted by man's misery.

I love tranquil solitude,
    And such society
As is quiet, wise, and good.
    Between thee and me
What diff'rence? but thou dost possess
The things I seek, not love them less.

I love Love – though he has wings,
And like light can flee,
But above all other things,
    Spirit, I love thee –
Thou art love and life! O come!
Make once more my heart thy home!

PERCY BYSSHE SHELLEY

My Love Is Like to Ice

My love is like to ice, and I to fire:
How comes it then that this her cold so great
Is not dissolved through my so hot desire,
But harder grows the more I her entreat?
Or how comes it that my exceeding heat
Is not allayed by her heart-frozen cold,
But that I burn much more in boiling sweat,
And feel my flames augmented manifold?
What more miraculous thing may be told,
That fire, which all things melts, should harden ice,
And ice, which is congeal'd with senseless cold,
Should kindle fire by wonderful device?
Such is the power of love in gentle mind,
That it can alter all the course of kind.

EDMUND SPENSER

Sonnet 129

Th' expense of Spirit in a waste of shame
Is lust in action; and till action, lust
Is perjured, murderous, bloody, full of blame,
Savage, extreme, rude, cruel, not to trust;
Enjoy'd no sooner but despisèd straight;
Past reason hunted; and, no sooner had,
Past reason hated, as a swallow'd bait
On purpose laid to make the taker mad:
Mad in pursuit, and in possession so;
Had, having, and in quest to have, extreme;
A bliss in proof, and proved, a very woe;
Before, a joy proposed; behind, a dream.
  All this the world well knows; yet none knows well
  To shun the heaven that leads men to this hell.

WILLIAM SHAKESPEARE

You Suck my Soul

You suck my soul through a straw.
I know it tastes bitter and intoxicating.
But I will not beg you to stop the torture.
For many weeks this has been my peaceful chamber.

Say when you're through. It is not sad
that my soul is not in this world.
I'll take the short road
to see the children playing.

The gooseberry bushes are in flower.
Beyond the fence they're carrying bricks.
Who are you: my brother or my lover?
I don't remember and do not need to.

How bright it is here, but homeless
the tired body rests.
The passers-by seem to be thinking:
she must be a recent widow.

ANNA AKHMATOVA 1889–1966
(Translated by Richard McKane.)

The Ballad of the Oysterman

It was a tall young oysterman lived by the river-side,
His shop was just upon the bank, his boat was on the tide;
The daughter of a fisherman, that was so straight and slim,
Lived over on the other bank, right opposite him.

It was the pensive oysterman that saw a lovely maid
Upon a moonlit evening, a-sitting in the shade;
He saw her wave her handkerchief, as much as if to say,
'I'm wide awake, you oysterman, and all the folks away.'

Then up arose the oysterman, and to himself said he,
'I guess I'll leave the skiff at home, for fear that folks should
      see;

106

I read it in the story-book, that, for to kiss his dear,
Leander swam the Hellespont, – and I will swim this here.'

And he has leaped into the waves, and crossed the shining
     stream,
And he has clambered up the bank, all in the moonlight
     gleam;
Oh, there were kisses sweet as dew, and words as soft as
     rain, –
But they have heard her father's step, and in he leaps again!

Out spoke the ancient fisherman: 'Oh, what was that, my
     daughter?'
''Twas nothing but a pebble, sir, I threw into the water.'
'And what is that, pray tell me, love, that paddles off so
     fast?'
'It's nothing but a porpoise, sir, that's been a-swimming
     past.'

Out spoke the ancient fisherman: 'Now, bring me my
     harpoon!
I'll get into my fishing-boat, and fix the fellow soon.'
Down fell the pretty innocent, as falls a snow-white lamb;
Her hair drooped round her pallid cheeks, like seaweed on
     a clam.

Alas for those two loving ones! She waked not from her
     swound,
And he was taken with a cramp, and in the waves was
     drowned;
But fate has metamorphosed them, in pity of their woe,
And now they keep an oyster-shop for mermaids down
     below.

OLIVER WENDELL HOLMES 1809–94

Gray

Looking at a half-gray opal
I remembered two beautiful gray eyes
I had seen; it must have been twenty years ago . . .

For a month we loved each other.
Then he went away, I believe to Smyrna,
to work there, and we never saw each other after that.

The gray eyes — if he is alive — must have grown ugly;
the handsome face must have spoiled.

Dear Memory, preserve them as they used to be.
And, Memory, bring back to me tonight all that you can,
of this love of mine, all that you can.

C. P. CAVAFY
(Translated by Rae Dalven.)

Counting the Beats

You, love, and I,
(He whispers) you and I,
And if no more than only you and I
What care you or I?

Counting the beats,
Counting the slow heart beats,
The bleeding to death of time in slow heart beats,
Wakeful they lie.

Cloudless day,
Night, and a cloudless day,
Yet the huge storm will burst upon their heads one
    day
From a bitter sky.

Where shall we be,
(She whispers) where shall we be,
When death strikes home, O when then shall we be
Who were you and I?

Not there but here,
(He whispers) only here,
As we are, here, together, now and here,
Always you and I.

Counting the beats,
Counting the slow heart beats,
The bleeding to death of time in slow heart beats,
Wakeful they lie.

ROBERT GRAVES 1895–1985

Lochinvar

from *Marmion*

O, young Lochinvar is come out of the west,
Through all the wide Border his steed was the best;
And save his good broadsword he weapons had none,
He rode all unarm'd, and he rode all alone.
So faithful in love, and so dauntless in war,
There never was knight like the young Lochinvar.

He staid not for brake, and he stopp'd not for stone,
He swam the Eske river where ford there was none;
But ere he alighted at Netherby gate,
The bride had consented, the gallant came late:
For a laggard in love, and a dastard in war,
Was to wed the fair Ellen of brave Lochinvar.

So boldly he enter'd the Netherby Hall,
Among bride's-men, and kinsmen, and brothers, and all:
Then spoke the bride's father, his hand on his sword,
(For the poor craven bridegroom said never a word,)
'O come ye in peace here, or come ye in war,
Or to dance at our bridal, young Lord Lochinvar?' –

'I long woo'd your daughter, my suit you denied; –
Love swells like the Solway, but ebbs like its tide –
And now am I come, with this lost love of mine,

To lead but one measure, drink one cup of wine.
There are maidens in Scotland more lovely by far,
That would gladly be bride to the young Lochinvar.'

The bride kiss'd the goblet: the knight took it up,
He quaff'd off the wine, and he threw down the cup.
She look'd down to blush, and she look'd up to sigh,
With a smile on her lips, and a tear in her eye.
He took her soft hand, ere her mother could bar, –
'Now tread we a measure!' said young Lochinvar.

SIR WALTER SCOTT 1771–1832

My Love is Like a Red, Red Rose

O, my luve's like a red, red rose,
    That's newly sprung in June:
O, my luve's like the melodie
    That's sweetly play'd in tune.

As fair art thou, my bonnie lass,
    So deep in luve am I;
And I will luve thee still, my dear,
    Till a' the seas gang dry.

Till a' the seas gang dry, my dear,
    And the rocks melt wi' the sun;
I will luve thee still, my dear,
    While the sands of life shall run.

And fare thee weel, my only luve!
    And fare thee weel a while!
And I will come again, my luve,
    Tho' it were ten thousand mile.

ROBERT BURNS 1759–96

The Clod and the Pebble

'Love seeketh not Itself to please,
Nor for Itself hath any care,
But for another gives its ease,
And builds a Heaven in Hell's despair.'

So sung a little Clod of Clay
Trodden with the cattle's feet,
But a Pebble of the brook
Warbled out these metres meet:

'Love seeketh only Self to please,
To bind another to Its delight,
Joys in another's loss of ease,
And builds a Hell in Heaven's despite.'

WILLIAM BLAKE 1757–1827

Poem

Love is for some a heavy cross,
But in you there is no contortion,
The key to life's enigma is
The charm that is your secret portion.

In spring rustling is heard again,
And news and truths that ripple running.
Your race has sprung from such a strain:
Like air, your mind is free from cunning.

Easy to wake, again to see,
To shake out the heart's wordy litter,
Nor henceforth choked in life to be, –
No need for still in such a matter.

BORIS PASTERNAK 1890–1960
(Translated by C. M. Bowra.)

111

Where Are You, My Prince?

Where are you, my prince?
On what plank bed?
(No, I won't cry: I promised, after all!)
My eyes are drier than a fire.
This is only the beginning.
How are you coping?
(No, I know:
Better than all the others. Oh, to take your hand!)
Winter's draughty curtain
Drives the winds round in a circle
To the point of despair,
The air was too exhausted
To leave its rags on the grille.
Are you falling asleep?
It's late.
I'll dream of you tonight.

IRINA RATUSHINSKAYA 1954–

If I Could Tell You

Time will say nothing but I told you so,
Time only knows the price we have to pay;
If I could tell you I would let you know.

If we should weep when clowns put on their show,
If we should stumble when musicians play,
Time will say nothing but I told you so.

There are no fortunes to be told, although,
Because I love you more than I can say,
If I could tell you I would let you know.

The winds must come from somewhere when they blow,
There must be reasons why the leaves decay;
Time will say nothing but I told you so.

112

Perhaps the roses really want to grow,
The vision seriously intends to stay;
If I could tell you I would let you know.

Suppose the lions all get up and go,
And all the brooks and soldiers run away;
Will Time say nothing but I told you so?
If I could tell you I would let you know.

W. H. AUDEN

A Farewell

For a while I shall still be leaving
Looking back at you as you slip away
Into the magic islands of the mind.
But for a while now all alive, believing
That in a single poignant hour
We did say all that we could ever say
In a great flowing out of radiant power.
It was like seeing and then going blind.

After a while we shall be cut in two
Between real islands where you live
And a far shore where I'll no longer keep
The haunting image of your eyes, and you,
As pupils widen, widen to deep black
And I am able neither to love or grieve
Between fulfilment and heartbreak.
The time will come when I can go to sleep.

But for a while still, centered at last,
Contemplate a brief amazing union,
Then watch you leave and then let you go.
I must not go back to the murderous past
Nor force a passage through to some safe landing.
But float upon this moment of communion
Entranced, astonished by pure understanding –
Passionate love dissolved like summer snow.

MAY SARTON 1912–

Lasca

It's all very well to write reviews,
And carry umbrellas, and keep dry shoes,
And say what everyone's saying here,
And wear what everyone else must wear;
But to-night I'm sick of the whole affair,
I want free life, and I want fresh air;
And I sigh for the canter after the cattle,
The crack of the whips like shots in a battle,
The mellay of hoofs and horns and heads
That wars and wrangles and scatters and spreads;
The green beneath, and the blue above,
And dash and danger, and life and love –
And Lasca!

　　　Lasca used to ride
On a mouse-gray mustang close to my side,
With blue *serape* and bright-belled spur;
I laughed with joy as I looked at her!
Little knew she of books or creeds;
An *Ave Maria* sufficed her needs;
Little she cared, save to be at my side,
To ride with me, and ever to ride,
From San Saba's shore to Lavaca's tide.
She was as bold as the billows that beat,
She was as wild as the breezes that blow:
From her little head to her little feet,
She was swayed in her suppleness to and fro
By each gust of passion; a sapling pine,
That grows on the edge of a Kansas bluff,
And wars with the wind when the weather is rough,
Is like this Lasca, this love of mine.

She would hunger that I might eat,
Would take the bitter and leave me the sweet;
But once, when I made her jealous for fun,
At something I'd whispered, or looked, or done,
One Sunday, in San Antonio,
To a glorious girl on the Alamo,
She drew from her garter a dear little dagger,

And – sting of a wasp! – it made me stagger!
An inch to the left, or an inch to the right,
And I shouldn't be maundering here to-night;
But she sobbed, and, sobbing, so swiftly bound
Her torn *rebosa* about the wound,
That I quickly forgave her. Scratches don't count
      In Texas, down by the Rio Grande.

Her eye was brown – a deep, deep brown;
Her hair was darker than her eye;
And something in her smile and frown,
Curled crimson lip and instep high,
Showed that there ran in each blue vein,
Mixed with the milder Aztec strain,
The vigorous vintage of Old Spain.
She was alive in every limb
With feeling, to the finger-tips;
And when the sun is like a fire,
And sky one shining, soft sapphire,
One does not drink in little sips.

Why did I leave the fresh and the free,
That suited her and suited me?
Listen awhile, and you will see;
But this be sure – in earth or air.
God and God's laws are everywhere,
And Nemesis comes with a foot as fleet
On the Texas trail as in Regent Street.

★ ★ ★

The air was heavy, the night was hot,
I sat by her side and forgot, – forgot:
Forgot the herd that were taking their rest,
Forgot that the air was close oppressed,
That the Texas norther comes sudden and soon,
In the dead of night, or the blaze of noon;
That once let the herd at its breath take fright,
Nothing on earth can stop their flight;
And woe to the rider, and woe to the steed,
Who fall in front of their mad stampede!

★ ★ ★

Was that thunder? No, by the Lord!
I sprang to my saddle without a word.
One foot on mine, and she clung behind.
Away! on a wild chase down the wind!
But never was fox-hunt half so hard,
And never was steed so little spared;
For we rode for our lives. You shall hear how we fared
    In Texas, down by the Rio Grande.

The mustang flew, and we urged him on;
There was one chance left, and you have but one –
Halt! jump to the ground, and shoot your horse;
Crouch under his carcass, and take your chance;
And if the steers in their frantic course
Don't batter you both to pieces at once,
You may thank your star; if not, goodbye
To the quickening kiss and the long-drawn sigh,
And the open air and the open sky,
    In Texas, down by the Rio Grande.

The cattle gained on us, and, just as I felt
For my old six-shooter behind in my belt,
Down came the mustang, and down came we,
Clinging together, and, – what was the rest?
A body that spread itself on my breast,
Two arms that shielded my dizzy head,
Two lips that hard to my lips were pressed;
Then came thunder in my ears,
As over us surged the sea of steers,
Blows that beat blood into my eyes;
And when I could rise –
Lasca was dead!

* * *

I hollowed a grave a few feet deep,
And there in Earth's arms I laid her to sleep;
And there she is lying, and no one knows;
And the summer shines, and the winter snows;
For many a day the flowers have spread
A pall of petals over her head;

And the little gray hawk hangs aloft in the air,
And the sly coyote trots here and there,
And the black-snake glides and glitters and slides
Into a rift in a cottonwood tree;
And the buzzard sails on,
And comes and is gone,
Stately and still, like a ship at sea;
And I wonder why I do not care
For the things that are, like the things that were.
Does half my heart lie buried there
    In Texas, down by the Rio Grande?
        FRANK DESPREZ 1853–1916

Where Be You Going, You Devon Maid?

Where be you going, you Devon maid?
    And what have ye there in the basket?
Ye tight little fairy, just fresh from the dairy,
    Will ye give me some cream if I ask it?

I love your hills and I love your dales,
    And I love your flocks a-bleating;
But oh, on the heather to lie together,
    With both our hearts a-beating!

I'll put your basket all safe in a nook;
    Your shawl I'll hang on a willow;
And we will sigh in the daisy's eye,
    And kiss on a grass-green pillow.
        JOHN KEATS 1795–1821

The Night has a Thousand Eyes

The night has a thousand eyes,
    And the day but one;
Yet the light of the bright world dies
    With the dying sun.

117

The mind has a thousand eyes,
    And the heart but one;
Yet the light of a whole life dies
    When love is done.
FRANCIS WILLIAM BOURDILLON 1852–1921

A Reflection

When Eve upon the first of Men
The apple press'd with specious cant
Oh! What a thousand pities then
That Adam was not adamant!
                    THOMAS HOOD

The Foggy, Foggy Dew

When I was a bachelor, I lived by myself
And I worked at the weaver's trade;
The only, only thing that I ever did wrong
Was to woo a fair young maid.
I wooed her in the winter time,
And in the summer too;
And the only, only thing that I ever did wrong
Was to keep her from the foggy, foggy dew.

One night she came to my bedside
Where I lay fast asleep;
She laid her head upon my bed,
And then began to weep.
She sighed, she cried, she damn near died,
She said – 'What shall I do?' –
So I hauled her into bed and I covered up her head,
Just to save her from the foggy, foggy dew.

Oh, I am a bachelor, I live with my son,
And we work at the weaver's trade;
And every, every time that I look into his eyes,

He reminds me of that maid.
He reminds me of the winter time,
And of the summer too;
And the many, many times that I held her in my arms,
Just to keep her from the foggy, foggy dew.

ANON.

Too Dear, Too Vague

Love by ambition
Of definition
Suffers partition
And cannot go
From yes to no,
For no is not love; no is no,
The shutting of a door,
The tightening jaw,
A wilful sorrow;
And saying yes
Turns love into success,
Views from the rail
Of land and happiness;
Assured of all,
The sofas creak,
And were this all, love were
But cheek to cheek
And dear to dear.

Voices explain
Love's pleasure and love's pain,
Still tap the knee
And cannot disagree,
Hushed for aggression
Of full confession,
Likeness to likeness
Of each old weakness;
Love is not there,
Love has moved to another chair,
Aware already

Of what stands next,
And is not vexed,
And is not giddy,
Leaves the North in place
With a good grace,
And would not gather
Another to another,
Designs his own unhappiness
Foretells his own death and is faithless.

W. H. AUDEN

La Belle Dame Sans Merci

O, what can ail thee, knight at arms,
    Alone and palely loitering;
The sedge has withered from the lake,
    And no birds sing.

O, what can ail thee, knight at arms,
    So haggard and so woe-begone?
The squirrel's granary is full,
    And the harvest's done.

I see a lily on thy brow
    With anguish moist and fever-dew,
And on thy cheeks a fading rose
    Fast withereth too.

I met a lady in the meads,
    Full beautiful – a faery's child,
Her hair was long, her foot was light,
    And her eyes were wild.

I made a garland for her head,
    And bracelets too, and fragrant zone,
She looked at me as she did love,
    And made sweet moan.

I set her on my pacing steed
   And nothing else saw all day long;
For sideways would she lean, and sing
   A faery's song.

She found me roots of relish sweet,
   And honey wild and manna dew;
And sure in language strange she said –
   I love thee true.

She took me to her elfin grot,
   And there she gazed and sighed full sore:
And there I shut her wild, wild eyes
   With kisses four.

And there she lullèd me asleep,
   And there I dreamed, ah woe betide,
The latest dream I ever dreamed
   On the cold hill side.

I saw pale kings and princes too,
   Pale warriors, death-pale were they all:
They cry'd – 'La belle Dame sans Merci
   Hath thee in thrall!'

I saw their starved lips in the gloam
   With horrid warning gapèd wide,
And I awoke, and found me here
   On the cold hill side.

And this is why I sojourn here
   Alone and palely loitering,
Though the sedge is withered from the lake,
   And no birds sing.

JOHN KEATS

The Speech of Silence

The solemn Sea of Silence lies between us;
   I know thou livest, and thou lovest me;
And yet I wish some white ship would come sailing
   Across the ocean, bearing word from thee.

The dead-calm awes me with its awful stillness.
   No anxious doubts or fears disturb my breast;
I only ask some little wave of language
   To stir this vast infinitude of rest.

I am oppressed with this great sense of loving;
   So much I give, so much receive from thee,
Like subtle incense, rising from a censer,
   So floats the fragrance of thy love round me.

All speech is poor, and written words unmeaning;
   Yet such I ask, blown hither by some wind,
To give relief to this too perfect knowledge,
   The Silence so impresses on my mind.

How poor the love that needeth word or message,
   To banish doubt or nourish tenderness!
I ask them but to temper love's convictions
   The Silence all too fully doth express.

Too deep the language which the spirit utters;
   Too vast the knowledge which my soul hath
     stirred;
Send some white ship across the Sea of Silence,
   And interrupt its utterance with a word.

ELLA WHEELER WILCOX 1850–1919

To One That Asked Me Why I Loved J.G.

Why do I love? go ask the glorious sun
Why every day it round the world doth run:
Ask Thames and Tiber why they ebb and flow:
Ask damask roses why in June they blow:
Ask ice and hail the reason why they're cold:
Decaying beauties, why they will grow old:
They'll tell thee, Fate, that everything doth move,
Inforces them to this, and me to love.
There is no reason for our love or hate.
'Tis irresistible as Death or Fate;
'Tis not his face; I've sense enough to see,
That is not good, though doated on by me:
Nor is't his tongue, that has this conquest won,
For that at least is equalled by my own:
His carriage can to none obliging be,
'Tis rude, affected, full of vanity:
Strangely ill natur'd, peevish and unkind,
Unconstant, false, to jealousy inclin'd:
His temper could not have so great a power,
'Tis mutable, and changes every hour:
Those vigorous years that women so adore
Are past in him: he's twice my age and more;
And yet I love this false, this worthless man,
With all the passion that a woman can;
Doat on his imperfections, though I spy
Nothing to love; I love, and know not why.
Since 'tis decreed in the dark book of Fate,
That I should love, and he should be ingrate.

EPHELIA 1679–?

Thou Shalt Dwell in Silence

Thou shalt dwell in silence in my heart like the
                full moon in the summer night.
Thy sad eyes shall watch over me in my wanderings.

The shadow of thy veil shall rest upon my heart.
Thy breath like the full moon in the summer night shall
   hover about my dreams making them fragrant.
RABINDRANATH TAGORE

A Man's Requirements

I

Love me Sweet, with all thou art,
 Feeling, thinking, seeing;
Love me in the lightest part,
 Love me in full being.

II

Love me with thine open youth
 In its frank surrender;
With the vowing of thy mouth,
 With its silence tender.

III

Love me with thine azure eyes,
 Made for earnest granting;
Taking colour from the skies,
 Can Heaven's truth be wanting?

IV

Love me with their lids, that fall
 Snow-like at first meeting;
Love me with thine heart, that all
 Neighbours then see beating.

V

Love me with thine hand stretched out
 Freely – open-minded:
Love me with thy loitering foot, –
 Hearing one behind it.

VI

Love me with thy voice, that turns
    Sudden faint above me;
Love me with thy blush that burns
    When I murmur *Love me!*

VII

Love me with thy thinking soul,
    Break it to love-sighing;
Love me with thy thoughts that roll
    On through living – dying.

VIII

Love me in thy gorgeous airs,
    When the world has crowned thee;
Love me, kneeling at thy prayers,
    With the angels round thee.

IX

Love me pure, as musers do,
    Up the woodlands shady:
Love me gaily, fast and true,
    As a winsome lady.

X

Through all hopes that keep us brave,
    Farther off or nigher,
Love me for the house and grave,
    And for something higher.

XI

Thus, if thou wilt prove me, Dear,
    Woman's love no fable,
I will love *thee* – half a year –
    As a man is able.

ELIZABETH BARRETT BROWNING

Lemon Haired Ladies

whatever you give me
i'll take as it comes
discarding self-pity
i'll manage with crumbs
i'll settle for moments
i won't ask for life
i'll not expect labels
like lover or wife
if showing affection
embarrasses you
i will not depend
and i will not pursue
for you are
younger than i
younger than i
younger than i
and i am
wiser than you
the one a.m. phone calls
you're here then you're gone
come when you need me
i won't carry on
i'll simply accept you
the way that you are
unsure and unstructured
my door is ajar
those lemon haired ladies
of twenty or so
of course you must see them
just don't let me know
don't let me know
whatever you do
for you are
younger than i
younger than i
younger than i
and i am
weaker than you
i'll give you a year

maybe two
maybe three
then what will happen?
where will i be?
you'll still be a boy
but what about me?
what about me?
what about me?
why must you treat me
with such little care
i've so much inside me
i'm aching to share
why am i constant
to someone like you?
children don't know
the meaning of 'true'
those lemon haired ladies
why must you see them?
all that i want in your eyes
is to be them
time is on their side
that's all i lack
i wish you would just
go away
no
come back
come back
go away
come back
go away
what in hell can i do?
i'm supposed to be wise
for i am
older than you
older than you
you so self-centered
the games that you play
do as you please
you will anyway
of course you will see them
no use to pretend

for they are
younger than i
younger than i
those lemon haired ladies
and they will
win in the end.

DORY PREVIN

Angels and Devils the Following Day

loved i two men
equally well
though they were diff'rent
as heaven and hell
one was an artist
one drove a truck
one would make love
the other would fuck
each treated me
the way he knew best
one held me lightly
one bruised my breast
and i responded
on two diff'rent levels
like children reacting
to angels and devils
one was a poet
who sang and read verse
one was a peasant
who drank and who cursed
before you decide
who's cruel and who's kind
let me explain
what i felt
in my heart and my mind . . .
the artist was tender
but suffered from guilt
making him sorry
the following day

and he made me feel guilty
the very same way
in his bed on the following day
the other would take me
and feel no remorse
he'd wake with a smile
in the bed where we lay
and he made me smile
in the very same way
in his bed on the following day
the blow to my soul
by fear and taboos
cut deeper far
than a bodily bruise
and the one who was gentle
hurt me much more
than the one who was rough
and made love on the floor.

DORY PREVIN

Lines from Endymion

A thing of beauty is a joy for ever:
Its loveliness increases, it will never
Pass into nothingness; but still will keep
A bower quiet for us, and a sleep
Full of sweet dreams, and health, and quiet breathing.
Therefore, on every morrow, are we wreathing
A flowery band to bind us to the earth,
Spite of despondence, of the inhuman dearth
Of noble natures, of the gloomy days,
Of all the unhealthy and o'er-darkened ways
Made of our searching; yes, in spite of all,
Some shape of beauty moves away the pall
From our dark spirits.

JOHN KEATS

i like my body when it is with your

i like my body when it is with your
body.   It is so quite new a thing.
Muscles better and nerves more.
i like your body.   i like what it does,
i like its hows.   i like to feel the spine
of your body and its bones,and the trembling
-firm-smooth ness and which i will
again and again and again
kiss,   i like kissing this and that of you,
i like,slowly stroking the,shocking fuzz
of your electric fur,and what-is-it comes
over parting flesh. . . .And eyes big love-crumbs,

and possibly i like the thrill

of under me you so quite new
                    e. e. cummings 1894–1962

Poor but Honest

She was poor, but she was honest,
     Victim of the squire's whim:
First he loved her, then he left her,
     And she lost her honest name.

Then she ran away to London,
     For to hide her grief and shame;
There she met another squire
     And she lost her name again.

See her riding in her carriage,
     In the Park and all so gay:
All the nibs and nobby persons
     Come to pass the time of day.

See the little old-world village
     Where her aged parents live,
Drinking the champagne she sends them;
     But they never can forgive.

In the rich man's arms she flutters,
    Like a bird with broken wing:
First he loved her, then he left her,
    And she hasn't got a ring.

See him in the splendid mansion,
    Entertaining with the best,
While the girl that he has ruined,
    Entertains a sordid guest.

See him in the House of Commons,
    Making laws to put down crime,
While the victim of his passions
    Trails her way through mud and slime.

Standing on the bridge, at midnight,
    She says: 'Farewell, blighted Love.'
There's a scream, a splash – Good Heavens!
    What is she a-doing of?

Then they drag her from the river,
    Water from her clothes they wrang,
For they thought that she was drownded;
    But the corpse got up and sang;

'It's the same the whole world over;
    It's the poor that gets the blame,
It's the rich that get the pleasure.
    Isn't it a blooming shame?'

ANON.

A Drinking Song

Wine comes in at the mouth
And love comes in at the eye;
That's all we shall know for truth
Before we grow old and die.
I lift the glass to my mouth,
I look at you, and I sigh.

W. B. YEATS

A Man That Looks on Glass

A man that looks on glass,
On it may stay his eye;
Or, if he pleaseth, through it pass,
And then the heaven espy.

GEORGE HERBERT 1593–1633

Frankie and Johnny

Frankie and Johnny were lovers. O Lordy, how they could love!
Swore to be true to each other, true as the stars above.
    He was her man, but he done her wrong.

Frankie she was a good woman, just like everyone knows.
She spent a hundred dollars for a suit of Johnny's clothes.
    He was her man, but he done her wrong.

Frankie and Johnny went walking, Johnny in a brand new suit.
'Oh, good Lord,' says Frankie, 'don't my Johnny look cute?'
    He was her man, but he done her wrong.

Frankie went down to Memphis, she went on the evening train.
She paid one hundred dollars for Johnny a watch and chain.
    He was her man, but he done her wrong.

Frankie lived in the crib-house, crib-house had only two doors;
Gave all her money to Johnny, he spent it on those parlor whores.
    He was her man, but he done her wrong.

Frankie went down to the corner to buy a glass of beer,
Says to the fat bartender, 'Has my lovingest man been here?
    He was my man, but he's doing me wrong.'

'Ain't going to tell you no story; ain't going to tell you no lie;
I seen your man 'bout an hour ago with a girl named Nellie Bly.
    If he's your man, he's doing you wrong.'

Frankie went down to the pawnshop, she didn't go there for fun;
She hocked all of her jewelry, bought a pearl-handled forty-four
    gun
        For to get her man who was doing her wrong.

Frankie went down to the hotel, she rang that hotel bell.
'Stand back, all you chippies, or I'll blow you all to hell.
    I want my man, who's doing me wrong.'

Frankie threw back her kimono, she took out her forty-four,
Root-a-toot-toot three times she shot right through that hotel door
    She was after her man who was doing her wrong.

Johnny grabbed off his Stetson, 'Oh, good Lord, Frankie, don't
      shoot!'
But Frankie pulled the trigger and the gun went root-a-toot-toot.
    He was her man, but she shot him down.

'Roll me over easy; roll me over slow;
Roll me over on my left side, for the bullet is hurting me so.
    I was her man, but I done her wrong.'

Oh, bring on your rubber-tired hearses; bring on your rubber-tired
      hacks;
They're taking Johnny to the cemetery, and they ain't a-bringing
      him back.
    He was her man, but he done her wrong

Now it was not murder in the second degree, it was not murder in
      the third.
That woman simply dropped her man, like a hunter drops his
      bird.
    He was her man and he done her wrong.

'Oh, put me in that dungeon. Oh, put me in that cell.
Put me where the northeast wind blows from the southwest corner
      of hell.
    I shot my man 'cause he done me wrong.'

Frankie walked up the scaffold, as calm as a girl can be,
And turning her eyes to heaven she said, 'Good Lord, I'm coming
      to thee.
    He was my man, and I done him wrong.'

This story has got no moral, this story has got no end.
This story only goes to show that there ain't no good in men.
    He was her man, but he done her wrong.

AMERICAN FOLK SONG – ANON.

Social Note

Lady, lady, should you meet
One whose ways are all discreet,
One who murmurs that his wife
Is the lodestar of his life,
One who keeps assuring you
That he never was untrue,
Never loved another one . . .
    Lady, lady, better run!
DOROTHY PARKER 1893–1967

One Perfect Rose

A single flow'r he sent me, since we met.
    All tenderly his messenger he chose;
Deep-hearted, pure, with scented dew still wet –
    One perfect rose.

I knew the language of the floweret;
    'My fragile leaves', it said, 'his heart enclose.'
Love long has taken for his amulet
    One perfect rose.

Why is it no one ever sent me yet
    One perfect limousine, do you suppose?
Ah no, it's always just my luck to get
    One perfect rose.
DOROTHY PARKER

Celia Celia

When I am sad and weary
When I think all hope has gone
When I walk along High Holborn
I think of you with nothing on
ADRIAN MITCHELL 1932–

134

I Loved You

I loved you; even now I may confess,
  Some embers of my love their fire retain;
But do not let it cause you more distress,
  I do not want to sadden you again.
Hopeless and tonguetied, yet I loved you dearly
  With pangs the jealous and the timid know,
So tenderly I loved you, so sincerely,
  I pray God grant another love you so.

ALEXANDER PUSHKIN 1799–1837
(Translated by Reginald Mainwaring Hewitt.)

The Hill

Breathless, we flung us on the windy hill,
Laughed in the sun, and kissed the lovely grass.
You said, 'Through glory and ecstasy we pass;
Wind, sun, and earth remain, the birds sing still,
When we are old, are old . . .' 'And when we die
All's over that is ours; and life burns on
Through other lovers, other lips,' said I,
'Heart of my heart, our heaven is now, is won!'

'We are Earth's best, that learnt her lesson here.
Life is our cry. We have kept the faith!' we said;
'We shall go down with unreluctant tread
Rose-crowned into the darkness!' . . . Proud we were,
And laughed, that had such brave true things to say.
– And then you suddenly cried, and turned away.

RUPERT BROOKE

Looking at Each Other

Yes, we were looking at each other
Yes we knew each other very well
Yes, we had made love with each other many times

135

Yes, we had heard music together
Yes, we had gone to the sea together
Yes, we had cooked and eaten together
Yes, we had laughed often day and night
Yes, we fought violence and knew violence
Yes, we hated the inner and outer oppression
Yes, that day we were looking at each other
Yes, we saw the sunlight pouring down
Yes, the corner of the table was between us
Yes, bread and flowers were on the table
Yes, our eyes saw each other's eyes
Yes, our mouths saw each other's mouth
Yes, our breasts saw each other's breasts
Yes, our bodies entire saw each other
Yes, it was beginning in each
Yes, it threw waves across our lives
Yes, the pulses were becoming very strong
Yes, the beating became very delicate
Yes, the calling   the arousal
Yes, the arriving   the coming
Yes, there it was for both entire
Yes, we were looking at each other

MURIEL RUKEYSER 1913–80

New Year's Eve

There are only two things now,
The great black night scooped out
And this fireglow.

This fireglow, the core,
And we the two ripe pips
That are held in store.

Listen, the darkness rings
As it circulates round our fire.
Take off your things.

Your shoulders, your bruised throat!
Your breasts, your nakedness!
This fiery coat!

As the darkness flickers and dips,
As the firelight falls and leaps
From your feet to your lips!

D. H. LAWRENCE 1885–1930

Green

The dawn was apple-green,
   The sky was green wine held up in the sun,
The moon was a golden petal between.

She opened her eyes, and green
   They shone, clear like flowers undone
For the first time, now for the first time seen.

D. H. LAWRENCE

To My Valentine

More than a catbird hates a cat,
Or a criminal hates a clue,
Or the Axis hates the United States,
That's how much I love you.

I love you more than a duck can swim,
And more than a grapefruit squirts,
I love you more than gin rummy is a bore
And more than a toothache hurts.

As a shipwrecked sailor hates the sea,
Or a juggler hates a shove,
As a hostess detests unexpected guests,
That's how much you I love.

I love you more than a wasp can sting,
And more than the subway jerks,
I love you as much as a beggar needs a crutch,
And more than a hangnail irks.

I swear to you by the stars above,
And below, if such there be,
As the High Court loathes perjurious oaths,
That's how you're loved by me.

OGDEN NASH

Administration

Day by day your estimation clocks up
Who deserves a smile and who a frown,
And girls you have to tell to pull their socks up
Are those whose pants you'd most like to pull down.

PHILIP LARKIN

In Praise of Cocoa, Cupid's Nightcap

*(Lines written upon hearing the startling news
that cocoa is, in fact, a mild aphrodisiac.)*

Half past nine – high time for supper;
'Cocoa, love?' 'Of course, my dear.'
Helen thinks it quite delicious,
John prefers it now to beer.
Knocking back the sepia potion,
Hubby winks, says, 'Who's for bed?'
'Shan't be long', says Helen softly,
Cheeks a faintly flushing red.
For they've stumbled on the secret

Of a love that never wanes,
Rapt beneath the tumbled bedclothes,
Cocoa coursing through their veins.

STANLEY J. SHARPLES 1910—

from IX. *A Last Confession*

What lively lad most pleasured me
Of all that with me lay?
I answer that I gave my soul
And loved in misery,
But had great pleasure with a lad
That I loved bodily.

Flinging from his arms I laughed
To think his passion such
He fancied that I gave a soul
Did but our bodies touch,
And laughed upon his breast to think
Beast gave beast as much.

I gave what other women gave
That stepped out of their clothes,
But when this soul, its body off,
Naked to naked goes,
He it has found shall find therein
What none other knows.

W. B. YEATS

After Love

Afterwards, the compromise.
Bodies resume their boundaries.

These legs, for instance, mine.
Your arms take you back in.

Spoons of our fingers, lips
admit their ownership.

The bedding yawns, a door
blows aimlessly ajar

and overhead, a plane
singsongs, coming down.

Nothing is changed, except
there was a moment when

the wolf, the mongering wolf
who stands outside the self

lay lightly down, and slept.

MAXINE KUMIN 1925–

Unfortunate Coincidence

By the time you swear you're his,
    Shivering and sighing,
And he vows his passion is
    Infinite, undying –
Lady, make a note of this:
    One of you is lying.

DOROTHY PARKER

There Was a Young Lady

There was a young lady named Bright
Whose speed was far faster than light;
She went out one day
In a relative way
And returned home the previous night.

ARTHUR BULLER 1874–1944

Polly Perkins

I am a broken-hearted milkman, in grief I'm arrayed,
Through keeping of the company of a young servant maid,
Who lived on board and wages the house to keep clean
In a gentleman's family near Paddington Green.

Chorus:

>> She was as beautiful as a butterfly
>> And as proud as a Queen
> Was pretty little Polly Perkins of
>> Paddington Green.

She'd an ankle like an antelope and a step like a deer,
A voice like a blackbird, so mellow and clear,
Her hair hung in ringlets so beautiful and long,
I thought that she loved me but I found I was wrong.

When I'd rattle in a morning and cry 'milk below',
At the sound of my milk-cans her face she would show
With a smile upon her countenance and a laugh in her eye,
If I thought she'd have loved me, I'd have laid down to die.

When I asked her to marry me she said 'Oh! what stuff',
And told me to 'drop it, for she had quite enough
Of my nonsense' – at the same time I'd been very kind,
But to marry a milkman she didn't feel inclined.

'Oh, the man that has me must have silver and gold,
A chariot to ride in and be handsome and bold,
His hair must be curly as any watch spring,
And his whiskers as big as a brush for clothing.'

The words that she uttered went straight through my heart,
I sobbed, I sighed, and straight did depart;
With a tear on my eyelid as big as a bean,
Bidding good-bye to Polly and Paddington Green.

In six months she married, – this hard-hearted girl, –
But it was not a Wi-count, and it was not a Nearl,
It was not a 'Baronite', but a shade or two wuss,
It was a bow-legged conductor of a twopenny bus.

ANON.

141

Song

from *The Vicar of Wakefield*

When lovely woman stoops to folly,
    And finds too late that men betray,
What charm can soothe her melancholy?
    What art can wash her guilt away?

The only art her guilt to cover,
    To hide her shame from every eye,
To give repentance to her lover,
    And wring his bosom, is – to die.

OLIVER GOLDSMITH 1728–74

A Subaltern's Love-song

Miss J. Hunter Dunn, Miss J. Hunter Dunn,
Furnish'd and burnish'd by Aldershot sun,
What strenuous singles we played after tea,
We in the tournament – you against me!

Love-thirty, love-forty, oh! weakness of joy,
The speed of a swallow, the grace of a boy,
With carefullest carelessness, gaily you won,
I am weak from your loveliness, Joan Hunter Dunn.

Miss Joan Hunter Dunn, Miss Joan Hunter Dunn,
How mad I am, sad I am, glad that you won.
The warm-handled racket is back in its press,
But my shock-headed victor, she loves me no less.

Her father's euonymus shines as we walk,
And swing past the summer-house, buried in talk,
And cool the verandah that welcomes us in
To the six-o'clock news and a lime-juice and gin.

The scent of the conifers, sound of the bath,
The view from my bedroom of moss-dappled path,
As I struggle with double-end evening tie,
For we dance at the Golf Club, my victor and I.

On the floor of her bedroom lie blazer and shorts
And the cream-coloured walls are be-trophied with sports,
And westering, questioning settles the sun
On your low-leaded window, Miss Joan Hunter Dunn.

The Hillman is waiting, the light's in the hall,
The pictures of Egypt are bright on the wall,
My sweet, I am standing beside the oak stair
And there on the landing's the light on your hair.

By roads 'not adopted', by woodlanded ways,
She drove to the club in the late summer haze,
Into nine-o'clock Camberley, heavy with bells
And mushroomy, pine-woody, evergreen smells.

Miss Joan Hunter Dunn, Miss Joan Hunter Dunn,
I can hear from the car-park the dance has begun.
Oh! full Surrey twilight! importunate band!
Oh! strongly adorable tennis-girl's hand!

Around us are Rovers and Austins afar,
Above us, the intimate roof of the car,
And here on my right is the girl of my choice,
With the tilt of her nose and the chime of her voice,

And the scent of her wrap, and the words never said,
And the ominous, ominous dancing ahead.
We sat in the car park till twenty to one
And now I'm engaged to Miss Joan Hunter Dunn.

JOHN BETJEMAN 1906–84

from *Trilogy for X*

When clerks and navvies fondle
　Beside canals their wenches,
In rapture or in coma
　The haunches that they handle,
And the orange moon sits idle
　Above the orchard slanted –
Upon such easy evenings
　We take our loves for granted.

But when, as now, the creaking
　Trees on the hills of London
Like bison charge their neighbours
　In wind that keeps us waking
And in the draught the scalloped
　Lampshade swings a shadow,
We think of love bound over –
　The mortgage on the meadow.

And one lies lonely, haunted
　By limbs he half remembers,
And one, in wedlock, wonders
　Where is the girl he wanted;
And some sit smoking, flicking
　The ash away and feeling
For love gone up like vapour
　Between the floor and ceiling.

But now when winds are curling
　The trees do you come closer,
Close as an eyelid fasten
　My body in darkness, darling;
Switch the light off and let me
　Gather you up and gather
The power of trains advancing
　Further, advancing further.

LOUIS MACNEICE 1907–63

144

My Young Man's a Cornishman

My young man's a Cornishman
He lives in Camborne town,
I met him going up the hill
As I was coming down.

His eye is bright as Dolcoath tin,
His body as china clay,
His hair is dark as Werrington Wood
Upon St Thomas's Day.

He plays the rugby football game
On Saturday afternoon,
And we shall walk on Wilsey Down
Under the bouncing moon.

My young man's a Cornishman,
Won't leave me in the lurch,
And one day we shall married be
Up to Trura church.

He's bought me a ring of Cornish gold,
A belt of copper made,
At Bodmin Fair for my wedding-dress
A purse of silver paid.

And I shall give him scalded cream
And starry-gazy pie,
And make him a saffron cake for tea
And a pasty for by and by.

My young man's a Cornishman,
A proper young man is he,
And a Cornish man with a Cornish maid
Is how it belongs to be.

CHARLES CAUSLEY

Rose Aylmer

Ah, what avails the sceptred race!
   Ah, what the form divine!
What every virtue, every grace!
   Rose Aylmer, all were thine.
Rose Aylmer, whom these wakeful eyes
   May weep, but never see,
A night of memories and sighs
   I consecrate to thee.

W. S. LANDOR 1775–1864

Now That I am Forever With Child

How the days went
while you were blooming within me
I remember each upon each –
the swelling changed planes of my body
and how you first fluttered, then jumped
and I thought it was my heart.

How the days wound down
and the turning of winter
I recall with you growing heavy
against the wind. I thought
now her hands
are formed, and her hair
has started to curl
now her teeth are done
now she sneezes.
Then the seed opened
I bore you one morning just before spring
My head rang like a fiery piston
my legs were towers between which
A new world was passing.

Since then
I can only distinguish

one thread within running hours
You, flowing through selves
toward You.

AUDRE LORDE 1934–

Safe Period

He will unlock the four-hooked gate of her bra,
Not noticing a kremlin built of lint,
With darkening scorch-marks where her arms press kisses.
She will pull back her arms, disturbing drifts
Of shallow, babyish hair, and let him drink,
Breathless, the heavy spirit smell, retreating
At length with a shy glance to grasp the chair-back,
And slightly stooped, tug out the darker bandage.
Her cupped palm will glow as she carries it
Quickly to the sink, like something burning.
He sees the bright beard on each inner thigh,
Carnations curling, ribboning in the bowl.
Her hands make soapy love. The laundered rag
Weeps swift pink tears from the washing-string.
He's stiffened with a shocked assent. She breathes
Against him, damp as a glass. A glass of red vodka.

CAROL RUMENS 1944–

Smokers for Celibacy

Some of us are a little tired of hearing that cigarettes kill.
We'd like to warn you about another way of making yourself ill:

we suggest that in view of AIDS, herpes, chlamydia, cystitis and NSU,
not to mention genital warts and cervical cancer and the proven
        connection between the two,

if you want to avoid turning into physical wrecks
what you should give up is not smoking but sex.

We're sorry if you're upset,
but think of the grisly things you might otherwise get.

We can't see much point in avoiding emphysema at sixty-five
if that's an age at which you have conspicuously failed to arrive,

and as for cancer, it is a depressing fact
that at least for women this disease is more likely to occur in the
        reproductive tract.

We could name friends of ours who died that way, if you insist,
but we feel sure you can each provide your own list.

You'll notice we don't mention syphilis and gonorrhea;
well, we have now, so don't get the idea

that, just because of antibiotics, quaint old clap and pox
are not still being generously spread around by men's cocks.

Some of us aren't too keen on the thought of micro-organisms
        travelling up into our brain
and giving us General Paralysis of the Insane.

We're opting out of one-night stands:
we'd rather have a cigarette in our hands.

If it's a choice between two objects of cylindrical shape
we go for the one that is seldom if ever guilty of rape.

Cigarettes just lie there quietly in their packs
waiting until you call on one of them to help you relax.

They aren't moody: they don't go in for sexual harassment and
        threats,
or worry about their performance as compared with that of other
        cigarettes,

nor do they keep you awake all night telling you the story of their life,
beginning with their mother and going on until morning about their
        first wife.

Above all, the residues they leave in your system are thoroughly
      sterilised and clean.
which is more than can be said for the products of the human
      machine.

Altogether, we've come to the conclusion that sex is a drag.
Just give us a fag.

FLEUR ADCOCK

A Code of Morals

Now Jones had left his new-wed bride to keep his house in order,
And hied away to the Hurrum Hills above the Afghan border,
To sit on a rock with a heliograph; but ere he left he taught
His wife the working of the Code that sets the miles at naught.

And Love had made him very sage, as Nature made her fair;
So Cupid and Apollo linked, *per* heliograph, the pair.
At dawn, across the Hurrum Hills, he flashed her counsel wise –
At e'en, the dying sunset bore her husband's homilies.

He warned her 'gainst seductive youths in scarlet clad and gold,
As much as 'gainst the blandishments paternal of the old;
But kept his gravest warnings for (hereby the ditty hangs)
That snowy-haired Lothario, Lieutenant-General Bangs.

'Twas General Bangs, with Aide and Staff, who tittupped on the way,
When they beheld a heliograph tempestuously at play.
They thought of Border risings, and of stations sacked and burnt –
So stopped to take the message down – and this is what they learnt –

'Dash dot dot, dot, dot dash, dot dash dot' twice. The General swore.
'Was ever General Officer addressed as "dear" before?
'"My Love," i' faith! "My Duck," Gadzooks! "My
      darling popsy-wop!"'
'Spirit of great Lord Wolseley, *who* is on that mountain-top?'

The artless Aide-de-camp was mute, the gilded Staff were still,
As, dumb with pent-up mirth, they booked that message from the
        hill;
For clear as summer lightning-flare, the husband's warning ran: –
'Don't dance or ride with General Bangs – a most immoral man.'

[At dawn, across the Hurrum Hills, he flashed her counsel wise –
But, howsoever Love be blind, the world at large hath eyes.]
With damnatory dot and dash he heliographed his wife
Some interesting details of the General's private life.

The artless Aide-de-camp was mute, the shining Staff were still,
And red and ever redder grew the General's shaven gill.
And this is what he said at last (his feelings matter not):–
'I think we've tapped a private line. Hi! Threes about there! Trot!'

All honour unto Bangs, for ne'er did Jones thereafter know
By word or act official who read off that helio.
But the tale is on the Frontier, and from Michni to Mool*tan*
They know the worthy General as 'that most immoral man.'

                                RUDYARD KIPLING

A Lover's Quarrel

We two were lovers, the Sea and I;
We plighted our troth 'neath a summer sky.

And all through the riotous, ardent weather
We dreamed and loved, and rejoiced together.

           ★ ★ ★

At times my lover would rage and storm.
I said: 'No matter, his heart is warm.'

Whatever his humour, I loved his ways,
And so we lived through the golden days.

I know not the manner it came about,
But in the autumn we two fell out.
Yet this I know – 'twas the fault of the Sea,
And was not my fault, that he changed to me.

*　*　*

I lingered as long as a woman may
To find what her lover will do or say.

But he met my smiles with a sullen frown,
And so I turned to the wooing Town.

Oh, bold was this suitor, and blithe as bold!
His look was as bright as the Sea's was cold.

As the Sea was sullen, the Town was gay;
He made me forget for a winter day.

For a winter day and a winter night
He laughed my sorrow away from sight.

And yet, in spite of his mirth and cheer,
I knew full well he was insincere.

And when the young buds burst on the tree,
The old love woke in my heart for the Sea.

Pride was forgotten – I knew, I knew,
That the soul of the Sea, like my own, was true.

I heard him calling, and lo! I came,
To find him waiting, for ever the same.

And when he saw me, with murmurs sweet
He ran to meet me, and fell at my feet.

And so again 'neath a summer sky
We have plighted our troth, the Sea and I.

ELLA WHEELER WILCOX

Daybreak

At dawn she lay with her profile at that angle
Which, when she sleeps, seems the carved face of an angel.
Her hair a harp, the hand of a breeze follows
And plays, against the white cloud of the pillows.
Then, in a flush of rose, she woke, and her eyes that opened
Swam in blue through her rose flesh that dawned.
From her dew of lips, the drop of one word
Fell like the first of fountains: murmured
'Darling' upon my ears the song of the first bird.
'My dream becomes my dream,' she said, 'come true.
I waken from you to my dream of you.'
Oh, my own wakened dream then dared assume
The audacity of her sleep. Our dreams
Poured into each other's arms, like streams.

STEPHEN SPENDER 1909—

from *Twelve Songs, IX*

Stop all the clocks, cut off the telephone,
Prevent the dog from barking with a juicy bone,
Silence the pianos and with muffled drum
Bring out the coffin, let the mourners come.

Let aeroplanes circle moaning overhead
Scribbling on the sky the message He Is Dead,
Put the crêpe bows round the white necks of the
    public doves,
Let the traffic policemen wear black cotton gloves.

He was my North, my South, my East and West,
My working week and my Sundays rest,
My noon, my midnight, my talk, my song;
I thought that love would last for ever: I was wrong.

The stars are not wanted now: put out every one;
Pack up the moon and dismantle the sun;
Pour away the ocean and sweep up the wood.
For nothing now can ever come to any good.

W. H. AUDEN

The Mermaid

A mermaid found a swimming lad,
Picked him for her own,
Pressed her body to his body,
Laughed; and plunging down
Forgot in cruel happiness
That even lovers drown.

W. B. YEATS

Episode

We walk by the sea-shore
holding firmly in our hands
the two ends of an antique dialogue
– do you love me?
– I love you

with furrowed eyebrows
I summarize all wisdom
of the two testaments
astrologers prophets
philosophers of the gardens
and cloistered philosophers

and it sounds about like this:
– don't cry
– be brave
– look how everybody

you pout your lips and say
– you should be a clergyman
and fed up you walk off
nobody loves moralists

what should I say on the shore of
a small dead sea

slowly the water fills
the shapes of feet which have vanished

ZBIGNIEW HERBERT 1924–
(Translated by Peter Dale Scott.)

Bloody Men

Bloody men are like bloody buses –
You wait for about a year
And as soon as one approaches your stop
Two or three others appear.

You look at them flashing their indicators,
Offering you a ride.
You're trying to read the destinations,
You haven't much time to decide.

If you make a mistake, there is no turning back.
Jump off and you'll stand there and gaze
While the cars and the taxis and lorries go by
And the minutes, the hours, the days.

WENDY COPE

The House

Far better never to have loved,
Better at least to break my vow,
– Anything rather than the shock
That jars me when I meet you now.

O those distant hands of yours!
Into this tedious condition
They bear their enchantment
Even now, in separation.

And now quite alone in my house
Empty and cold, I am not free
Even in sleep; I dream
Only of things that used to be . . .

I dream only of the old times,
Dream only of the bygone years . . .
You have me under lock and key
For good now, it appears . . .

Whoever should come calling now,
I would not change this bleak unease,
For a foolish affair, and so
I turn the key, and hold my peace.

ALEXANDER BLOK 1880–1921
(Translated by Geoffrey Thurley.)

Poem for Blok

Your name is a   bird on my hand
a piece of   ice on the tongue
a single movement of the lips
Your name is: five signs,
a ball caught in flight, a
silver bell in the mouth

a stone, cast in a quiet pool
makes the splash of your name, and
the sound is in the clatter of
night hooves, loud as a thunderclap
or it speaks straight into my forehead,
shrill as the click of a gun cock

Your name   is impossible it
is a kiss in the eyes on
motionless eyelashes, chill and sweet.
Your name is a kiss of snow
a gulp of icy spring water, blue
as a dove. About your name is: sleep

MARINA TSVETAYEVA 1892–1941

(An experimental poet who deliberately breaks lines and even words. Translated by Elaine Feinstein.)

Love

Two thousand cigarettes.
A hundred miles
from wall to wall.
An eternity and a half of vigils
blanker than snow.

Tons of words
old as the tracks
of a platypus in the sand.

A hundred books we didn't write.
A hundred pyramids we didn't build.

Sweepings.
Dust.

Bitter
as the beginning of the world.

Believe me when I say
it was beautiful.

MIROSLAV HOLUB 1923—
(Translated by Ian Milner.)

1704. *Unto a Broken Heart*

Unto a broken heart
No other one may go
Without the high prerogative
Itself hath suffered too.

EMILY DICKINSON

Naked

Naked, you are simple as a hand,
minimal, supple, earthy, transparent, round.
The lunar markings, the pathways, through the apple,
are yours; naked, you are slender as the wheat.

The Cuban blue of midnight is your color,
naked, I trace stars and tendrils in your skin;
naked, you stand tawny and tremendous,
a summer's wholeness in cathedral gold.

PABLO NERUDA 1904–73

The Saddest Lines

Tonight I can write the saddest lines.

Write, for example, 'The night is shattered
and the blue stars shiver in the distance.'

The night wind revolves in the sky and sings.

Tonight, I can write the saddest lines.
I loved her, and sometimes she loved me too.

Through nights like this one, I held her in my arms.
I kissed her again and again under the endless sky.

She loved me, sometimes I loved her too.
How could one not have loved her great still eyes.

Tonight I can write the saddest lines.
To think that I do not have her. To feel that I have lost her.

To hear the immense night, still more immense without her.
And the verse falls to the soul like dew to the pasture.

What does it matter that my love could not keep her.
The night is shattered and she is not with me.

This is all. In the distance someone is singing. In the distance.
My soul is not satisfied that it has lost her.

PABLO NERUDA

Marriage

'My wife and I – we're *pals*. Marriage is *fun*.'
Yes: two can live as stupidly as one.

PHILIP LARKIN

157

A Dedication to My Wife

To whom I owe the leaping delight
That quickens my senses in our wakingtime
And the rhythm that governs the repose of our sleepingtime,
    The breathing in unison

Of lovers whose bodies smell of each other
Who think the same thoughts without need of speech
And babble the same speech without need of meaning.

No peevish winter wind shall chill
No sullen tropic sun shall wither
The roses in the rose-garden which is ours and ours only

But this dedication is for others to read:
These are private words addressed to you in public.

T. S. ELIOT

Song by the Subconscious Self

I know not what my secret is,
I know but it is mine,
I know to dwell with it were bliss,
To die for it divine,
I cannot yield it in a kiss,
Nor breathe it in a sigh;
Enough that I have lived for this,
For this, my love, I die.

A. LANG

SOLDIER

Then a soldier,
Full of strange oaths, and bearded like the pard,
Jealous in honour, sudden and quick in quarrel,
Seeking the bubble reputation
Even in the cannon's mouth.

Make Bright the Arrows

Make bright the arrows; gather the
shields: the Lord hath raised up the spirit of
the kings of the Medes.

JEREMIAH, CHAPTER 51, VERSE 11

Make Bright the Arrows

Make bright the arrows,
  Gather the shields:
Conquest narrows
  The peaceful fields.

Stock well the quiver
  With arrows bright:
The bowman feared
  Need never fight.

Make bright the arrows,
  O peaceful and wise!
Gather the shields
  Against surprise.

EDNA ST VINCENT MILLAY

The Destruction of Sennacherib

The Assyrian came down like the wolf on the fold,
And his cohorts were gleaming in purple and gold;
And the sheen of their spears was like stars on the sea,
When the blue wave rolls nightly on deep Galilee.

Like the leaves of the forest when Summer is green,
That host with their banners at sunset were seen:
Like the leaves of the forest when Autumn hath blown,
That host on the morrow lay withered and strown.

For the Angel of Death spread his wings on the blast,
And breathed in the face of the foe as he passed;
And the eyes of the sleepers waxed deadly and chill,
And their hearts but once heaved, and for ever grew still!

And there lay the steed with his nostril all wide,
But through it there rolled not the breath of his pride:
And the foam of his gasping lay white on the turf
And cold as the spray of the rock-beating surf.

And there lay the rider distorted and pale,
With the dew on his brow and the rust on his mail;
And the tents were all silent, the banners alone,
The lances unlifted, the trumpet unblown.

And the widows of Ashur are loud in their wail,
And the idols are broke in the temple of Baal;
And the might of the Gentile, unsmote by the sword,
Hath melted like snow in the glance of the Lord!

LORD BYRON 1788–1824

Prologue

from *King Henry V*

O for a Muse of fire, that would ascend
The brightest heaven of invention,
A kingdom for a stage, princes to act,
And monarchs to behold the swelling scene!
Then should the warlike Harry, like himself,
Assume the port of Mars; and at his heels,
Leash'd in like hounds, should famine, sword, and fire,
Crouch for employment. But pardon, gentles all,
The flat unraised spirits that hath dar'd
On this unworthy scaffold to bring forth
So great an object. Can this cockpit hold
The vasty fields of France? Or may we cram
Within this wooden O the very casques
That did affright the air at Agincourt?
O, pardon! since a crooked figure may

Attest in little place a million;
And let us, ciphers to this great accompt,
On your imaginary forces work.
Suppose within the girdle of these walls
Are now confin'd two mighty monarchies,
Whose high upreared and abutting fronts
The perilous narrow ocean parts asunder.
Piece out our imperfections with your thoughts:
Into a thousand parts divide one man,
And make imaginary puissance;
Think, when we talk of horses, that you see them
Printing their proud hoofs i' th' receiving earth;
For 'tis your thoughts that now must deck our kings,
Carry them here and there, jumping o'er times,
Turning th' accomplishment of many years
Into an hour-glass; for the which supply,
Admit me Chorus to this history;
Who, prologue-like, your humble patience pray
Gently to hear, kindly to judge, our play.

WILLIAM SHAKESPEARE

Once to Every Man and Nation

Once to every man and nation
   Comes the moment to decide,
In the strife of truth with falsehood,
   For the good or evil side:
Some great cause, God's new Messiah,
   Offering each the bloom or blight;
And the choice goes by for ever
   'Twixt that darkness and that light.

Then to side with truth is noble,
   When we share her wretched crust,
Ere her cause bring fame and profit,
   And 'tis prosperous to be just;

Then it is the brave man chooses,
    While the coward stands aside,
Till the multitude make virtue
    Of the faith they had denied.

By the light of burning martyrs,
    Christ, thy bleeding feet we track,
Toiling up new Calvaries ever
    With the cross that turns not back.
New occasions teach new duties;
    Time makes ancient good uncouth;
They must upward still and onward
    Who would keep abreast of truth.

Though the cause of evil prosper,
    Yet 'tis truth alone is strong;
Though her portion be the scaffold,
    And upon the throne be wrong,
Yet that scaffold sways the future,
    And, behind the dim unknown,
Standeth God within the shadow,
    Keeping watch above his own.
                JAMES RUSSELL LOWELL 1819–91

Rendezvous

I have a rendezvous with Death
At some disputed barricade,
When Spring comes back with rustling shade
And apple-blossoms fill the air –
I have a rendezvous with Death
When Spring brings back blue days and fair.

It may be he shall take my hand
And lead me into his dark land
And close my eyes and quench my breath –
It may be I shall pass him still.

I have a rendezvous with Death
On some scarred slope of battered hill,
When Spring comes round again this year
And the first meadow-flowers appear.

God knows 'twere better to be deep
Pillowed in silk and scented down,
Where love throbs out in blissful sleep,
Pulse nigh to pulse, and breath to breath,
Where hushed awakenings are dear . . .
But I've a rendezvous with Death
At midnight in some flaming town,
When Spring trips north again this year,
And I to my pledged word am true,
I shall not fail that rendezvous.

ALAN SEEGER 1888–1916

Elegy in a Country Churchyard

The men that worked for England
They have their graves at home:
And bees and birds of England
About the cross can roam.

But they that fought for England,
Following a falling star,
Alas, alas for England
They have their graves afar.

And they that rule in England,
In stately conclave met,
Alas, alas for England
They have no graves as yet.

G. K. CHESTERTON

Luck

I suppose they'll say his last thoughts were of simple things,
Of April back at home, and the late sun on his wings;
Or that he murmured someone's name
As earth reclaimed him sheathed in flame.
Oh God! Let's have no more of empty words,
Lip service ornamenting death!
The worms don't spare the hero;
Nor can children feed upon resounding praises of his deed.
'He died who loved to live,' they'll say,
'Unselfishly so we might have today!'
Like hell! He fought because he had to fight;
He died that's all. It was his unlucky night.

DENNIS MCHARRIE

An Irish Airman Foresees His Death

I know that I shall meet my fate
Somewhere among the clouds above;
Those that I fight I do not hate,
Those that I guard I do not love;
My country is Kiltartan Cross,
My countrymen Kiltartan's poor,
No likely end could bring them loss
Or leave them happier than before.
Nor law, nor duty bade me fight,
Nor public men, nor cheering crowds,
A lonely impulse of delight
Drove to this tumult in the clouds;
I balanced all, brought all to mind,
The years to come seemed waste of breath,
A waste of breath the years behind
In balance with this life, this death.

W. B. YEATS

A Dead Statesman

from *Epitaphs of the War 1914–18*

I could not dig: I dared not rob:
Therefore I lied to please the mob.
Now all my lies are proved untrue
And I must face the men I slew.
What tale shall serve me here among
Mine angry and defrauded young?

RUDYARD KIPLING

When Statesmen Gravely Say

When Statesmen gravely say – 'We must be realistic –'
The chances are they're weak and, therefore, pacifistic,
But when they speak of Principles, look out: perhaps
Their generals are already poring over maps.

W. H. AUDEN

A Ballad of Glyn Dŵr's Rising

My son, the mist is clearing and the moon will soon be high,
And then we'll hear the thudding hooves, the horsemen
      speeding by,
With murmurs coming nearer, carried over on the breeze
Of the men who march in secret through the cloisters of the trees:
Tonight we two go riding, for the threads of fate are spun,
And we join Glyn Dŵr at Corwen at the rising of the sun.

For yesterday our leader was proclaimed the Prince of Wales,
His call to arms is sounding now among the hills and vales,
And Owain, heir of dynasties, in this auspicious year
May be our great deliverer, foretold by bard and seer:
And rumour runs that Arthur's voice is heard along the west
Acclaiming this descendant of Cadwaladr the Blest.

At last shall I unsheath again my father's two-edged sword,
And hand you mine to strike amain at Ruthin's tyrant lord,

Because I've waited, waited long throughout the bitter years
For this hour of freedom's challenge and the flashing of the
    spears:
So now we two must face as one the hazards of the night
To pledge our lives to Owain at the breaking of the light.

My son, go kiss your mother, kiss her gently, she'll not wake,
For an older mother calls you, though you perish for her sake:
The fabled Dragon banner flies once more above the Dee
Where the sons of Wales are gathering to set our people free
From wrong and dire oppression: pray, my son, for strength
    anew,
For widows will be weeping at the falling of the dew.

A. G. PRYS-JONES 1888–1986

from *Horatius*

I

Lars Porsena of Clusium
    By the Nine Gods he swore
That the great house of Tarquin
    Should suffer wrong no more.
By the Nine Gods he swore it,
    And named a trysting day,
And bade his messengers ride forth,
East and west and south and north,
    To summon his array.

II

East and west and south and north
    The messengers ride fast,
And tower and town and cottage
    Have heard the trumpet's blast.
Shame on the false Etruscan
    Who lingers in his home,
When Porsena of Clusium
    Is on the march for Rome.

III

The horsemen and the footmen
   Are pouring in amain
From many a stately market-place;
   From many a fruitful plain;
From many a lonely hamlet,
   Which, hid by beech and pine,
Like an eagle's nest, hangs on the crest
   Of purple Apennine; . . .

XI

And now hath every city
   Sent up her tale of men;
The foot are fourscore thousand,
   The horse are thousands ten:
Before the gates of Sutrium
   Is met the great array.
A proud man was Lars Porsena
   Upon the trysting day.

XII

For all the Etruscan armies
   Were ranged beneath his eye,
And many a banished Roman,
   And many a stout ally;
And with a mighty following
   To join the muster came
The Tusculan Mamilius,
   Prince of the Latian name.

XIII

But by the yellow Tiber
   Was tumult and affright:
From all the spacious champaign
   To Rome men took their flight.
A mile around the city,
   The throng stopped up the ways;
A fearful sight it was to see
   Through two long nights and days. . . .

XIX

They held a council standing
  Before the River-Gate;
Short time was there, ye well may guess,
  For musing or debate.
Out spake the Consul roundly:
  'The bridge must straight go down;
For, since Janiculum is lost,
  Nought else can save the town.'

XX

Just then a scout came flying,
  All wild with haste and fear;
'To arms! to arms! Sir Consul:
  Lars Porsena is here.'
On the low hills to westward
  The Consul fixed his eye,
And saw the swarthy storm of dust
  Rise fast along the sky.

XXI

And nearer fast and nearer
  Doth the red whirlwind come;
And louder still and still more loud,
From underneath that rolling cloud,
Is heard the trumpet's war-note proud,
  The trampling, and the hum.
And plainly and more plainly
  Now through the gloom appears,
Far to left and far to right,
In broken gleams of dark-blue light,
The long array of helmets bright,
  The long array of spears.

XXII

And plainly and more plainly,
  Above that glimmering line,
Now might ye see the banners
  Of twelve fair cities shine;

But the banner of proud Clusium
  Was highest of them all,
The terror of the Umbrian,
  The terror of the Gaul. . . .

XXVI

But the Consul's brow was sad,
  And the Consul's speech was low,
And darkly looked he at the wall,
  And darkly at the foe.
'Their van will be upon us
  Before the bridge goes down;
And if they once may win the bridge,
  What hope to save the town?'

XXVII

Then out spake brave Horatius,
  The Captain of the Gate:
'To every man upon this earth
  Death cometh soon or late.
And how can man die better
  Than facing fearful odds,
For the ashes of his fathers,
  And the temples of his Gods,

XXVIII

'And for the tender mother
  Who dandled him to rest,
And for the wife who nurses
  His baby at her breast,
And for the holy maidens
  Who feed the eternal flame,
To save them from false Sextus
  That wrought the deed of shame?

XXIX

'Hew down the bridge, Sir Consul,
  With all the speed ye may;

I, with two more to help me,
  Will hold the foe in play.
In yon strait path a thousand
  May well be stopped by three.
Now who will stand on either hand,
  And keep the bridge with me?'

XXX

Then out spake Spurius Lartius;
  A Ramnian proud was he:
'Lo, I will stand at thy right hand,
  And keep the bridge with thee.'
And out spake strong Herminius;
  Of Titian blood was he:
'I will abide on thy left side,
  And keep the bridge with thee.'

XXXI

'Horatius,' quoth the Consul,
  'As thou sayest, so let it be.'
And straight against that great array
  Forth went the dauntless Three.
For Romans in Rome's quarrel
  Spared neither land nor gold,
Nor son nor wife, nor limb nor life,
  In the brave days of old.

XXXII

Then none was for a party;
  Then all were for the state;
Then the great man helped the poor,
  And the poor man loved the great;
Then lands were fairly portioned;
  Then spoils were fairly sold:
The Romans were like brothers
  In the brave days of old.

XXXIII

Now Roman is to Roman
  More hateful than a foe,

And the Tribunes beard the high,
   And the Fathers grind the low.
As we wax hot in faction,
   In battle we wax cold:
Wherefore men fight not as they fought
   In the brave days of old.

XXXIV

Now while the Three were tightening
   Their harness on their backs,
The Consul was the foremost man
   To take in hand an axe:
And Fathers mixed with Commons
   Seized hatchet, bar, and crow,
And smote upon the planks above,
   And loosed the props below.

XXXV

Meanwhile the Tuscan army,
   Right glorious to behold,
Came flashing back the noonday light,
Rank behind rank, like surges bright
   Of a broad sea of gold. . . .

Four hundred trumpets sounded
   A peal of warlike glee,
As that great host, with measured tread,
And spears advanced, and ensigns spread,
Rolled slowly towards the bridge's head,
   Where stood the dauntless Three.

L

Was none who would be foremost
   To lead such dire attack:
But those behind cried 'Forward!'
   And those before cried 'Back!'
And backward now and forward
   Wavers the deep array;
And on the tossing sea of steel,
   To and fro the standards reel;

And the victorious trumpet-peal
　　Dies fitfully away.

LI

Yet one man for one moment
　　Stood out before the crowd;
Well known was he to all the Three,
　　And they gave him greeting loud,
'Now welcome, welcome, Sextus!
　　Now welcome to thy home!
Why dost thou stay, and turn away?
　　Here lies the road to Rome.'

LII

Thrice looked he at the city;
　　Thrice looked he at the dead;
And thrice came on in fury,
　　And thrice turned back in dread:
And, white with fear and hatred,
　　Scowled at the narrow way
Where, wallowing in a pool of blood,
　　The bravest Tuscans lay.

LIII

But meanwhile axe and lever
　　Have manfully been plied;
And now the bridge hangs tottering
　　Above the boiling tide.
'Come back, come back, Horatius!'
　　Loud cried the Fathers all.
'Back, Lartius! back, Herminius!
　　Back, ere the ruin fall!'

LIV

Back darted Spurius Lartius;
　　Herminius darted back:
And as they passed, beneath their feet
　　They felt the timbers crack.

But when they turned their faces,
  And on the farther shore
Saw brave Horatius stand alone,
  They would have crossed once more.

LV

But with a crash like thunder
  Fell every loosened beam,
And, like a dam, the mighty wreck
  Lay right athwart the stream:
And a long shout of triumph
  Rose from the walls of Rome,
As to the highest turret-tops
  Was splashed the yellow foam.

LVI

And, like a horse unbroken
  When first he feels the rein,
The furious river struggled hard,
  And tossed his tawny mane,
And burst the curb, and bounded,
  Rejoicing to be free,
And whirling down, in fierce career,
Battlement, and plank, and pier,
  Rushed headlong to the sea.

LVII

Alone stood brave Horatius,
  But constant still in mind;
Thrice thirty thousand foes before,
  And the broad flood behind.
'Down with him!' cried false Sextus,
  With a smile on his pale face.
'Now yield thee,' cried Lars Porsena,
  'Now yield thee to our grace.'

LVIII

Round turned he, as not deigning
  Those craven ranks to see;

Nought spake he to Lars Porsena,
  To Sextus nought spake he;
But he saw on Palatinus
  The white porch of his home;
And he spake to the noble river
  That rolls by the towers of Rome.

LIX

'Oh, Tiber! father Tiber!
  To whom the Romans pray,
A Roman's life, a Roman's arms,
  Take thou in charge this day!'
So he spake, and speaking sheathed
  The good sword by his side,
And with his harness on his back,
  Plunged headlong in the tide.

LX

No sound of joy or sorrow
  Was heard from either bank;
But friends and foes in dumb surprise,
With parted lips and straining eyes,
  Stood gazing where he sank;
And when above the surges
  They saw his crest appear,
All Rome sent forth a rapturous cry,
And even the ranks of Tuscany
  Could scarce forbear to cheer.

LXI

But fiercely ran the current,
  Swollen high by months of rain:
And fast his blood was flowing;
  And he was sore in pain,
And heavy with his armour,
  And spent with changing blows;
And oft they thought him sinking,
  But still again he rose.

LXII

Never, I ween, did swimmer,
   In such an evil case,
Struggle through such a raging flood
   Safe to the landing place:
But his limbs were borne up bravely
   By the brave heart within,
And our good father Tiber
   Bore bravely up his chin.

LXIII

'Curse on him!' quoth false Sextus;
   'Will not the villain drown?
But for this stay, ere close of day
   We should have sacked the town!'
'Heaven help him!' quoth Lars Porsena,
   'And bring him safe to shore;
For such a gallant feat of arms
   Was never seen before.'

LXIV

And now he feels the bottom;
   Now on dry earth he stands;
Now round him throng the Fathers
   To press his gory hands;
And now, with shouts and clapping,
   And noise of weeping loud,
He enters through the River-Gate,
   Borne by the joyous crowd.

LXV

They gave him of the corn-land,
   That was of public right,
As much as two strong oxen
   Could plough from morn till night;
And they made a molten image,
   And set it up on high,
And there it stands unto this day
   To witness if I lie.

LXVI

It stands in the Comitium,
    Plain for all folk to see;
Horatius in his harness,
    Halting upon one knee:
And underneath is written,
    In letters all of gold,
How valiantly he kept the bridge
    In the brave days of old.

THOMAS BABINGTON MACAULAY 1800–59

Scots, Wha Hae

Scots, wha hae wi' Wallace bled,
Scots, wham Bruce has aften led,
Welcome to your gory bed,
    Or to victory!

Now's the day, and now's the hour;
See the front o' battle lour,
See approach proud Edward's power –
    Chains and slaverie!

Wha will be a traitor knave?
Wha can fill a coward's grave?
Wha sae base as be a slave? –
    Let him turn, and flee!

Wha for Scotland's King and Law
Freedom's sword will strongly draw,
Freeman stand or freeman fa',
    Let him follow me!

By Oppression's woes and pains,
By your sons in servile chains,
We will drain our dearest veins,
    But they shall be free!

Lay the proud usurpers low!
Tyrants fall in every foe!
Liberty's in every blow!
Let us do, or die!

ROBERT BURNS
(This commemorates the defeat of the English at Bannockburn, 1314.)

Before Harfleur

from *King Henry V*, Act III, Scene i

Once more unto the breach, dear friends, once more;
Or close the wall up with our English dead.
In peace there's nothing so becomes a man
As modest stillness and humility;
But when the blast of war blows in our ears,
Then imitate the action of the tiger;
Stiffen the sinews, summon up the blood,
Disguise fair nature with hard-favour'd rage;
Then lend the eye a terrible aspect;
Let it pry through the portage of the head
Like the brass cannon; let the brow o'erwhelm it
As fearfully as doth a gallèd rock
O'erhang and jutty his confounded base,
Swill'd with the wild and wasteful ocean.
Now set the teeth and stretch the nostril wide;
Hold hard the breath, and bend up every spirit
To his full height. On, on, you noblest English,
Whose blood is fet from fathers of warproof –
Fathers that like so many Alexanders
Have in these parts from morn till even fought,
And sheath'd their swords for lack of argument.
Dishonour not your mothers; now attest
That those whom you call'd fathers did beget you.
Be copy now to men of grosser blood,
And teach them how to war. And you, good yeomen,
Whose limbs were made in England, show us here
The mettle of your pasture; let us swear

179

That you are worth your breeding – which I doubt not;
For there is none of you so mean and base
That hath not noble lustre in your eyes.
I see you stand like greyhounds in the slips,
Straining upon the start. The game's afoot:
Follow your spirit; and upon this charge
Cry 'God for Harry, England, and Saint George!'

WILLIAM SHAKESPEARE

Before Agincourt

from *King Henry V*, Act IV, Scene iii

This day is called the feast of Crispian:
He that outlives this day and comes safe home,
Will stand a tip-toe when this day is named,
And rouse him at the name of Crispian.
He that shall see this day, and live old age,
Will yearly on the vigil feast his neighbours,
And say, 'to-morrow is Saint Crispian':
Then will he strip his sleeve and show his scars,
And say 'These wounds I had on Crispin's day.'
Old men forget; yet all shall be forgot,
But he'll remember, with advantages,
What feats he did that day: then shall our names,
Familiar in his mouth as household words,
Harry the king, Bedford and Exeter,
Warwick and Talbot, Salisbury and Gloucester,
Be in their flowing cups freshly remembered:
This story shall the good man teach his son;
And Crispin Crispian shall ne'er go by,
From this day to the ending of the world,
But we in it shall be remembered:
We few, we happy few, we band of brothers;
For he to-day that sheds his blood with me
Shall be my brother; be he ne'er so vile
This day shall gentle his condition:

And gentlemen in England, now a-bed,
Shall think themselves accursed they were not here;
And hold their manhoods cheap, while any speaks
That fought with us upon Saint Crispin's day.

WILLIAM SHAKESPEARE

Say not the Struggle Nought Availeth

Say not the struggle nought availeth,
   The labour and the wounds are vain,
The enemy faints not, nor faileth,
   And as things have been, things remain.

If hopes were dupes, fears may be liars;
   It may be, in yon smoke concealed,
Your comrades chase e'en now the fliers,
   And, but for you, possess the field.

For while the tired waves, vainly breaking,
   Seem here no painful inch to gain,
Far back through creeks and inlets making
   Comes, silent, flooding in, the main,

And not by eastern windows only,
   When daylight comes, comes in the light,
In front the sun climbs slow, how slowly,
   But westward, look, the land is bright.

ARTHUR HUGH CLOUGH 1819–61

(This last line was quoted by Winston Churchill in April 1941 at the end of a speech.)

Lepanto

White founts falling in the courts of the sun,
And the Soldan of Byzantium is smiling as they run;
There is laughter like the fountains in that face of all men feared,
It stirs the forest darkness, the darkness of his beard,
It curls the blood-red crescent, the crescent of his lips,
For the inmost sea of all the earth is shaken with his ships.
They have dared the white republics up the capes of Italy,
They have dashed the Adriatic round the Lion of the Sea,
And the Pope has cast his arms abroad for agony and loss,
And called the kings of Christendom for swords about the
    Cross,
The cold queen of England is looking in the glass;
The shadow of the Valois is yawning at the Mass;
From evening isles fantastical rings faint the Spanish gun,
And the Lord upon the Golden Horn is laughing in the sun.
Dim drums throbbing, in the hills half heard,
Where only on a nameless throne a crownless prince has stirred,
Where, risen from a doubtful seat and half-attainted stall,
The last knight of Europe takes weapons from the wall,
The last and lingering troubadour to whom the bird has sung,
That once went singing southward when all the world was
    young,
In that enormous silence, tiny and unafraid,
Comes up along a winding road the noise of the Crusade.
Strong gongs groaning as the guns boom far,
Don John of Austria is going to the war,
Stiff flags straining in the night-blasts cold
In the gloom black-purple, in the glint old-gold,
Torchlight crimson on the copper kettle-drums,
Then the tuckets, then the trumpets, then the cannon, and he
    comes.
Don John laughing in the brave beard curled,
Spurning of his stirrups like the thrones of all the world,
Holding his head up for a flag of all the free.
Love-light of Spain – hurrah!
Death-light of Africa!
Don John of Austria
Is riding to the sea.

G. K. CHESTERTON

Drake's Drum

Drake he's in his hammock an' a thousand mile away,
  (Capten, art tha sleepin' there below?),
Slung atween the round shot in Nombre Dios Bay,
  An' dreamin' arl the time o' Plymouth Hoe.
Yarnder lumes the Island, yarnder lie the ships,
  Wi' sailor lads a dancin' heel-an'-toe,
An' the shore-lights flashin', an' the night-tide dashin',
  He sees et arl so plainly as he saw et long ago.

Drake he was a Devon man, an' rüled the Devon seas,
  (Capten, art tha sleepin' there below?),
Rovin' tho' his death fell, he went wi' heart at ease,
  An' dreamin' arl the time o' Plymouth Hoe.
'Take my drum to England, hang et by the shore,
  Strike et when your powder's runnin' low;
If the Dons sight Devon, I'll quit the port o' Heaven,
  An' drum them up the Channel as we drummed them
    long ago.'

Drake he's in his hammock till the great Armadas come,
  (Capten, art tha sleepin' there below?),
Slung atween the round shot, listenin' for the drum,
  An' dreamin' arl the time o' Plymouth Hoe.
Call him on the deep sea, call him up the Sound,
  Call him when ye sail to meet the foe;
Where the old trades' plyin' an' the old flag flyin'
  They shall find him ware an' wakin', as they found him long
    ago!

SIR HENRY NEWBOLT 1862–1938

Valiant-for-Truth's Song

Who would true Valour see
Let him come hither;
One here will Constant be,
Come Wind, come Weather.
There's no *Discouragement*
Shall make him once *Relent*,
His first avow'd *Intent*,
To be a Pilgrim.

Who so beset him round,
With dismal *Storys*,
Do but themselves Confound;
His Strength the *more is*.
No *Lyon* can him fright,
He'l with a *Gyant* Fight,
But he will have a right,
To be a Pilgrim.

Hobgoblin, nor foul *Fiend*,
Can *daunt* his Spirit:
He knows, he *at the end*,
Shall Life Inherit.
Then Fancies fly away,
He'l fear not what men say,
He'l labour Night and Day,
To be a Pilgrim.

JOHN BUNYAN 1628–88

The Gift Outright

The land was ours before we were the land's.
She was our land more than a hundred years
Before we were her people. She was ours
In Massachusetts, in Virginia,
But we were England's, still colonials,
Possessing what we still were unpossessed by,
Possessed by what we now no more possessed.

Something we were withholding made us weak
Until we found out that it was ourselves
We were withholding from our land of living,
And forthwith found salvation in surrender.
Such as we were we gave ourselves outright
(The deed of gift was many deeds of war)
To the land vaguely realizing westward,
But still unstoried, artless, unenhanced,
Such as she was, such as she would become.

ROBERT FROST 1874–1963

The Star-Spangled Banner

O say, can you see, by the dawn's early light,
    What so proudly we hailed at the twilight's last gleaming –
Whose broad stripes and bright stars, through the clouds of the
        fight,
    O'er the ramparts we watched were so gallantly streaming!
And the rocket's red glare, the bombs bursting in air,
Gave proof through the night that our flag was still there;
O! say, does that star-spangled banner yet wave
O'er the land of the free, and the home of the brave?

On that shore dimly seen through the mists of the deep,
    Where the foe's haughty host in dread silence reposes,
What is that which the breeze, o'er the towering steep,
    As it fitfully blows, now conceals, now discloses?
Now it catches the gleam of the morning's first beam,
In full glory reflected now shines on the stream;
'Tis the star-spangled banner; O long may it wave
O'er the land of the free, and the home of the brave!

And where is that band who so vauntingly swore
    That the havoc of war and the battle's confusion
A home and a country should leave us no more?
    Their blood has washed out their foul footsteps' pollution.
No refuge could save the hireling and slave
From the terror of flight, or the gloom of the grave;

And the star-spangled banner in triumph doth wave
O'er the land of the free, and the home of the brave.

O! thus be it ever, when freemen shall stand
    Between their loved homes and the war's desolation!
Blest with victory and peace, may the heav'n-rescued land
    Praise the power that hath made and preserved us a nation.
Then conquer we must, when our cause it is just,
And this be our motto – '*In God is our trust*':
And the star-spangled banner in triumph shall wave
O'er the land of the free, and the home of the brave.

FRANCIS SCOTT KEY 1780–1843

(The American flag, then with only fifteen stars, flew over Fort McHenry, Baltimore
during the attack by the British fleet in the War of 1812.)

A March in the Ranks Hard-Prest, and the Road Unknown

A march in the ranks hard-prest, and the road unknown;
A route through a heavy wood, with muffled steps in the
    darkness;
Our army foil'd with loss severe, and the sullen remnant
    retreating;
Till after midnight glimmer upon us, the lights of a dim-
    lighted building;
We come to an open space in the woods, and halt by the
    dim-lighted building;
'Tis a large old church, at the crossing roads – 'tis now
    an impromptu hospital;
– Entering but for a minute, I see a sight beyond all the
    pictures and poems ever made:
Shadows of deepest, deepest black, just lit by moving
    candles and lamps,
And by one great pitchy torch, stationary, with wild red
    flame, and clouds of smoke;
By these, crowds, groups of forms, vaguely I see, on the
    floor, some in the pews laid down;
At my feet more distinctly, a soldier, a mere lad, in dan-
    ger of bleeding to death, (he is shot in the abdomen;)

I staunch the blood temporarily, (the youngster's face is
    white as a lily;)
Then before I depart I sweep my eyes o'er the scene, fain
    to absorb it all;
Faces, varieties, postures beyond description, most in
    obscurity, some of them dead;
Surgeons operating, attendants holding lights, the smell
    of ether, the odor of blood;
The crowd, O the crowd of the bloody forms of soldiers
    – the yard outside also fill'd;
Some on the bare ground, some on planks or stretchers,
    some in the death-spasm sweating;
An occasional scream or cry, the doctor's shouted orders
    or calls;
The glisten of the little steel instruments catching the
    glint of the torches;
These I resume as I chant – I see again the forms, I
    smell the odor;
Then hear outside the orders given, *Fall in, my men,*
    Fall in;
But first I bend to the dying lad – his eyes open – a
    half-smile gives he me;
Then the eyes close, calmly close, and I speed forth to
    the darkness,
Resuming, marching, as ever in darkness marching, on in
    the ranks,
The unknown road still marching.

WALT WHITMAN 1819–92

Address at Gettysburg

Fourscore and seven years ago our fathers brought
forth on this continent, a new nation, conceived in
Liberty, and dedicated to the proposition that all
men are created equal.

    Now we are engaged in a great civil war, testing
whether that nation or any nation so conceived
and so dedicated can long endure. We are met on
a great battlefield of that war. We have come to
dedicate a portion of that field, as a final resting

place for those who here gave their lives that that nation might live. It is altogether fitting and proper that we should do this.

But, in a larger sense, we cannot dedicate – we cannot consecrate – we cannot hallow – this ground. The brave men, living and dead, who struggled here, have consecrated it far above our poor power to add or detract. The world will little note nor long remember what we say here, but it can never forget what they did here. It is for us, the living, rather to be dedicated here to the unfinished work which they who fought here have thus far so nobly advanced. It is rather for us to be here dedicated to the great task remaining before us – that from these honored dead we take increased devotion to that cause for which they gave the last full measure of devotion; that we here highly resolve that these dead shall not have died in vain; that this nation, under God, shall have a new birth of freedom; and that government of the people, by the people, for the people, shall not perish from the earth.

ABRAHAM LINCOLN 19 NOVEMBER 1863

The Martyr

Good Friday was the day
  Of the prodigy and crime,
When they killed him in his pity,
  When they killed him in his prime
Of clemency and calm
When with yearning he was filled
    To redeem the evil-willed,
And, though conqueror, be kind;
  But they killed him in his kindness,
  In their madness and their blindness,
And they killed him from behind.

There is sobbing of the strong,
  And a pall upon the land;

188

But the People in their weeping
   Bare the iron hand;
Beware the People weeping
   When they bare the iron hand.

He lieth in his blood –
   The father in his face;
They have killed him, the Forgiver –
   The Avenger takes his place,
The Avenger wisely stern,
      Who in righteousness shall do
      What the heavens call him to,
And the parricides remand;
   For they killed him in his kindness,
   In their madness and their blindness,
And his blood is on their hand.

There is sobbing of the strong,
   And a pall upon the land;
But the People in their weeping
   Bare the iron hand;
Beware the People weeping
   When they bare the iron hand.

HERMAN MELVILLE 1819–91
(Indicative of the passion of the people on the
15 April 1865, after the assassination of Lincoln.)

O Captain! My Captain!

I

O captain! my captain! our fearful trip is done;
The ship has weather'd every rack, the prize we sought
   is won;
The port is near, the bells I hear, the people all exulting,
While follow eyes the steady keel, the vessel grim and
   daring:
      But O heart! heart! heart!
        Leave you not the little spot,
          Where on the deck my captain lies,
          Fallen cold and dead.

O captain! my captain! rise up and hear the bells;
Rise up – for you the flag is flung – for you the bugle
   trills;
For you bouquets and ribbon'd wreaths – for you the
   shores a–crowding;
For you they call, the swaying mass, their eager faces
   turning;
            O captain! dear father!
                  This arm I push beneath you;
                        It is some dream that on the deck,
                              You've fallen cold and dead.

My captain does not answer, his lips are pale and still;
My father does not feel my arm, he has no pulse nor will:
But the ship, the ship is anchor'd safe, its voyage closed
   and done;
From fearful trip, the victor ship, comes in with object
   won:
            Exult, O shores, and ring, O bells!
                  But I, with silent tread,
                        Walk the spot my captain lies,
                              Fallen cold and dead.

WALT WHITMAN

Let America Be America Again

Let America be America again.
Let it be the dream it used to be.
Let it be the pioneer on the plain
Seeking a home where he himself is free.

(America never was America to me.)

Let America be the dream the dreamers dreamed –
Let it be that great strong land of love

Where never kings connive nor tyrants scheme
That any man be crushed by one above.

(It never was America to me.)

O, let my land be a land where Liberty
Is crowned with no false patriotic wreath,
But opportunity is real, and life is free,
Equality is in the air we breathe.

(There's never been equality for me,
Nor freedom in this 'homeland of the free.')

Say who are you that mumbles in the dark?
And who are you that draws your veil across the stars?

I am the poor white, fooled and pushed apart,
I am the Negro bearing slavery's scars.
I am the red man driven from the land,
I am the immigrant clutching the hope I seek –
And finding only the same old stupid plan
Of dog eat dog, of mighty crush the weak.

I am the young man, full of strength and hope,
Tangled in that ancient endless chain
Of profit, power, gain, of grab the land!
Of grab the gold! Of grab the ways of satisfying need!
Of work the men! Of take the pay!
Of owning everything for one's own greed!

I am the farmer, bondsman to the soil.
I am the worker sold to the machine.
I am the Negro, servant to you all.
I am the people, humble, hungry, mean –
Hungry yet today despite the dream.
Beaten yet today – O, Pioneers!
I am the man who never got ahead,
The poorest worker bartered through the years.

Yet I'm the one who dreamt our basic dream
In that Old World while still a serf of kings,
Who dreamt a dream so strong, so brave, so true,
That even yet its mighty daring sings
In every brick and stone, in every furrow turned
That's made America the land it has become.
O, I'm the man who sailed those early seas
In search of what I meant to be my home –
For I'm the one who left dark Ireland's shore,
And Poland's plain, and England's grassy lea,
And torn from Black Africa's strand I came
To build a 'homeland of the free.'

The free?

Who said the free? Not me?
Surely not me? The millions on relief today?
The millions shot down when we strike?

The millions who have nothing for our pay?
For all the dreams we've dreamed
And all the songs we've sung
And all the hopes we've held
And all the flags we've hung,
The millions who have nothing for our pay –
Except the dream that's almost dead today.

O, let America be America again –
The land that never has been yet –
And yet must be – the land where *every* man is free.
The land that's mine – the poor man's, Indian's, Negro's, ME –
Who made America,
Whose sweat and blood, whose faith and pain,
Whose hand at the foundry, whose plow in the rain,
Must bring back our mighty dream again.

Sure, call me any ugly name you choose –
The steel of freedom does not stain.
From those who live like leeches on the people's lives,
We must take back our land again,
America!

O, yes,
I say it plain,
America never was America to me,
And yet I swear this oath –
America will be!

Out of the rack and ruin of our gangster death,
The rape and rot of graft, and stealth, and lies,
We, the people, must redeem
The land, the mines, the plants, the rivers,
The mountains and the endless plain –
All, all the stretch of these great green states –
And make America again!

LANGSTON HUGHES 1902–67

The Song of the Western Men

A good sword and a trusty hand!
   A merry heart and true!
King James's men shall understand
   What Cornish lads can do.

And have they fixed the where and when?
   And shall Trelawny die?
Here's twenty thousand Cornish men
   Will know the reason why!

Out spake their captain brave and bold,
   A merry wight was he:
'If London Tower were Michael's hold,
   We'd set Trelawny free!

'We'll cross the Tamar, land to land,
   The Severn is no stay,
With "one and all," and hand in hand,
   And who shall bid us nay?

'And when we come to London Wall,
  A pleasant sight to view,
Come forth! come forth! ye cowards all,
  Here's men as good as you.

'Trelawny he's in keep and hold,
  Trelawny he may die;
But here's twenty thousand Cornish bold
  Will know the reason why!'

ROBERT S. HAWKER 1803–75

The Charge of the Light Brigade

Half a league, half a league,
Half a league onward,
All in the valley of Death
  Rode the six hundred.
  'Forward, the Light Brigade!
Charge for the guns!' he said.
Into the valley of Death
  Rode the six hundred.

'Forward, the Light Brigade!'
Was there a man dismayed?
Not though the soldier knew
  Some one had blundered.
Theirs not to make reply,
Theirs not to reason why,
Theirs but to do and die.
Into the valley of Death
  Rode the six hundred.

Cannon to right of them,
Cannon to left of them,
Cannon in front of them
  Volleyed and thundered;
Stormed at with shot and shell,
Boldly they rode and well,
Into the jaws of Death,
Into the mouth of Hell
  Rode the six hundred.

Flashed all the sabres bare,
Flashed as they turned in air
Sabring the gunners there,
Charging an army, while
    All the world wondered:
Plunged in the battery-smoke
Right through the line they broke:
Cossack and Russian
Reeled from the sabre-stroke
    Shattered and sundered.
Then they rode back, but not,
    Not the six hundred.

Cannon to right of them,
Cannon to left of them,
Cannon behind them
    Volleyed and thundered;
Stormed at with shot and shell,
While horse and hero fell,
They that had fought so well
Came through the jaws of Death,
Back from the mouth of Hell,
All that was left of them,
    Left of six hundred.

When can their glory fade?
O the wild charge they made!
    All the world wondered.
Honour the charge they made!
Honour the Light Brigade,
    Noble six hundred!
ALFRED, LORD TENNYSON 1809–92

The Burial of Sir John Moore
After Corunna

Not a drum was heard, not a funeral note,
    As his corse to the rampart we hurried;

Not a soldier discharged his farewell shot
  O'er the grave where our hero we buried.

We buried him darkly at dead of night,
  The sods with our bayonets turning,
By the struggling moonbeam's misty light
  And the lantern dimly burning.

No useless coffin enclosed his breast,
  Not in sheet or in shroud we wound him;
But he lay like a warrior taking his rest
  With his martial cloak around him.

Few and short were the prayers we said,
  And we spoke not a word of sorrow;
But we steadfastly gazed on the face that was dead,
  And we bitterly thought of the morrow.

We thought, as we hollowed his narrow bed
  And smoothed down his lonely pillow,
That the foe and the stranger would tread o'er his head,
  And we far away on the billow!

Lightly they'll talk of the spirit that's gone,
  And o'er his cold ashes upbraid him –
But little he'll reck, if they let him sleep on
  In the grave where a Briton has laid him.

But half of our heavy task was done
  When the clock struck the hour for retiring;
And we heard the distant and random gun
  That the foe was sullenly firing.

Slowly and sadly we laid him down,
  From the field of his fame fresh and gory;
We carved not a line, and we raised not a stone,
  But we left him alone with his glory!

CHARLES WOLFE 1791–1823

Drummer Hodge

I

They throw in Drummer Hodge, to rest
   Uncoffined – just as found:
His landmark is a kopje-crest
   That breaks the veldt around;
And foreign constellations west
   Each night above his mound.

II

Young Hodge the Drummer never knew –
   Fresh from his Wessex home –
The meaning of the broad Karoo,
   The Bush, the dusty loam,
And why uprose to nightly view
   Strange stars amid the gloam.

III

Yet portion of that unknown plain
   Will Hodge for ever be;
His homely Northern breast and brain
   Grow to some Southern tree,
And strange-eyed constellations reign
   His stars eternally.

THOMAS HARDY

The Wearing of the Green

Oh Paddy dear, and did you hear the news that's
   going round?
The shamrock is forbid by law to grow on Irish ground:
Saint Patrick's day no more we'll keep, his colour can't be
   seen,
For there's a cruel law agin the wearing of the Green.
I met with Napper Tandy and he took me by the hand,
And said he, How's poor old Ireland, and how does she
   stand?

She's the most distressful country that ever yet was seen;
They're hanging men and women for the wearing of the
        Green.
Then since the colour we must wear is England's cruel
        Red,
'Twill serve us to remind us of the blood that has been shed;
You may take the shamrock from your hat and cast it on
        the sod,
But never fear, 'twill take root there, though underfoot 'tis
        trod.
When laws can stop the blades of grass from growing as
        they grow,
And when the leaves in summertime their verdure dare not
        show,
Then I will change the colour that I wear in my caubeen;
But till that day, please God, I'll stick to wearing of the
        Green.

ANON.

Ulster

1912

('Their webs shall not become garments, neither shall they cover themselves with their works: their works are works of iniquity and the act of violence is in their hands.' – ISAIAH lix. 6.)

The dark eleventh hour
Draws on and sees us sold
To every evil power
We fought against of old.
Rebellion, rapine, hate,
Oppression, wrong and greed
Are loosed to rule our fate,
By England's act and deed.

The Faith in which we stand,
The laws we made and guard –
Our honour, lives, and land –
Are given for reward

To Murder done by night,
To Treason taught by day,
To folly, sloth, and spite,
And we are thrust away.

The blood our fathers spilt,
Our love, our toils, our pains,
Are counted us for guilt,
And only bind our chains.
Before an Empire's eyes
The traitor claims his price.
What need of further lies?
We are the sacrifice.

We asked no more than leave
To reap where we had sown,
Through good and ill to cleave
To our own flag and throne.
Now England's shot and steel
Beneath that flag must show
How loyal hearts should kneel
To England's oldest foe.

We know the wars prepared
On every peaceful home,
We know the hells declared
For such as serve not Rome –
The terror, threats, and dread
In market, hearth, and field –
We know, when all is said,
We perish if we yield.

Believe, we dare not boast,
Believe, we do not fear –
We stand to pay the cost
In all that men hold dear.
What answer from the North?
One Law, one Land, one Throne.
If England drive us forth
We shall not fall alone!

RUDYARD KIPLING

Whatever You Say,
Say Nothing

I

I'm writing just after an encounter
With an English journalist in search of 'views
On the Irish thing'. I'm back in winter
Quarters where bad news is no longer news,

Where media-men and stringers sniff and point,
Where zoom lenses, recorders and coiled leads
Litter the hotels. The times are out of joint
But I incline as much to rosary beads

As to the jottings and analyses
Of politicians and newspapermen
Who've scribbled down the long campaign from gas
And protest to gelignite and sten,

Who proved upon their pulses 'escalate',
'Backlash' and 'crack down', 'the provisional wing',
'Polarization' and 'long-standing hate'.
Yet I live here, I live here too, I sing,

Expertly civil tongued with civil neighbours
On the high wires of first wireless reports,
Sucking the fake taste, the stony flavours
Of those sanctioned, old, elaborate retorts:

'Oh, it's disgraceful, surely, I agree,'
'Where's it going to end?' 'It's getting worse.'
'They're murderers.' 'Internment, understandably . . .'
The 'voice of sanity' is getting hoarse.

II

Men die at hand. In blasted street and home
The gelignite's a common sound effect:
As the man said when Celtic won, 'The Pope of Rome
's a happy man this night.' His flock suspect

In their deepest heart of hearts the heretic
Has come at last to heel and to the stake.
We tremble near the flames but want no truck
With the actual firing. We're on the make

As ever. Long sucking the hind tit
Cold as a witch's and as hard to swallow
Still leaves us fork-tongued on the border bit:
The liberal papist note sounds hollow

When amplified and mixed in with the bangs
That shake all hearts and windows day and night.
(It's tempting here to rhyme on 'labour pangs'
And diagnose a rebirth in our plight

But that would be to ignore other symptoms.
Last night you didn't need a stethoscope
To hear the eructation of Orange drums
Allergic equally to Pearse and Pope.)

On all sides 'little platoons' are mustering –
The phrase is Cruise O'Brien's via that great
Blacklash, Burke – while I sit here with a pestering
Drouth for words at once both gaff and bait

To lure the tribal shoals to epigram
And order. I believe any of us
Could draw the line through bigotry and sham
Given the right line, *aere perennius*.

III

'Religion's never mentioned here,' of course.
'You know them by their eyes,' and hold your tongue.
'One side's as bad as the other,' never worse.
Christ, it's near time that some small leak was sprung

In the great dykes the Dutchman made
To dam the dangerous tide that followed Seamus.
Yet for all this art and sedentary trade
I am incapable. The famous

201

Northern reticence, the tight gag of place
And times: yes, yes. Of the 'wee six' I sing
Where to be saved you only must save face
And whatever you say, say nothing.

Smoke-signals are loud-mouthed compared with us:
Manoeuvrings to find out name and school,
Subtle discrimination by addresses
With hardly an exception to the rule

That Norman, Ken and Sidney signalled Prod
And Seamus (call me Sean) was sure-fire Pape.
O land of password, handgrip, wink and nod,
Of open minds as open as a trap,

Where tongues lie coiled, as under flames lie wicks,
Where half of us, as in a wooden horse
Were cabin'd and confined like wily Greeks,
Besieged within the siege, whispering morse.

IV

This morning from a dewy motorway
I saw the new camp for the internees:
A bomb had left a crater of fresh clay
In the roadside, and over in the trees

Machine-gun posts defined a real stockade.
There was that white mist you get on a low ground
And it was déjà-vu, some film made
Of Stalag 17, a bad dream with no sound.

Is there a life before death? That's chalked up
In Ballymurphy. Competence with pain,
Coherent miseries, a bite and sup,
We hug our little destiny again.

SEAMUS HEANEY 1939–

The Soldier

If I should die, think only this of me:
    That there's some corner of a foreign field
That is for ever England. There shall be
    In that rich earth a richer dust concealed;
A dust whom England bore, shaped, made aware,
    Gave, once, her flowers to love, her ways to roam,
A body of England's, breathing English air,
    Washed by the rivers, blessed by suns of home.

And think, this heart, all evil shed away,
    A pulse in the eternal mind, no less
        Gives somewhere back the thoughts by England given;
Her sights and sounds; dreams happy as her day;
    And laughter, learnt of friends; and gentleness,
        In hearts at peace, under an English heaven.

RUPERT BROOKE

from *Into Battle*

The thundering line of the battle stands,
    And in the air death moans and sings;
But Day shall clasp him with strong hands,
    And Night shall fold him in soft wings.

JULIAN GRENFELL 1888–1915

The Dead-Beat

He dropped, – more sullenly than wearily,
Lay stupid like a cod, heavy like meat,
And none of us could kick him to his feet;
Just blinked at my revolver, blearily;
– Didn't appear to know a war was on,
Or see the blasted trench at which he stared.
'I'll do 'em in,' he whined. 'If this hand's spared,
I'll murder them, I will.'

                            A low voice said,

'It's Blighty, p'raps, he sees; his pluck's all gone,

Dreaming of all the valiant, that aren't dead:
Bold uncles, smiling ministerially;
Maybe his brave young wife, getting her fun
In some new home, improved materially.
It's not these stiffs have crazed him; nor the Hun.'

We sent him down at last, out of the way.
Unwounded; – stout lad, too, before that strafe.
Malingering? Stretcher-bearers winked, 'Not half'
Next day I heard the Doc.'s well-whiskied laugh:
'That scum you sent last night soon died. Hooray.'

WILFRED OWEN 1893–1918

'I can see no excuse for deceiving you about these last 4 days. I have suffered seventh hell.
I have not been at the front. I have been in front of it. I held an advanced post, that is, a
'dug-out' in the middle of No Man's Land. We had a march of 3 miles over shelled
road, then nearly 3 along a flooded trench. After that we came to where the trenches had
been blown flat out and had to go over the top. It was of course dark, too dark, and the
ground was not mud, not sloppy mud, but an octopus of sucking clay, 3, 4, and 5 feet
deep, relieved only by craters full of water. Men have been known to drown in them.'

Part of a letter from the front by WILFRED OWEN

Pre-existence

I laid me down upon the shore
   And dreamed a little space;
I heard the great waves break and roar
   The sun was on my face.

My idle hands and fingers brown
   Played with the pebbles grey;
The waves came up, the waves went down,
   Both thundering and gay.

The pebbles smooth and salt and round
   Were warm upon my hands,
Like little people I had found
   Sitting among the sands.

The grains of sand completely small
   Soft through my fingers ran;
The sun shone down upon us all,
   And so my dream began:

How all of this had been before,
　　How ages far away
I lay on some forgotten shore
　　As here I lie today.
FRANCES CORNFORD 1886–1960

In Flanders Fields

In Flanders fields the poppies blow
Between the crosses, row on row
　　That mark our place; and in the sky
　　The larks, still bravely singing, fly
Scarce heard amid the guns below.

We are the Dead. Short days ago
We lived, felt dawn, saw sunset glow,
　　Loved and were loved, and now we lie
　　　　In Flanders fields.

Take up our quarrel with the foe:
To you from failing hands we throw
　　The torch; be yours to hold it high.
　　If ye break faith with us who die
We shall not sleep, though poppies grow
　　　　In Flanders fields.
JOHN MCCREA 1872–1918

Magpies in Picardy

The magpies in Picardy
Are more than I can tell.
They flicker down the dusty roads
And cast a magic spell
On the men who march through Picardy,
Through Picardy to hell.

(The blackbird flies with panic,
The swallow goes with light,

The finches move like ladies,
The owl floats by at night;
But the great and flashing magpie
He flies as artists might.)

A magpie in Picardy
Told me secret things –
Of the music in white feathers,
And the sunlight that sings
And dances in deep shadows –
He told me with his wings.

(The hawk is cruel and rigid,
He watches from a height;
The rook is slow and sombre,
The robin loves to fight;
But the great and flashing magpie
He flies as lovers might.)

He told me that in Picardy,
An age ago or more,
While all his fathers still were eggs,
These dusty highways bore
Brown, singing soldiers marching out
Through Picardy to war.

He said that still through chaos
Works on the ancient plan,
And two things have altered not
Since first the world began –
The beauty of the wild green earth
And the bravery of man.

(For the sparrow flies unthinking
And quarrels in his flight;
The heron trails his legs behind,
The lark goes out of sight;
But the great and flashing magpie
He flies as poets might.)

T. P. CAMERON WILSON 1889–1918

Perhaps

(To R.A.L. Died of Wounds in France, 23 December 1915)

Perhaps some day the sun will shine again,
    And I shall see that still the skies are blue,
And feel once more I do not live in vain,
    Although bereft of You.

Perhaps the golden meadows at my feet
    Will make the sunny hours of Spring seem gay,
And I shall find the white May blossoms sweet,
    Though You have passed away.

Perhaps the summer woods will shimmer bright,
    And crimson roses once again be fair,
And autumn harvest fields a rich delight,
    Although You are not there.

Perhaps some day I shall not shrink in pain
    To see the passing of the dying year,
And listen to the Christmas songs again,
    Although You cannot hear.

But, though kind Time may many joys renew,
    There is one greatest joy I shall not know
Again, because my heart for loss of You
    Was broken, long ago.

VERA BRITTAIN 1893–1970

Insensibility

I

Happy are men who yet before they are killed
Can let their veins run cold.
Whom no compassion fleers
Or makes their feet
Sore on the alleys cobbled with their brothers.

207

The front line withers,
But they are troops who fade, not flowers
For poets' tearful fooling:
Men, gaps for filling:
Losses who might have fought
Longer, but no one bothers.

II

And some cease feeling
Even themselves or for themselves.
Dullness best solves
The tease and doubt of shelling,
And Chance's strange arithmetic
Comes simpler than the reckoning of their shilling.
They keep no check on armies' decimation.

III

Happy are these who lose imagination:
They have enough to carry with ammunition.
Their spirit drags no pack,
Their old wounds save with cold can not more ache.
Having seen all things red,
Their eyes are rid
Of the hurt of the colour of blood for ever.
And terror's first constriction over,
Their hearts remain small-drawn.
Their senses in some scorching cautery of battle
Now long since ironed,
Can laugh among the dying, unconcerned.

IV

Happy the soldier home, with not a notion
How somewhere, every dawn, some men attack,
And many sighs are drained.
Happy the lad whose mind was never trained:
His days are worth forgetting more than not.
He sings along the march
Which we march taciturn, because of dusk,
The long, forlorn, relentless trend
From larger day to huger night.

V

We wise, who with a thought besmirch
Blood over all our soul,
How should we see our task
But through his blunt and lashless eyes?
Alive, he is not vital overmuch;
Dying, not mortal overmuch;
Nor sad, nor proud,
Nor curious at all.
He cannot tell
Old men's placidity from his.

VI

But cursed are dullards whom no cannon stuns,
That they should be as stones;
Wretched are they, and mean
With paucity that never was simplicity.
By choice they made themselves immune
To pity and whatever moans in man
Before the last sea and the hapless stars;
Whatever mourns when many leave these shores;
Whatever shares
The eternal reciprocity of tears.

WILFRED OWEN

Lamplight

We planned to shake the world together, you and I,
Being young, and very wise;
Now in the light of the green shaded lamp
Almost I see your eyes
Light with the old gay laughter; you and I
Dreamed greatly of an Empire in those days,
Setting our feet upon laborious ways,
And all you asked of fame
Was crossed swords in the Army List,
My Dear, against your name.

We planned a great Empire together, you and I,
Bound only by the sea;
Now in the quiet of a chill Winter's night
Your voice comes hushed to me
Full of forgotten memories: you and I
Dreamed great dreams of our future in those days,
Setting our feet on undiscovered ways,
And all I asked of fame
A scarlet cross on my breast, my Dear,
For the swords by your name.

We shall never shake the world together, you and I,
For you gave your life away;
And I think my heart was broken by the war,
Since on a summer day
You took the road we never spoke of: you and I
Dreamed greatly of an Empire in those days;
You set your feet upon the Western ways
And have no need of fame –
There's a scarlet cross on my breast, my Dear,
And a torn cross with your name.

MAY WEDDERBURN CANNAN

Anthem for Doomed Youth

What passing-bells for these who die as cattle?
 Only the monstrous anger of the guns.
 Only the stuttering rifles' rapid rattle
Can patter out their hasty orisons.
No mockeries for them from prayers or bells,
 Nor any voice of mourning save the choirs, –
The shrill, demented choirs of wailing shells;
 And bugles calling for them from sad shires.

What candles may be held to speed them all?
 Not in the hands of boys, but in their eyes
Shall shine the holy glimmers of good-byes.
 The pallor of girls' brows shall be their pall;

Their flowers the tenderness of silent minds,
And each slow dusk a drawing-down of blinds.

WILFRED OWEN

Dulce Et Decorum Est

Bent double, like old beggars under sacks,
Knock-kneed, coughing like hags, we cursed through
    sludge,
Till on the haunting flares we turned our backs,
And towards our distant rest began to trudge.
Men marched asleep. Many had lost their boots,
But limped on, blood-shod. All went lame, all blind;
Drunk with fatigue; deaf even to the hoots
Of gas-shells dropping softly behind.

Gas! GAS! Quick, boys! – An ecstasy of fumbling,
Fitting the clumsy helmets just in time,
But someone still was yelling out and stumbling
And floundering like a man in fire or lime. –
Dim through the misty panes and thick green light,
As under a green sea, I saw him drowning.

In all my dreams before my helpless sight
He plunges at me, guttering, choking, drowning.

If in some smothering dreams, you too could pace
Behind the wagon that we flung him in,
And watch the white eyes writhing in his face,
His hanging face, like a devil's sick of sin;
If you could hear, at every jolt, the blood
Come gargling from the froth-corrupted lungs,
Bitter as the cud
Of vile, incurable sores on innocent tongues, –
My friend, you would not tell with such high zest
To children ardent for some desperate glory,
The old Lie: Dulce et decorum est
Pro patria mori.

WILFRED OWEN

Pluck

Crippled for life at seventeen,
  His great eyes seem to question why:
With both legs smashed it might have been
  Better in that grim trench to die
  Than drag maimed years out helplessly.

A child – so wasted and so white,
  He told a lie to get his way,
To march, a man with men, and fight
  While other boys are still at play.
  A gallant lie your heart will say.

So broke with pain, he shrinks in dread
  To see the 'dresser' drawing near;
And winds the clothes about his head
  That none may see his heart-sick fear.
  His shaking, strangled sobs you hear.

But when the dreaded moment's there
  He'll face us all, a soldier yet,
Watch his bared wounds with unmoved air,
  (Though tell-tale lashes still are wet),
  And smoke his woodbine cigarette.

EVA DOBELL

Clearing Station

Every morning there is war again.
Naked wounded, as in old paintings.
Festered dressings hang like garlands from their shoulders.
The curiously dark, mysterious head wounds.
The quivering nose-wings of the chest wounds.
The pallor of suppuration.

Whiteness in the quarter-open eyes of those near death.
The rhythmical groaning of those with a stomach wound.
The terrified expression on dead faces.
The ventriloquist voices of the tetanus cases.

Their frozen, agonized grinning, their wooden grimaces.
The ribbons of spilt blood, on which one loses one's
    footing.
The gamut of odours.
The great pitchers full of pus, cotton-wool, blood,
    amputated limbs,
the dressings full of maggots. The wounds full of bone
    and straw.
One man raises himself on his stinking bed,
a great, sick, naked bird. Another
weeps like a child: 'Comrade, help me!'

The careful gait of the ones with broken arms and
    shoulders.
The hopping of those with foot and calf wounds, the
    stiff stilting
of those with buttock wounds; the crawling on all fours.

Intestines hang out. From a ripped saddle of flesh
the spleen and stomach have welled. A rump-bone gapes
    round an arse-hole.
On the amputated stump flesh foams into the air.

Proliferating like fungi, streams of bright green pus
flow; jutting out over flesh
pulses the tree of arteries tied underneath.

The fearful, clonic tottering of the whole stump,
and the howling, whining and crying, the yammering and
    begging,
the silent heroism and the moving 'For the Fatherland'.

Until a gasping for breath comes, – and the pearls of sweat,
when the night sinks on grey faces –
a soldier's grave – two laths tied in a cross.

WILHELM KLEMM 1881–1968
(Translated by David McDuff.)

The Kite

Above the field drowses the kite
in ring turned through unbroken ring,
eyeing the grass. It's desolate.
 A cottage where a mother's loss
frets at her son. Here, feed and suck,
grow to your suffering: the cross.

Age changes time, war tears the form
that nurses it: the village burns.
Earth of my earth itself returns
an ancient beauty that tears stain.
For how long must the mother fret
and the kite's circling time remain?

ALEXANDER BLOK
(Translated by David McDuff and Jon Silkin.)

Greater Love

Red lips are not so red
   As the stained stones kissed by the English dead.
Kindness of wooed and wooer
Seems shame to their love pure.
O Love, your eyes lose lure
   When I behold eyes blinded in my stead!

Your slender attitude
   Trembles not exquisite like limbs knife-skewed,
Rolling and rolling there
Where God seems not to care;
Till the fierce Love they bear
   Cramps them in death's extreme decrepitude.

Your voice sings not so soft, –
   Though even as wind murmuring through raftered
         loft, –
Your dear voice is not dear,
Gentle, and evening clear,

214

As theirs whom none now hear,
  Now earth has stopped their piteous mouths that
    coughed.

Heart, you were never hot,
  Nor large, nor full like hearts made great with shot;
And though your hand be pale,
Paler are all which trail
Your cross through flame and hail:
  Weep, you may weep, for you may touch them not.

WILFRED OWEN

Grass

Pile the bodies high at Austerlitz and Waterloo.
Shovel them under and let me work –
    I am the grass; I cover all.

And pile them high at Gettysburg
And pile them high at Ypres and Verdun.
Shovel them under and let me work.
Two years, ten years, and passengers ask the conductor:
    What place is this?
    Where are we now?

    I am the grass.
    Let me work.

CARL SANDBURG 1878–1967

The Fabulists
1914–18

When all the world would keep a matter hid,
  Since Truth is seldom friend to any crowd,
Men write in fable as old Æsop did,
  Jesting at that which none will name aloud.
And this they needs must do, or it will fall
Unless they please they are not heard at all.

When desperate Folly daily laboureth
    To work confusion upon all we have,
When diligent Sloth demandeth Freedom's death,
    And banded Fear commandeth Honour's grave –
Even in that certain hour before the fall,
Unless men please they are not heard at all.

Needs must all please, yet some not all for need,
    Needs must all toil, yet some not all for gain,
But that men taking pleasure may take heed,
    Whom present toil shall snatch from later pain.
Thus some have toiled, but their reward was small
Since, though they pleased, they were not heard at all.

This was the lock that lay upon our lips,
    This was the yoke that we have undergone,
Denying us all pleasant fellowships
    As in our time and generation.
Our pleasures unpursued age past recall,
And for our pains – we are not heard at all.

What man hears aught except the groaning guns?
    What man heeds aught save what each instant brings
When each man's life all imaged life outruns,
    What man shall pleasure in imaginings?
So it has fallen, as it was bound to fall,
We are not, nor we were not, heard at all.

RUDYARD KIPLING

The Cenotaph
September 1919

Not yet will those measureless fields be green again
Where only yesterday the wild sweet blood of wonderful youth
    was shed;
There is a grave whose earth must hold too long, too deep a stain,
Though for ever over it we may speak as proudly as we may
    tread.
But here, where the watchers by lonely hearths from the thrust of
    an inward sword have more slowly bled,
We shall build the Cenotaph: Victory, winged, with Peace,
    winged too, at the column's head.
And over the stairway, at the foot – oh! here, leave desolate,
    passionate hands to spread
Violets, roses, and laurel, with the small, sweet, twinkling
    country things
Speaking so wistfully of other Springs,
From the little gardens of little places where son or sweetheart
    was born and bred.
In splendid sleep, with a thousand brothers
                    To lovers – to mothers
                    Here, too, lies he:
Under the purple, the green, the red,
It is all young life: it must break some women's hearts to see
Such a brave, gay coverlet to such a bed!
Only, when all is done and said,
God is not mocked and neither are the dead.
For this will stand in our Market-place –
                    Who'll sell, who'll buy
                    (Will you or I
Lie each to each with the better grace)?
While looking into every busy whore's and huckster's face
As they drive their bargains, is the Face
Of God: and some young, piteous, murdered face.

CHARLOTTE MEW 1869–1928

217

Afterwards

Oh, my beloved, shall you and I
Ever be young again, be young again?
The people that were resigned said to me
—Peace will come and you will lie
Under the larches up in Sheer,
Sleeping,
And eating strawberries and cream and cakes —
      O cakes, O cakes, O cakes, from Fuller's!
And quite forgetting there's a train to town,
Plotting in an afternoon the new curves for the world.

And peace came. And lying in Sheer
I look round at the corpses of the larches
Whom they slew to make pit-props
For mining the coal for the great armies.
And think, a pit-prop cannot move in the wind,
Nor have red manes hanging in spring from its branches,
And sap making the warm air sweet.
Though you planted it out on the hill again it would be dead.

And if these years have made you into a pit-prop,
To carry the twisting galleries of the world's reconstruction
(Where you may thank God, I suppose
That they set you the sole stay of a nasty corner)
What use is it to you? What use
To have your body lying here
In Sheer, underneath the larches?

MARGARET POSTGATE COLE

from *In Memory of W. B. Yeats*

In the nightmare of the dark
All the dogs of Europe bark,
And the living nations wait,
Each sequestered in its hate;

Intellectual disgrace
Stares from every human face,

And the seas of pity lie
Locked and frozen in each eye.

Follow, poet, follow right
To the bottom of the night,
With your unconstraining voice
Still persuade us to rejoice;

With the farming of a verse
Make a vineyard of the curse,
Sing of human unsuccess
In a rapture of distress;

In the deserts of the heart
Let the healing fountain start,
In the prison of his days
Teach the free man how to praise.

W. H. AUDEN

Their Finest Hour

I expect that the battle of Britain is about to begin. Upon this battle
depends the survival of Christian civilisation. Upon it depends our
own British life, and the long continuity of our institutions and our
Empire. The whole fury and might of the enemy must very soon
be turned on us. Hitler knows that he will have to break us in this
island or lose the war. If we can stand up to him, all Europe may be
free and the life of the world may move forward into broad, sunlit
uplands. But if we fail, then the whole world, including the United
States, including all that we have known and cared for, will sink
into the abyss of a new Dark Age made more sinister, and perhaps
more protracted, by the lights of perverted science. Let us therefore
brace ourselves to our duties, and so bear ourselves that, if the
British Empire and its Commonwealth last for a thousand years,
men will still say, 'This was their finest hour.'

WINSTON CHURCHILL, 18 June 1940

Long, Dark Months

Long, dark months of trials and tribulations lie before us. Not only great dangers, but many more misfortunes, many shortcomings, many mistakes, many disappointments will surely be our lot. Death and sorrow will be the companions of our journey; hardship our garment; constancy and valour our only shield. We must be united, we must be undaunted, we must be inflexible. Our qualities and deeds must burn and glow through the gloom of Europe until they become the veritable beacon of its salvation.

WINSTON CHURCHILL, 8 October 1940

To the French People

Good night then: sleep to gather strength for the morning. For the morning will come. Brightly will it shine on the brave and true, kindly upon all who suffer for the cause, glorious upon the tombs of heroes. Thus will shine the dawn. *Vive la France!* Long live also the forward march of the common people in all the lands towards their just and true inheritance, and towards the broader and fuller age.

WINSTON CHURCHILL, 21 October 1940

At a War Grave

No grave is rich, the dust that herein lies
Beneath this white cross mixing with the sand
Was vital once, with skill of eye and hand
And speed of brain. These will not re-arise
These riches, nor will they be replaced;
They are lost and nothing now, and here is left
Only a worthless corpse of sense bereft,
Symbol of death, and sacrifice and waste.

El Alamein, 30 October 1942

JOHN JARMAIN

El Alamein

There are flowers now, they say, at Alamein;
Yes, flowers in the minefields now.
So those that come to view that vacant scene,
Where death remains and agony has been
Will find the lilies grow –
Flowers, and nothing that we know.

So they rang the bells for us and Alamein,
Bells which we could not hear.
And to those that heard the bells what could it mean,
The name of loss and pride, El Alamein?
– Not the murk and harm of war.
But their hope, their own warm prayer.

It will become a staid historic name,
That crazy sea of sand!
Like Troy or Agincourt its single fame
Will be the garland for our brow, our claim,
On us a fleck of glory to the end;
And there our dead will keep their holy ground.

But this is not the place that we recall,
The crowded desert crossed with foaming tracks,
The one blotched building, lacking half a wall,
The grey-faced men, sand-powdered over all;
The tanks, the guns, the trucks,
The black, dark-smoking wrecks.

So be it; none but us has known that land;
El Alamein will still be only ours
And those ten days of chaos in the sand.
Others will come who cannot understand,
Will halt beside the rusty minefield wires
And find there, flowers.

JOHN JARMAIN

Chief Petty Officer

He is older than the naval side of British history,
And sits
More permanent than the spider in the enormous wall.
His barefoot, coal-burning soul,
Expands, puffs like a toad, in the convict air
Of the Royal Naval Barracks at Devonport.
Here, in depôt, is his stone Nirvana:
More real than the opium-pipes,
The uninteresting relics of his Edwardian foreign-commission.
And, from his thick stone box,
He surveys with a prehistoric eye the hostilities-only ratings.

He has the face of the dinosaur
That sometimes stares from old Victorian naval photographs:
That of some elderly lieutenant
With boots and a celluloid Crippen-collar,
Brass buttons and cruel ambitious eyes of almond.

He was probably made a Freemason in Hong Kong.
He has a son (on War Work) in the Dockyard,
And an appalling daughter
In the W.R.N.S.
He writes on your draft-chit,
Tobacco-permit or request-form
In a huge antique Borstal hand,
And pins notices on the board in the Chiefs' Mess
Requesting his messmates not to
Lay on the billiard-table.
He is an anti-Semite, and has somewhat reactionary views,
And reads the pictures in the daily news.

And when you return from the nervous Pacific
Where the seas
Shift like sheets of plate-glass in the dazzling morning;
Or when you return
Browner than Alexander, from Malta,
Where you have leaned over the side, in harbour,
And seen in the clear water
The salmon-tins, wrecks and tiny explosions of crystal fish,

A whole war later
He will still be sitting under a pusser's clock
Waiting for tot-time,
His narrow forehead ruffled by the Jutland wind.

CHARLES CAUSLEY

('Hostilities–only ratings' were those in the Royal Navy for the duration of the war. Naval property is 'pusser's', as issued by the 'Pusser' or Paymaster.)

Save the Tot

In the Navy of the seventies
The beginning of the rot
The Day that killed the Andrew
Was the day they stopped the 'Tot'

Oh they don't go East of Suez,
Or West of Panama –
When your belly's full of limers
You can't go very far

The legend on the Rumtub
Is still there to be seen
But the motto looks quite silly
On the side of a 'goffa' machine

You will hear old sailors saying
'It will never be the same'
And when they talk of bubbly
They don't mean French champagne

Did Jack flinch at Trafalgar
As he faced the shot and shell?
With a 'Tot' inside his belly
Our Jack would sail through hell

At ten to twelve each forenoon
Since the Andrew first began
Jack drinks the health of Nelson
From Jutland to Japan

Their Lordships sip their sherry
And cry 'more efficiency'
But what works fine on paper
Doesn't always work at sea.

Now Jack's a humble sailor
Who doesn't ask a lot
And after Trafalgar and Jutland
Who dares to stop his 'Tot'

He's always done his duty
To country and to throne
And all he asks in fairness
Is: leave his 'Tot' alone.

ANON.

The Flying Bum: 1944

In the vegetarian guest-house
All was frolic, feast and fun,
Eager voices were enquiring
'Are the nettle cutlets done?'
Peals of vegetarian laughter,
Husky wholesome wholemeal bread,
Will the evening finish with a
Rush of cocoa to the head?

Yes, you've guessed; it's Minnie's birthday,
Hence the frolic, hence the feast.
Are there calories in custard?
There are vitamins in yeast.
Kate is here and Tom her hubby,
Ex-commissioner for oaths,
She is mad on Christian Science,
Parsnip flan he simply loathes.
And Mr Croaker, call him Arthur,
Such a keen philatelist,
Making sheep's-eyes at Louisa

(After dinner there'll be whist) –
Come, sit down, the soup is coming,
All of docks and darnels made,
Drinks a health to dear old Minnie
In synthetic lemonade.

Dentures champing juicy lettuce,
Champing macerated bran,
Oh the imitation rissoles!
Oh the food untouched by man!
Look, an imitation sausage
Made of monkey-nuts and spice,
Prunes tonight and semolina,
Wrinkled prunes, unpolished rice.

Yards of guts absorbing jellies,
Bellies filling up with nuts,
Carbohydrates jostling proteins
Out of intestinal ruts;
Peristalsis calls for roughage,
Haulms and fibres, husks and grit,
Nature's way to open bowels,
Maybe – let them practise it.

'Hark, I hear an air-raid warning!'
'Take no notice, let 'em come.'
'Who'll say grace?' 'Another walnut?'
'Listen, what's that distant hum?'
'Bomb or no bomb,' stated Minnie,
'Lips unsoiled by beef or beer
We shall use to greet our Maker
When he sounds the Great All-Clear.'

When the flying bomb exploded
Minnie's wig flew off her pate,
Half a curtain, like a tippet,
Wrapped itself round bony Kate,
Plaster landed on Louisa,
Tom fell headlong on the floor,
And a spurt of lukewarm custard
Lathered Mr Croaker's jaw.

All were spared by glass and splinters
But, the loud explosion past,
Greater was the shock impending
Even than the shock of blast –
Blast we veterans know as freakish
Gave this feast its final course,
Planted bang upon the table
A lightly roasted rump of horse.

WILLIAM PLOMER 1903–73

Punishment Enough

They say that women, in a bombing-raid,
Retire to sleep in brand-new underwear
Lest they be tumbled out of doors, displayed
In shabby garments to the public stare.

You've often seen a house, sliced like cheese,
Displaying its poor secrets – peeling walls
And warping cupboards. Of such tragedies
It is the petty scale that most appals.

When you confess your sins before a parson,
You find it no great effort to disclose
Your crimes of murder, bigamy and arson,
But can you tell him that you pick your nose?

If after death you pay for your misdeeds,
Surely the direst and most just requital
Would be to listen while an angel reads
Before a crowd your endless, mean recital:

Golf scorecards faked, thefts from your mother's purse . . .
But why should Doomsday bother with such stuff?
This is the Hell that you already nurse
Within you. You've had punishment enough.

NORMAN CAMERON 1905–53

Handbag

My mother's old leather handbag,
crowded with letters she carried
all through the war. The smell
of my mother's handbag: mints
and lipstick and Coty powder.
The look of those letters, softened
and worn at the edges, opened,
read, and refolded so often.
Letters from my father. Odour
of leather and powder, which ever
since then has meant womanliness,
and love, and anguish, and war.

RUTH FAINLIGHT 1931–

Salvage Song (or: The Housewife's Dream)

'Women of Britain, give us your aluminium. We want it
and we want it now . . . We will turn your pots and
pans into Spitfires and Hurricanes, Blenheims and
Wellingtons . . .' (Lord Beaverbrook, July 1940)

My saucepans have all been surrendered,
The teapot is gone from the hob,
The colander's leaving the cabbage
For a very much different job.
So now, when I hear on the wireless
Of Hurricanes showing their mettle,
I see, in a vision before me,
A Dornier chased by my kettle.

ELSIE CAWSER 1915–

The Dying Airman

A handsome young airman lay dying,
And as on the aerodrome he lay,
To the mechanics who round him came sighing,
These last dying words he did say:

227

'Take the cylinders out of my kidneys,
The connecting-rod out of my brain,
Take the cam-shaft from out of my backbone,
And assemble the engine again.'

ANON.

The Englishman's Home

I was playing golf the day
  That the Germans landed;
All our troops had run away,
  All our ships were stranded;
And the thought of England's shame
Altogether spoilt my game.

HARRY GRAHAM

The Dead in Europe

After the planes unloaded, we fell down
Buried together, unmarried men and women;
Not crown of thorns, not iron, not Lombard crown,
Not grilled and spindle spires pointing to heaven
Could save us. Raise us, Mother, we fell down
Here hugger-mugger in the jellied fire:
Our sacred earth in our day was our curse.

Our Mother, shall we rise on Mary's day
In Maryland, wherever corpses married
Under the rubble, bundled together? Pray
For us whom the blockbusters married and buried;
When Satan scatters us on Rising-day,
O Mother, snatch our bodies from the fire:
Our sacred earth in our day was our curse.

Mother, my bones are trembling and I hear
The earth's reverberations and the trumpet
Bleating into my shambles. Shall I bear,

(O Mary!) unmarried man and powder-puppet,
Witness to the Devil? Mary, hear,
O Mary, marry earth, sea, air and fire;
Our sacred earth in our day is our curse.

ROBERT LOWELL 1917–77

Royal Naval Air Station

The piano, hollow and sentimental, plays,
And outside, falling in a moonlit haze,
The rain is endless as the empty days.

Here in the mess, on beds, on benches, fall
The blue serge limbs in shapes fantastical:
The photographs of girls are on the wall.

And the songs of the minute walk into our ears;
Behind the easy words are difficult tears:
The pain which stabs is dragged out over years.

A ghost has made uneasy every bed.
You are not you without me and *The dead
Only are pleased to be alone* it said.

And hearing it silently the living cry
To be again themselves, or sleeping try
To dream it is impossible to die.

ROY FULLER

Written with a Pencil in a Sealed Wagon

Here, in this transport,
I, Eve,
With my son Abel.
If you see my older son, Cain,

229

Son of Adam,
Tell him that I am.

DAN PAGIS 1930–
(Translated by Amos Oz.)

(Cattle wagons were used during the Second World War to transport Jews to the concentration camps and gas chambers.)

Dover Beach

The sea is calm to-night.
The tide is full, the moon lies fair
Upon the straits; – on the French coast the light
Gleams and is gone; the cliffs of England stand,
Glimmering and vast, out in the tranquil bay.
Come to the window, sweet is the night air!
Only, from the long line of spray
Where the ebb meets the moon-blanch'd sand,
Listen! you hear the grating roar
Of pebbles which the waves draw back, and fling,
At their return, up the high strand,
Begin, and cease, and then again begin,
With tremulous cadence slow, and bring
The eternal note of sadness in.

Sophocles long ago
Heard it on the Ægæan, and it brought
Into his mind the turbid ebb and flow
Of human misery; we
Find also in the sound a thought,
Hearing it by this distant northern sea.

The Sea of Faith
Was once, too, at the full, and round earth's shore
Lay like the folds of a bright girdle furl'd;
But now I only hear
Its melancholy, long, withdrawing roar,
Retreating to the breath
Of the night-wind down the vast edges drear
And naked shingles of the world.

Ah, love, let us be true
To one another! for the world, which seems
To lie before us like a land of dreams,
So various, so beautiful, so new,
Hath really neither joy, nor love, nor light,
Nor certitude, nor peace, nor help for pain:
And we are here as on a darkling plain
Swept with confused alarms of struggle and fight,
Where ignorant armies clash by night!

MATTHEW ARNOLD 1822–88

Drink, Britannia

Drink, Britannia, Britannia, drink your Tea,
For Britons, Boars and butter'd Toast; they all begin with B.

THOMAS LOVELL BEDDOES

England

from *The Return*

If England were what England seems
   An' not the England of our dreams
But only putty, brass an' paint
   'Ow quick we'd drop 'er. But she ain't.

RUDYARD KIPLING

from **The White Cliffs**

I have loved England, dearly and deeply,
Since that first morning, shining and pure,
The white cliffs of Dover I saw rising steeply
Out of the sea that once made her secure.

I had no thought then of husband or lover,
I was a traveller, the guest of a week;

Yet when they pointed 'the white cliffs of Dover',
Startled I found there were tears on my cheek.

I have loved England, and still as a stranger,
Here is my home and I still am alone,
Now in her hour of trial and danger,
Only the English are really her own.

I am American bred,
I have seen much to hate here – much to forgive,
But in a world where England is finished and dead
I do not wish to live.

ALICE DUER MILLER

Think of Europe

> 'When I hear his steps outside my door I lie
> down on my bed, close my eyes, open my legs
> and think of England.' – Lady Hillingdon's
> journal for 1912, quoted in *Brewer's Twentieth
> Century Phrase & Fable*, published by Cassell

Once, when Britain's power was massive
And the map was mostly red,
Well-bred ladies who were passive
Thought of England when in bed.
Now, no longer high and mighty,
Forced to sing Beethoven Nine,
When Britannia lifts her nightie
She submits to foreign swine.

What a tune! We love to hum it,
Glory be to Ludwig van!
Women at the Maastricht summit
Underpin the rights of man.
Cuddled in the spoons position,
Sitting up or on her back,
Britain, faithful to her mission,
Still will wave the Union Jack.

ROGER WODDIS 1917–

The Secret People

Smile at us, pay us, pass us; but do not quite forget;
For we are the people of England, that never have spoken yet.
There is many a fat farmer that drinks less cheerfully,
There is many a free French peasant who is richer and sadder than
    we.
There are no folk in the whole world so helpless or so wise.
There is hunger in our bellies, there is laughter in our eyes;
You laugh at us and love us, both mugs and eyes are wet:
Only you do not know us. For we have not spoken yet.

The fine French kings came over in a flutter of flags and dames.
We liked their smiles and battles, but we never could say their
    names.
The blood ran red to Bosworth and the high French lords went
    down;
There was naught but a naked people under a naked crown.
And the eyes of the King's Servants turned terribly every way,
And the gold of the King's Servants rose higher every day.
They burnt the homes of the shaven men, that had been quaint and
    kind,
Till there was no bed in monk's house, nor food that man could
    find.
The inns of God where no man paid, that were the wall of the
    weak,
The King's Servants ate them all. And still we did not speak.

And the face of the King's Servants grew greater than the King:
He tricked them, and they trapped him, and stood round him in a
    ring.
The new grave lords closed round him, that had eaten the abbey's
    fruits,
And the men of the new religion, with their bibles in their boots,
We saw their shoulders moving, to menace or discuss,
And some were pure and some were vile; but none took heed of us.
We saw the King as they killed him, and his face was proud and pale;
And a few men talked of freedom, while England talked of ale.

A war that we understood not came over the world and woke

Americans, Frenchmen, Irish; but we know not the things they
    spoke.
They talked about rights and nature and peace and the people's
    reign:
And the squires, our masters, bade us fight; and scorned us never
    again.
Weak if we be for ever, could none condemn us then;
Men called us serfs and drudges; men knew that we were men.
In foam and flame at Trafalgar, on Albuera plains,
We did and died like lions, to keep ourselves in chains
We lay in living ruins; firing and fearing not
The strange fierce face of the Frenchmen who knew for what they
    fought,
And the man who seemed to be more than man we strained against
    and broke;
And we broke our own rights with him. And still we never spoke.

Our patch of glory ended; we never heard guns again.
But the squire seemed struck in the saddle; he was foolish, as if in
    pain.
He leaned on a staggering lawyer, he clutched a cringing Jew,
He was stricken; it may be, after all, he was stricken at Waterloo.
Or perhaps the shades of the shaven men, whose spoil is in his
    house,
Come back in shining shapes at last to spoil his last carouse:
We only know the last sad squires ride slowly towards the sea,
And a new people takes the land: and still it is not we.

They have given us into the hand of new unhappy lords,
Lords without anger and honour, who dare not carry their swords.
They fight by shuffling papers; they have bright dead alien eyes;
They look at our labour and laughter as a tired man looks at flies.
And the load of their loveless pity is worse than the ancient
    wrongs,
Their doors are shut in the evening; and they know no songs.

We hear men speaking for us of new laws strong and sweet,
Yet is there no man speaketh as we speak in the street.
It may be we shall rise the last as Frenchmen rose the first,
Our wrath come after Russia's wrath and our wrath be the worst.

It may be we are meant to mark with our riot and our rest
God's scorn for all men governing. It may be beer is best.
But we are the people of England; and we have not spoken yet.
Smile at us, pay us, pass us. But do not quite forget.

G. K. CHESTERTON

No Man is an Iland

No man is an Iland, intire of it selfe; every man is a peece of the Continent, a part of the maine; if a Clod bee washed away by the Sea, Europe is the lesse, as well as if a Promontorie were, as well as if a Mannor of thy friends or of thine own were. Any mans death diminishes me, because I am involved in Mankinde. And therefore never send to know for whom the bell tolls. It tolls for thee.

JOHN DONNE 1572–1631

WISDOM

And then the justice,
In fair round belly with good capon lined,
With eyes severe and beard of formal cut,
Full of wise saws and modern instances;
And so he plays his part.

The Price of Wisdom

Surely there is a vein for the silver,
And a place for gold where they fine it.
Iron is taken out of the earth,
And brass is molten out of the stone.
He setteth an end to darkness,
And searcheth out all perfection:
The stones of darkness, and the shadow of death.
The flood breaketh out from the inhabitant;
Even the waters forgotten of the foot:
They are dried up, they are gone away from men.
As for the earth, out of it cometh bread:
And under it is turned up as it were fire.
The stones of it are the place of sapphires:
And it hath dust of gold.
There is a path which no fowl knoweth,
And which the vulture's eye hath not seen:
The lion's whelps have not trodden it,
Nor the fierce lion passed by it.
He putteth forth his hand upon the rock;
He overturneth the mountains by the roots.
He cutteth out rivers among the rocks;
And his eye seeth every precious thing.
He bindeth the floods from overflowing;
And the thing that is hid bringeth he forth to light.
But where shall wisdom be found?
And where is the place of understanding?
Man knoweth not the price thereof;
Neither is it found in the land of the living.
The depth saith, It is not in me:
And the sea saith, It is not with me.
It cannot be gotten for gold,
Neither shall silver be weighed for the price thereof.
It cannot be valued with the gold of Ophir,
With the precious onyx, or the sapphire.
The gold and the crystal cannot equal it:
And the exchange of it shall not be for jewels of fine gold.
No mention shall be made of coral, or of pearls:
For the price of wisdom is above rubies.
The topaz of Ethiopia shall not equal it,

Neither shall it be valued with pure gold.
Whence then cometh wisdom?
And where is the place of understanding?
Seeing it is hid from the eyes of all living,
And kept close from the fowls of the air.
Destruction and death say,
We have heard the fame thereof with our ears.
God understandeth the way thereof,
And he knoweth the place thereof.
For he looketh to the ends of the earth,
And seeth under the whole heaven;
To make the weight for the winds;
And he weigheth the waters by measure.
When he made a decree for the rain,
And a way for the lightning of the thunder:
Then did he see it, and declare it;
He prepared it, yea, and searched it out.
And unto man he said,
Behold, the fear of the Lord, that is wisdom;
And to depart from evil is understanding.

JOB CHAPTER 28, VERSES 6–28

The Quality of Mercy

from *The Merchant of Venice*, Act IV, Scene i

The quality of mercy is not strain'd,
It droppeth as the gentle rain from heaven
Upon the place beneath; it is twice blest;
It blesseth him that gives and him that takes:
'Tis mightiest in the mightiest: it becomes
The thronèd monarch better than his crown;
His sceptre shows the force of temporal power,
The attribute to awe and majesty,
Wherein doth sit the dread and fear of kings;
But mercy is above this sceptred sway;
It is enthronèd in the hearts of kings,
It is an attribute to God himself;

240

And earthly power doth then show likest God's
When mercy seasons justice. . . .

WILLIAM SHAKESPEARE

Whatsoever Things Are True

Whatsoever things are true,
whatsoever things are honest,
whatsoever things are just,
whatsoever things are pure,
whatsoever things are lovely,
whatsoever things are of good report;
if there be any virtue,
and if there be any praise,
think on these things.

PHILIPPIANS CHAPTER 4, VERSE 8

What is Good

'What is the real good?'
I asked in musing mood.

Order, said the law court;
Knowledge, said the school;
Truth, said the wise man;
Pleasure, said the fool;
Love, said the maiden;
Beauty, said the page;
Freedom, said the dreamer;
Home, said the sage;
Fame, said the soldier;
Equity, the seer; –

Speak my heart full sadly,
'The answer is not here.'

Then within my bosom
Softly this I heard:

'Each heart holds the secret;
Kindness is the word.'
JOHN BOYLE O'REILLY 1844–90

Four Things

Four things a man must learn to do
If he would make his record true:
To think without confusion clearly;
To love his fellow-men sincerely;
To act from honest motives purely;
To trust in God and Heaven securely.
HENRY VAN DYKE 1852–1933

Leaves of Grass

Here is the test of wisdom,
Wisdom is not finally tested in schools,
Wisdom cannot be passed from one having it, to an-
     other not having it,
Wisdom is of the Soul, is not susceptible of proof, is
     its own proof,
Applies to all stages and objects and qualities, and is
     content,
Is the certainty of the reality and immortality of
     things, and the excellence of things;
Something there is in the float of the sight of things
     that provokes it out of the Soul.
WALT WHITMAN

New Eyes Each Year

New eyes each year
Find old books here,

242

And new books, too,
Old eyes renew;
So youth and age
Like ink and page
In this house join,
Minting new coin.

PHILIP LARKIN

Addendum to the Ten Commandments

Thou shalt not covet thy neighbour's wife,
Nor the ox her husband bought her;
But thank the Lord you're not forbidden
To covet your neighbour's daughter.

ANON.

Once I was Young

Once I was young
And filled with winged ideas,
With songs unsung
To echo down the years.

The old men smiled
'We sang those selfsame songs
Once on a time –
Convinced we could right all wrongs.'

Thinking them blind
I kept my faith unfurled:
Made up my mind
Youth would convert the world.

The years have passed
And I am older now,
Youth does not last,
The blossom leaves the bough.

Yet wiser now
I know a wider truth,
I have learned how
Hope is the spirit's youth.

A. C. S. GIMSON 1919–82

A Student

from *The Canterbury Tales*

A Student came from Oxford town also,
Wedded to lore and logic long ago.
The horse he rode was lean as any rake;
Himself was scarcely fat, I'll undertake,
But hollow in his sad sobriety.
His overcoat was threadbare, too; for he
Was yet to win a single benefice,
And worldly thoughts of office were not his.
For he would rather have at his bed's head
Twenty great books, all bound in black or red,
Of Aristotle and his philosophy
Than rich robes, fiddle, or gay psaltery.
Though a philosopher, he could not proffer
A treasury of gold from his scant coffer;
Anything he could borrow from a friend
On books and learning he would quickly spend,
And constantly he prayed for those who'd give
Help for the means by which his soul might live.
He gave most care to study and most heed;
Never a word he spoke beyond his need.
His speech was framed in form and reverence,
Pointed and quick and always packed with sense.
Moral his mind, and virtuous his speech;
And gladly would he learn, and gladly teach.

GEOFFREY CHAUCER 1340?–1400

Solitude

Happy the man, whose wish and care
A few paternal acres bound,

Content to breathe his native air
    In his own ground.
Whose herds with milk, whose fields with bread,
Whose flocks supply him with attire;
Whose trees in summer yield him shade,
    In winter, fire.
Blest, who can unconcernedly find
Hours, days, and years slide soft away
In health of body, peace of mind;
    Quiet by day.
Sound sleep by night; study and ease
Together mixed, sweet recreation,
And innocence, which most does please
    With meditation.
Thus let me live, unseen, unknown;
Thus unlamented let me die,
Steal from the world, and not a stone
    Tell where I lie.

                    ALEXANDER POPE 1688–1744
                    (Written at the age of twelve.)

The Greatest of These

Though I speak with the tongues of men and of angels,
And have not charity,
I am become as sounding brass,
Or a tinkling cymbal.

And though I have the gift of prophecy,
And understand all mysteries, and all knowledge;
And though I have all faith,
So that I could remove mountains,
And have not charity,
I am nothing.

And though I bestow all my goods to feed the poor,
And though I give my body to be burned,
And have not charity,
It profiteth me nothing.

Charity suffereth long, and is kind;
Charity envieth not;
Charity vaunteth not itself, is not puffed up,

Doth not behave itself unseemly,
Seeketh not her own,
Is not easily provoked,
Thinketh no evil;

Rejoiceth not in iniquity, but rejoiceth in the truth;

Beareth all things,
Believeth all things,
Hopeth all things,
Endureth all things.

Charity never faileth:
But whether there be prophecies, they shall fail;
Whether there be tongues, they shall cease;
Whether there be knowledge, it shall vanish away.

For we know in part and we prophesy in part.
But when that which is perfect is come,
Then that which is in part shall be done away.

When I was a child,
I spake as a child,
I understood as a child,
I thought as a child.
But when I became a man,
I put away childish things.

For now we see through a glass, darkly;
But then face to face:
Now I know in part;
But then shall I know even as also I am known.

And now abideth faith, hope, charity,
These three;
But the greatest of these is charity.

CORINTHIANS, CHAPTER 13, VERSES 1–13

Abou Ben Adhem

Abou Ben Adhem (may his tribe increase!)
Awoke one night from a deep dream of peace,
And saw, within the moonlight in his room,
Making it rich, and like a lily in bloom,
An angel writing in a book of gold:
Exceeding peace had made Ben Adhem bold,
And to the presence in the room he said,
　　'What writest thou?' – The vision raised its head,
And with a look made of all sweet accord,
Answered, 'The names of those who love the Lord.'
'And is mine one?' said Abou. 'Nay, not so,'
Replied the angel. Abou spoke more low,
But cheerly still; and said, 'I pray thee, then,
Write me as one that loves his fellow men.'

　　The angel wrote, and vanished. The next night
It came again with a great wakening light,
And showed the names whom love of God had blest,
And lo! Ben Adhem's name led all the rest.

JAMES LEIGH HUNT 1784–1859

The Lord is Full of Mercy

The Lord is full of mercy
Were He not so full of mercy,
There could have been some mercy
In the World,
Not just in Him.

YEHUDA AMICHAI 1924–
(Translated by Amos Oz.)

The Cave Man's Prayer

This is the prayer the cave-man prayed,
When first the household fires he lit,
And saw the solemn stars o'erhead
Contemptuously looked down on it
The sweep and silence of the night,
The brooding dusk on every side

Oppressed his simple mind with fright
And 'Heaven send me friends' he cried

'Wise friends who know what track will lure
The wounded mammoth to defeat.
And cunning friends who have the cure
For pains inside me when I eat.
Strong friends who know how spears are hurled,
Bold friends that charge and drive them in.
It takes all sorts to make a world,
But give me friends and I'll begin.'

The gods considered his distress
And guided to his lonely blaze
Companions in loneliness
The cave-men of the elder days
With twitching nose and eyes astare,
They crouched and watched him for a spell,
Till to his caution 'who goes there?'
They grunted 'Friend' and all was well.

And when at last their leave they took
Refreshed by meat and drink and talk,
For lack of any proper book,
They scratched their Totems on the chalk,
And host and hostess at the door
Bade them goodbye and made their plans
Next Saturday to ask some more
And that was how the world began.

The wash tub and the kitchen range
Electric lighting paper pens,
Affect the life but do not change
The heart of Homo Sapiens.
O long, long may the record run,
And you enjoy until it ends,
The four best gifts beneath the sun;
Love peace and health, and honest friends.

(I have never seen this poem in print before. It was copied by a friend of mine from a
visitors' book in a house in Sussex where it was thought to be written in Rudyard
Kipling's own hand but I have never been able to verify this story and have left the
poem unattributed in the index.)

The Agnostic's Creed

At last I have ceased repining, at last I accept my fate;
I have ceased to beat at the Portal, I have ceased to knock
　　at the Gate;
I have ceased to work at the Puzzle, for the Secret has ended
　　my search,
And I know that the Key is entrusted to never a creed nor
　　church.

They have threatened with lakes of fire, they have threa-
　　tened with fetters of hell;
They have offered me heights of heaven with their fields of
　　asphodel;
But the Threat and the Bribe are useless if Reason be strong
　　and stout,
And an honest man can never surrender an honest doubt.

The fables of hell and of heaven are but worn-out Christmas
　　toys
To coax or to bribe or to frighten the grown-up girls and
　　boys;
I have ceased to be an infant, I have travelled beyond their
　　span –
It may do for women and children, but it never will do for
　　a man.

They are all alike, these churches: Mohammedan, Christian,
　　Parsee;
You are vile, you are curst, you are outcast, if you be not
　　as they be;
But my Reason stands against them, and I go as it bids
　　me go;
Its commands are as calls of a trumpet, and I follow for
　　weal or woe.

But oh! it is often cheerless, and oh! it is often chill,
And I often sigh to heaven as my path grows steep and still.
I have left behind my comrades, with their prattle and
　　childish noise;
My boyhood now is behind me, with all of its broken toys!

Oh! that God of gods is glorious, the emperor of every land;
He carries the moon and the planets in the palm of His
    mighty hand;
He is girt with the belt of Orion, he is Lord of the suns and
    stars,
A wielder of constellations, Canopus, Arcturus, and Mars!

I believe in Love and Duty, I believe in the True and Just:
I believe in the common kinship of everything born from
    dust.
I hope that the Right will triumph, that the sceptered
    Wrong will fall;
That Death will at last be defeated, that the Grave will not
    end all.

I believe in the martyrs and heroes who have died for the
    sake of Rig¹ ,
And I promise, like them, to follow in my Reason's faithful
    light;
If my Reason errs in Judgment, I but honestly strive as
    I can;
If a God decrees my downfall, I shall stand it like a man.

WALTER MALONE 1866–1915

On Woman

May God be praised for woman
That gives up all her mind,
A man may find in no man
A friendship of her kind
That covers all he has brought
As with her flesh and bone,
Nor quarrels with a thought
Because it is not her own.

Though pedantry denies,
It's plain the Bible means
That Solomon grew wise

While talking with his queens,
Yet never could, although
They say he counted grass,
Count all the praises due
When Sheba was his lass,
When she the iron wrought, or
When from the smithy fire
It shuddered in the water:
Harshness of their desire
That made them stretch and yawn,
Pleasure that comes with sleep,
Shudder that made them one.
What else He give or keep
God grant me – no, not here,
For I am not so bold
To hope a thing so dear
Now I am growing old,
But when, if the tale's true,
The Pestle of the moon
That pounds up all anew
Brings me to birth again –
To find what once I had
And know what once I have known,
Until I am driven mad,
Sleep driven from my bed,
By tenderness and care,
Pity, an aching head,
Gnashing of teeth, despair;
And all because of some one
Perverse creature of chance,
And live like Solomon
That Sheba led a dance.

W. B. YEATS

The Female of the Species

When the Himalayan peasant meets the he-bear in his
          pride,
He shouts to scare the monster, who will often turn aside.

But the she-bear thus accosted rends the peasant tooth and
       nail.
For the female of the species is more deadly than the male.

When Nag the basking cobra hears the careless foot of
       man,
He will sometimes wriggle sideways and avoid it if he
       can.
But his mate makes no such motion where she camps beside
       the trail.
For the female of the species is more deadly than the male.

When the early Jesuit fathers preached to Hurons and
       Choctaws,
They prayed to be delivered from the vengeance of the
       squaws.
'Twas the women, not the warriors, turned those stark
       enthusiasts pale.
For the female of the species is more deadly than the male.

Man's timid heart is bursting with the things he must not say,
For the Woman that God gave him isn't his to give away;
But when hunter meets with husband, each confirms the
       other's tale –
The female of the species is more deadly than the male.

Man, a bear in most relations – worm and savage otherwise, –
Man propounds negotiations, Man accepts the compromise.
Very rarely will he squarely push the logic of a fact
To its ultimate conclusion in unmitigated act.

Fear, or foolishness, impels him, ere he lay the wicked low,
To concede some form of trial even to his fiercest foe.
Mirth obscene diverts his anger – Doubt and Pity oft perplex
Him in dealing with an issue – to the scandal of The Sex!

But the Woman that God gave him, every fibre of her frame
Proves her launched for one sole issue, armed and engined for
       the same;
And to serve that single issue, lest the generations fail,
The female of the species must be deadlier than the male.

She who faces Death by torture for each life beneath her
  breast
May not deal in doubt or pity – must not swerve for fact or
  jest.
These be purely male diversions – not in these her honour
  dwells.
She the Other Law we live by, is that Law and nothing else.

She can bring no more to living than the powers that make
  her great
As the Mother of the Infant and the Mistress of the Mate.
And when Babe and Man are lacking and she strides
  unclaimed to claim
Her right as femme (and baron), her equipment is the same.

She is wedded to convictions – in default of grosser ties;
Her contentions are her children, Heaven help him who
  denies! –
He will meet no suave discussion, but the instant, white-hot,
  wild,
Wakened female of the species warring as for spouse and
  child.

Unprovoked and awful charges – even so the she-bear fights,
Speech that drips, corrodes, and poisons – even so the cobra
  bites,
Scientific vivisection of one nerve till it is raw
And the victim writhes in anguish – like the Jesuit with the
  squaw!

So it comes that Man, the coward, when he gathers to confer
With his fellow-braves in council, dare not leave a place for
  her
Where, at war with Life and Conscience, he uplifts his erring
  hands
To some God of Abstract Justice – which no woman under-
  stands.

And Man knows it! Knows, moreover, that the Woman
  that God gave him

253

Must command but may not govern – shall enthral but not
    enslave him.
And *She* knows, because She warns him, and Her instincts
    never fail,
That the Female of Her Species is more deadly than the
    Male.

RUDYARD KIPLING

Trial and Error

A lady is smarter than a gentleman, maybe.
She can sew a fine seam, she can have a baby,
She can use her intuition instead of her brain,
But she can't fold a paper on a crowded train.

PHYLLIS MCGINLEY 1905–78

The Song of Hiawatha

INTRODUCTION

Should you ask me, whence these stories?
Whence these legends and traditions,
With the odours of the forest,
With the dew and damp of meadows,
With the curling smoke of wigwams,
With the rushing of great rivers,
With their frequent repetitions,
And their wild reverberations,
As of thunder in the mountains?
   I should answer, I should tell you,
'From the forest and the prairies,
From the great lakes of the Northland,
From the land of the Ojibways,
From the land of the Dacotahs,
From the mountains, moors, and fen-lands,
Where the heron, the Shuh-shuh-gah,
Feeds among the reeds and rushes,

I repeat them as I heard them
From the lips of Nawadaha,
The musician, the sweet singer.'
    Should you ask where Nawadaha
Found these songs, so wild and wayward,
Found these legends and traditions,
I should answer, I should tell you,
'In the birds'-nests of the forest,
In the lodges of the beaver,
In the hoof-prints of the bison,
In the eyrie of the eagle!
    'All the wild-fowl sang them to him,
In the moorlands and the fen-lands,
In the melancholy marshes;
Chetowaik, the plover, sang them,
Mahng, the loon, the wild goose, Wawa,
The blue heron, the Shuh-shuh-gah,
And the grouse, the Mushkodasa!'
    If still further you should ask me,
Saying, 'Who was Nawadaha?
Tell us of this Nawadaha,'
I should answer your inquiries
Straightway in such words as follow.
    'In the vale of Tawasentha,
In the green and silent valley,
By the pleasant water-courses,
Dwelt the singer Nawadaha.
Round about the Indian village
Spread the meadows and the corn-fields,
And beyond them stood the forest,
Stood the groves of singing pine-trees,
Green in Summer, white in Winter,
Ever sighing, ever singing.
    'And the pleasant water-courses,
You could trace them through the valley,
By the rushing in the Spring-time,
By the alders in the Summer,
By the white fog in the Autumn,
By the black line in the Winter;
And beside them dwelt the singer.
In the vale of Tawasentha,

In the green and silent valley.
   'There he sang of Hiawatha,
Sang the song of Hiawatha,
Sang his wondrous birth and being,
How he prayed and how he fasted,
How he lived, and toiled, and suffered,
That the tribes of men might prosper,
That he might advance his people!'
   Ye who love the haunts of Nature,
Love the sunshine of the meadow,
Love the shadow of the forest,
Love the wind among the branches,
And the rain-shower and the snow-storm,
And the rushing of great rivers
Through their palisades of pine-trees,
And the thunder in the mountains,
Whose innumerable echoes
Flap like eagles in their eyries; –
Listen to these wild traditions,
To this Song of Hiawatha!
   Ye who love a nation's legends,
Love the ballads of a people,
That like voices from afar off
Call to us to pause and listen,
Speak in tones so plain and childlike,
Scarcely can the ear distinguish
Whether they are sung or spoken; –
Listen to this Indian legend,
To this Song of Hiawatha!
   Ye whose hearts are fresh and simple,
Who have faith in God and Nature,
Who believe, that in all ages
Every human heart is human,
That in even savage bosoms
There are longings, yearnings, strivings,
For the good they comprehend not,
That the feeble hands and helpless,
Groping blindly in the darkness,
Touch God's right hand in that darkness,
 And are lifted up and strengthened: –
 Listen to this simple story,

To this Song of Hiawatha!
   Ye, who sometimes, in your rambles
Through the green lanes of the country,
Where the tangled barberry-bushes
Hang their tufts of crimson berries
Over stone walls grey with mosses,
Pause by some neglected graveyard,
For a while to muse, and ponder
On a half-effaced inscription,
Written with little skill of song-craft,
Homely phrases, but each letter
Full of hope and yet of heart-break,
Full of all the tender pathos
Of the Here and the Hereafter; –
Stay and read this rude inscription!
Read this Song of Hiawatha!
     HENRY WADSWORTH LONGFELLOW

My Heart Leaps Up

My heart leaps up when I behold
   A rainbow in the sky:
So was it when my life began;
So is it now I am a man;
So be it when I shall grow old,
   Or let me die!
The Child is father of the Man;
And I could wish my days to be
Bound each to each by natural piety.
WILLIAM WORDSWORTH 1770–1850

Song of the Open Road

I think that I shall never see
A billboard lovely as a tree.

Perhaps unless the billboards fall,
I'll never see a tree at all.

OGDEN NASH

Auguries of Innocence

To see a World in a Grain of Sand
And a Heaven in a Wild Flower,
Hold Infinity in the palm of your hand
And Eternity in an hour.

A Robin Red breast in a Cage
Puts all Heaven in a Rage,
A dove house fill'd with doves & Pigeons
Shudders Hell thro' all its regions.
A dog starv'd at his Master's Gate
Predicts the ruin of the State.
A Horse misus'd upon the Road
Calls to Heaven for Human blood.
Each outcry of the hunted Hare
A fibre from the Brain does tear.
A Skylark wounded in the wing,
A Cherubim does cease to sing.
The Game Cock clip'd & arm'd for fight
Does the Rising Sun affright.
Every Wolf's & Lion's howl
Raises from Hell a Human Soul.
The wild deer, wand'ring here & there,
Keeps the Human Soul from Care.
The Lamb misus'd breeds Public strife
And yet forgives the Butcher's Knife.
The Bat that flits at close of Eve
Has left the Brain that won't Believe.
The Owl that calls upon the Night
Speaks the Unbeliever's fright.
He who shall hurt the little Wren
Shall never be belov'd by Men.
He who the Ox to wrath has mov'd
Shall never be by Woman lov'd.

The wanton Boy that kills the Fly
Shall feel the Spider's enmity.
He who torments the Chafer's sprite
Weaves a Bower in endless Night.
The Catterpiller on the Leaf
Repeats to thee thy Mother's grief.
Kill not the Moth nor Butterfly,
For the Last Judgment draweth nigh.
He who shall train the Horse to War
Shall never pass the Polar Bar.
The Beggar's Dog & Widow's Cat
Feed them & thou wilt grow fat.
The Gnat that sings his Summer's song
Poison gets from Slander's tongue.
The poison of the Snake & Newt
Is the sweat of Envy's Foot.
The Poison of the Honey Bee
Is the Artist's Jealousy.
The Prince's Robes & Beggar's Rags
Are Toadstools on the Miser's Bags.
A truth that's told with bad intent
Beats all the Lies you can invent.
It is right it should be so;
Man was made for Joy & Woe;
And when this we rightly know
Thro' the World we safely go.
Joy & Woe are woven fine,
A Clothing for the Soul divine;
Under every grief & pine
Runs a joy with silken twine.
The Babe is more than swadling Bands;
Throughout all these Human Lands
Tools were made, & Born were hands,
Every Farmer Understands.
Every Tear from Every Eye
Becomes a Babe in Eternity;
This is caught by Females bright
And return'd to its own delight.
The Bleat, the Bark, Bellow & Roar
Are Waves that Beat on Heaven's Shore.
The Babe that weeps the Rod beneath

Writes Revenge in realms of death.
The Beggar's Rags, fluttering in Air,
Does to Rags the Heaven tear.
The Soldier, arm'd with Sword & Gun,
Palsied strikes the Summer's Sun.
The poor Man's Farthing is worth more
Than all the Gold on Afric's Shore.
One Mite wrung from the Labrer's hands
Shall buy & sell the Miser's Lands:
Or, if protected from on high,
Does that whole Nation sell & buy.
He who mocks the Infant's Faith
Shall be mock'd in Age & Death.
He who shall teach the Child to Doubt
The rotting Grave shall ne'er get out.
He who respects the Infant's faith
Triumphs over Hell & Death.
The Child's Toys & the Old Man's Reasons
Are the Fruits of the Two seasons.
The Questioner, who sits so sly,
Shall never know how to Reply.
He who replies to words of Doubt
Doth put the Light of Knowledge out.
The Strongest Poison ever known
Came from Caesar's Laurel Crown.
Nought can deform the Human Race
Like to the Armour's iron brace.
When Gold & Gems adorn the Plow
To peaceful Arts shall Envy Bow.
A Riddle or the Cricket's Cry
Is to Doubt a fit Reply.
The Emmet's Inch & Eagle's Mile
Make Lame Philosophy to smile.
He who Doubts from what he sees
Will ne'er Believe, do what you Please.
If the Sun & Moon should doubt,
They'd immediately Go out.
To be in a Passion you Good may do,
But no Good if a Passion is in you.
The Whore & Gambler, by the State
Licenc'd, build that Nation's Fate.

The Harlot's cry from Street to Street
Shall weave Old England's winding Sheet.
The Winner's Shout, the Loser's Curse,
Dance before dead England's Hearse.
Every Night & every Morn
Some to Misery are Born.
Every Morn & every Night
Some are Born to sweet delight.
Some are Born to sweet delight,
Some are Born to Endless Night.
We are led to Believe a Lie
When we see not Thro' the Eye
Which was Born in a Night to perish in a Night
When the Soul Slept in Beams of Light.
God Appears & God is Light
To those poor Souls who dwell in Night,
But does a Human Form Display
To those who Dwell in Realms of day.

WILLIAM BLAKE

Monarch of All I Survey

I am monarch of all I survey,
  My right there is none to dispute;
From the centre all round to the sea,
  I am lord of the fowl and the brute.
Oh, solitude! where are the charms
  That sages have seen in thy face?
Better dwell in the midst of alarms,
  Than reign in this horrible place.

I am out of humanity's reach,
  I must finish my journey alone,
Never hear the sweet music of speech;
  I start at the sound of my own.
The beasts, that roam over the plain,
  My form with indifference see;
They are so unacquainted with man,
  Their tameness is shocking to me.

261

Society, friendship, and love,
  Divinely bestowed upon man,
Oh, had I the wings of a dove,
  How soon would I taste you again!
My sorrows I then might assuage
  In the ways of religion and truth,
Might learn from the wisdom of age,
  And be cheered by the sallies of youth.

Religion! what treasure untold
  Resides in that heavenly word!
More precious than silver and gold,
  Or all that this earth can afford,
But the sound of the church-going bell
  These valleys and rocks never heard,
Ne'er sighed at the sound of a knell,
  Or smiled when a sabbath appeared.

Ye winds, that have made me your sport,
  Convey to this desolate shore
Some cordial endearing report
  Of a land I shall visit no more.
My friends, do they now and then send
  A wish or a thought after me?
O tell me I yet have a friend,
  Though a friend I am never to see.

How fleet is a glance of the mind!
  Compared with the speed of its flight,
The tempest itself lags behind,
  And the swift-winged arrows of light.
When I think of my own native land,
  In a moment I seem to be there;
But alas! recollection at hand
  Soon hurries me back to despair.

But the sea-fowl is gone to her nest,
  The beast is laid down in his lair,
Ev'n here is a season of rest,
  And I to my cabin repair.

There is mercy in every place;
    And mercy, encouraging thought!
Gives even affliction a grace,
    And reconciles man to his lot.
      ALEXANDER SELKIRK 1676–1721

(Supposed to have been written during his solitary stay in the island of Juan Fernández.)

664. *Of All the Souls That Stand Create*

Of all the souls that stand create
I have elected one.
When sense from spirit files away,
And subterfuge is done;

When that which is and that which was
Apart, intrinsic, stand,
And this brief tragedy of flesh
Is shifted like a sand;

When figures show their royal front
And mists are carved away –
Behold the atom I preferred
To all the lists of clay!
      EMILY DICKINSON 1830–86

The Listeners

'Is there anybody there?' said the Traveller,
    Knocking on the moonlit door;
And his horse in the silence champed the grasses
    Of the forest's ferny floor:
And a bird flew up out of the turret,
    Above the Traveller's head:
And he smote upon the door again a second time;
    'Is there anybody there?' he said.
But no one descended to the Traveller;
    No head from the leaf-fringed sill

Leaned over and looked into his grey eyes,
  Where he stood perplexed and still.
But only a host of phantom listeners
  That dwelt in the lone house then
Stood listening in the quiet of the moonlight
  To that voice from the world of men:
Stood thronging the faint moonbeams on the dark stair,
  That goes down to the empty hall,
Hearkening in an air stirred and shaken
  By the lonely Traveller's call.
And he felt in his heart their strangeness,
  Their stillness answering his cry,
While his horse moved, cropping the dark turf,
  'Neath the starred and leafy sky;
For he suddenly smote on the door, even
  Louder, and lifted his head: –
'Tell them I came, and no one answered,
  That I kept my word,' he said.
Never the least stir made the listeners,
  Though every word he spake
Fell echoing through the shadowiness of the still house
  From the one man left awake:
Ay, they heard his foot upon the stirrup,
  And the sound of iron on stone,
And how the silence surged softly backward,
  When the plunging hoofs were gone.

WALTER DE LA MARE 1873–1956

Dream-Pedlary

I

If there were dreams to sell,
  What would you buy?
Some cost a passing bell;
  Some a light sigh,
That shakes from Life's fresh crown
Only a rose-leaf down.
If there were dreams to sell,
Merry and sad to tell,

And the crier rung the bell,
  What would you buy?

II

A cottage lone and still,
  With bowers nigh,
Shadowy, my woes to still,
  Until I die.
Such pearl from Life's fresh crown
Fain would I shake me down.
Were dreams to have at will,
This would best heal my ill,
  This would I buy.

III

But there were dreams to sell
  Ill didst thou buy;
Life is a dream, they tell,
  Waking, to die.
Dreaming a dream to prize,
Is wishing ghosts to rise:
  And, if I had the spell
  To call the buried well,
    Which one would I?

IV

If there are ghosts to raise,
  What shall I call,
Out of hell's murky haze,
  Heaven's blue pall?
Raise my loved long-lost boy
To lead me to his joy.
  There are no ghosts to raise;
  Out of death lead no ways;
    Vain is the call.

V

Know'st thou not ghosts to sue?
  No love thou hast.

Else lie, as I will do,
    And breathe thy last.

So out of Life's fresh crown
Fall like a rose-leaf down.
    Thus are the ghosts to woo;
    Thus are all dreams made true,
        Ever to last!
        THOMAS LOVELL BEDDOES

from *The Hound of Heaven*

I fled Him, down the nights and down the days;
    I fled Him, down the arches of the years;
I fled Him, down the labyrinthine ways
    Of my own mind, and in the mist of tears

I hid from Him, and under running laughter.
            Up vistaed hopes I sped;
            And shot, precipitated,
Adown Titanic glooms of chasmèd fears,
    From those strong Feet that followed, followed after.

            But with unhurrying chase,
            And unperturbèd pace,
    Deliberate speed, majestic instancy,
            They beat — and a Voice beat
            More instant than the Feèt —
    'All things betray thee, who betrayest Me.'

            I pleaded, outlaw-wise,
By many a hearted casement, curtained red,
    Trellised with intertwining charities;
(For, though I knew His love Who followèd,
            Yet was I sore adread
Lest, having Him, I must have naught beside).
But, if one little casement parted wide,
    The gust of His approach would clash it to.
    Fear wist not to evade, as Love wist to pursue.
Across the margent of the world I fled,

And troubled the gold gateways of the stars,
　　Smiting for shelter on their clangèd bars;
　　　　Fretted to dulcet jars
And silvern clatter the pale ports o' the moon.
I said to Dawn: Be sudden – to Eve: Be soon;
　　With thy young skiey blossoms heap me over
　　　　From this tremendous Lover –
Float thy vague veil about me, lest He see!
　　I tempted all His servitors, but to find
My own betrayal in their constancy,
In faith to Him their fickleness to me,
　　Their traitorous trueness, and their loyal deceit.
To all swift things for swiftness did I sue;
　　Clung to the whistling mane of every wind.
　　　　But whether they swept, smoothly fleet,
　　The long savannahs of the blue;
　　　　Or whether, Thunder-driven,
　　They clanged his chariot 'thwart a heaven,
Plashy with flying lightnings round the spurn o' their feet: –
Fear wist not to evade as Love wist to pursue.

　　　　Still with unhurrying chase,
　　　　And unperturbèd pace,
　　Deliberate speed, majestic instancy,
　　　　Came on the following Feet,
　　　　And a Voice above their beat –
　　'Naught shelters thee, who wilt not shelter Me.'

★　★　★

　　　　Nigh and nigh draws the chase,
　　　　With unperturbèd pace,
　　Deliberate speed, majestic instancy;
　　　　And past those noisèd Feet
　　　　A voice comes yet more fleet –
　　'Lo! naught contents thee, who content'st not Me.'

Naked I wait Thy love's uplifted stroke!
My harness piece by piece Thou hast hewn from me,
　　　　And smitten me to my knee;
　　　　I am defenceless utterly.
　　　　I slept, methinks, and woke,
And, slowly gazing, find me stripped in sleep.

In the rash lustihead of my young powers,
            I shook the pillaring hours
And pulled my life upon me; grimed with smears,
I stand amid the dust o' the moulded years –
My mangled youth lies dead beneath the heap.
My days have crackled and gone up in smoke,
Have puffed and burst as sun-starts on a stream.
            Yea, faileth now even dream
The dreamer, and the lute the lutanist;
Even the linked fantasies, in whose blossomy twist
I swung the earth a trinket at my wrist,
Are yielding; cords of all too weak account
For earth with heavy griefs so overplussed.

★ ★ ★

            Halts by me that footfall:
            Is my gloom, after all,
Shade of His hand, outstretched caressingly?
            'Ah, fondest, blindest, weakest,
            I am He Whom thou seekest!
Thou dravest love from thee, who dravest Me.'

FRANCIS THOMPSON 1859–1907

The Nightmare

When you're lying awake with a dismal headache, and
            repose is taboo'd by anxiety,
I conceive you may use any language you choose to
            indulge in, without impropriety;
For your brain is on fire – the bedclothes conspire of usual
            slumber to plunder you:
First your counterpane goes, and uncovers your toes, and
            your sheet slips demurely from under you;
Then the blanketing tickles – you feel like mixed pickles –
            so terribly sharp is the pricking,
And you're hot, and you're cross, and you tumble and toss
            till there's nothing 'twixt you and the ticking.
Then the bedclothes all creep to the ground in a heap, and
            you pick 'em all up in a tangle;

Next your pillow resigns and politely declines to remain at
    its usual angle!
Well, you get some repose in the form of a doze, with hot
    eye-balls and head ever aching,
But your slumbering teems with such horrible dreams that
    you'd very much better be waking;
For you dream you are crossing the Channel, and tossing
    about in a steamer from Harwich –
Which is something between a large bathing machine and
    a very small second-class carriage –
And you're giving a treat (penny ice and cold meat) to a
    party of friends and relations –
They're a ravenous horde – and they all came on board at
    Sloane Square and South Kensington Stations.
And bound on that journey you find your attorney (who
    started that morning from Devon);
He's a bit undersized, and you don't feel surprised when he
    tells you he's only eleven.
Well, you're driving like mad with this singular lad
    (by-the-bye the ship's now a four-wheeler),
And you're playing round games, and he calls you bad
    names when you tell him that 'ties pay the dealer';
But this you can't stand, so you throw up your hand, and
    you find you're as cold as an icicle,
In your shirt and your socks (the black silk with gold
    clocks), crossing Salisbury Plain on a bicycle:
And he and the crew are on bicycles too – which they've
    somehow or other invested in –
And he's telling the tars, all the particu*lars* of a company
    · he's interested in –
It's a scheme of devices, to get at low prices, all goods from
    cough mixtures to cables
(Which tickled the sailors) by treating retailers, as though
    they were all vege*t*ables –
You get a good spadesman to plant a small tradesman,
    (first take off his boots with a boot-tree),
And his legs will take root, and his fingers will shoot, and
    they'll blossom and bud like a fruit-tree –
From the greengrocer tree you get grapes and green pea,
    cauliflower, pineapple, and cranberries, ·

While the pastrycook plant, cherry brandy will grant,
    apple puffs, and three-corners, and banberries –
The shares are a penny, and ever so many are taken by
    Rothschild and Baring,
And just as a few are allotted to you, you awake with a
    shudder despairing –
You're a regular wreck, with a crick in your neck, and no
    wonder you snore, for your head's on the floor, and
    you've needles and pins from your soles to your shins,
    and your flesh is a-creep for your left leg's asleep, and
    you've cramp in your toes, and a fly on your nose,
    and some fluff in your lung, and a feverish tongue,
    and a thirst that's intense, and a general sense that you
    haven't been sleeping in clover;
But the darkness has passed, and it's daylight at last, and
    the night has been long – ditto ditto my song – and
    thank goodness they're both of them over!

W. S. GILBERT

Solitude

Laugh, and the world laughs with you,
    Weep, and you weep alone,
For sad old earth must borrow its mirth,
    But has trouble enough of its own.
Sing, and the hills will answer;
    Sigh, it is lost on the air,
The echoes bound to a joyful sound,
    But shrink from voicing care.
Rejoice, and men will seek you;
    Grieve, and they turn and go.
They want full measure of all your pleasure.
    But they do not need your woe.
Be glad, and your friends are many,
    Be sad, and you lose them all;
There are none to decline your nectared wine,
    But alone you must drink life's gall.
Feast, and your halls are crowded,
    Fast, and the world goes by.
Succeed and give – and it helps you live,

But no man can help you die;
There is room in the halls of pleasure
For a large and lordly train,
But one by one we must all file on
Through the narrow aisles of pain.

ELLA WHEELER WILCOX

Leap Before You Look

The sense of danger must not disappear:
The way is certainly both short and steep,
However gradual it looks from here;
Look if you like, but you will have to leap.

Tough-minded men get mushy in their sleep
And break the by-laws any fool can keep;
It is not the convention but the fear
That has a tendency to disappear.

The worried efforts of the busy heap,
The dirt, the imprecision, and the beer
Produce a few smart wisecracks every year;
Laugh if you can, but you will have to leap.

The clothes that are considered right to wear
Will not be either sensible or cheap,
So long as we consent to live like sheep
And never mention those who disappear.

Much can be said for social savoir-faire,
But to rejoice when no one else is there
Is even harder than it is to weep;
No one is watching, but you have to leap.

A solitude ten thousand fathoms deep
Sustains the bed on which we lie, my dear:
Although I love you, you will have to leap;
Our dream of safety has to disappear.

W. H. AUDEN

The Tyger

Tyger, Tyger, burning bright,
In the forests of the night:
What immortal hand or eye,
Could frame thy fearful symmetry?

In what distant deeps or skies
Burnt the fire of thine eyes?
On what wings dare he aspire?
What the hand dare seize the fire?

And what shoulder, & what art
Could twist the sinews of thy heart?
And when thy heart began to beat,
What dread hand? & what dread feet?

What the hammer? what the chain,
In what furnace was thy brain?
What the anvil? what dread grasp
Dare its deadly terrors clasp?

When the stars threw down their spears
And water'd heaven with their tears,
Did he smile his work to see?
Did he who made the Lamb make thee?

Tyger, Tyger, burning bright
In the forests of the night:
What immortal hand or eye
Dare frame thy fearful symmetry?

WILLIAM BLAKE

Bagpipe Music

It's no go the merrygoround, it's no go the rickshaw,
All we want is a limousine and a ticket for the peepshow.
Their knickers are made of crêpe-de-chine, their shoes are made
of python,
Their halls are lined with tiger rugs and their walls with heads
of bison.

John MacDonald found a corpse, put it under the sofa,
Waited till it came to life and hit it with a poker,
Sold its eyes for souvenirs, sold its blood for whisky,
Kept its bones for dumb-bells to use when he was fifty.

It's no go the Yogi-Man, it's no go Blavatsky,
All we want is a bank balance and a bit of skirt in a taxi.

Annie MacDougall went to milk, caught her foot in the heather,
Woke to hear a dance record playing of Old Vienna.
It's no go your maidenheads, it's no go your culture,
All we want is a Dunlop tyre and the devil mend the puncture.

The Laird o' Phelps spent Hogmanay declaring he was sober,
Counted his feet to prove the fact and found he had one foot over.
Mrs Carmichael had her fifth, looked at the job with repulsion,
Said to the midwife 'Take it away; I'm through with
    over-production'.

It's no go the gossip column, it's no go the ceilidh,
All we want is a mother's help and a sugar-stick for the baby.

Willie Murray cut his thumb, couldn't count the damage.
Took the hide of an Ayrshire cow and used it for a bandage.
His brother caught three hundred cran when the seas were lavish,
Threw the bleeders back in the sea and went upon the parish.

It's no go the Herring Board, it's no go the Bible,
All we want is a packet of fags when our hands are idle.
It's no go the picture palace, it's no go the stadium,
It's no go the country cot with a pot of pink geraniums,
It's no go the Government grants, it's no go the elections,
Sit on your arse for fifty years and hang your hat on a pension.

It's no go my honey love, it's no go my poppet;
Work your hands from day to day, the winds will blow the
    profit.
The glass is falling hour by hour, the glass will fall for ever,
But if you break the bloody glass you won't hold up the
    weather.

LOUIS MACNEICE

Jazz Fantasia

Drum on your drums, batter on your banjoes,
sob on the long cool winding saxophones.
Go to it, O jazzmen.

Sling your knuckles on the bottoms of the happy
tin pans, let your trombones ooze, and go husha-
husha-hush with the slippery sand-paper.

Moan like an autumn wind high in the lonesome treetops, moan
soft like you wanted somebody terrible, cry like a racing car slipping
away from a motor-cycle cop, bang-bang! you jazzmen, bang alto-
gether drums, traps, banjoes, horns, tin cans – make two people
fight on the top of a stairway and scratch each other's eyes in a
clinch tumbling down the stairs.

Can the rough stuff . . . now a Mississippi steamboat pushes up the
night river with a hoo-hoo-hoo-oo . . . and the green lanterns
calling to the high soft stars . . . a red moon rides on the humps of
the low river hills . . . go to it, O jazzmen.

CARL SANDBURG

A Bookshop Idyll

Between the GARDENING and the COOKERY
    Comes the brief POETRY shelf;
By the Nonesuch Donne, a thin anthology
    Offers itself.

Critical, and with nothing else to do,
    I scan the Contents page,
Relieved to find the names are mostly new;
    No one my age.

Like all strangers, they divide by sex:
    Landscape near Parma
Interests a man, so does *The Double Vortex*,
    So does *Rilke* and *Buddha*.

274

'I travel, you see', 'I think' and 'I can read'
  These titles seem to say;
But *I Remember You, Love is my Creed,*
  Poem for J.,

The ladies' choice, discountenance my patter
  For several seconds;
From somewhere in this (as in any) matter
  A moral beckons.

Should poets bicycle-pump the human heart
  Or squash it flat?
Man's love is of man's life a thing apart;
  Girls aren't like that.

We men have got love well weighed up; our stuff
  Can get by without it.
Women don't seem to think that's good enough;
  They write about it,

And the awful way their poems lay them open
  Just doesn't strike them.
Women are really much nicer than men;
  No wonder we like them.

Deciding this, we can forget those times
  We sat up half the night
Chockfull of love, crammed with bright thoughts, names,
    rhymes,
  And couldn't write.

                              KINGSLEY AMIS 1922–

Chorus of Spirits

from *Prometheus Unbound*

    We come from the mind
    Of human kind
  Which was late so dusk, and obscene, and blind,
    Now 'tis an ocean

Of clear emotion,
A heaven of serene and mighty motion.
From that deep abyss
Of wonder and bliss,
Whose caverns are crystal palaces;
From those skiey towers
Where Thought's crowned powers
Sit watching your dance, ye happy Hours!
From the dim recesses
Of woven caresses,
Where lovers catch ye by your loose tresses;
From the azure isles,
Where sweet Wisdom smiles,
Delaying your ships with her siren wiles.
From the temples high
Of Man's ear and eye,
Roofed over Sculpture and Poesy;
From the murmurings
Of the unsealed springs
Where Science bedews her Dædal wings.
Years after years,
Through blood, and tears,
And a thick hell of hatreds, and hopes, and fears;
We waded and flew,
And the islets were few
Where the bud-blighted flowers of happiness grew.
Our feet now, every palm,
Are sandalled with calm,
And the dew of our wings is a rain of balm;
And, beyond our eyes,
The human love lies
Which makes all it gazes on Paradise.

PERCY BYSSHE SHELLEY

It's the First of January

It's the first of January –
Yet we don't have to sweep out a single fir-needle!
And my neighbour grumbles all morning

Trying to sweep out her frustration.
And then suddenly gives a roar.
I don't go to her: what help can I give her?
'Exercise!'
The red carpet.
The drunken faces of the guards.
To get along the corridor as quickly as possible
(Through the chlorine, bits of food, urine, putty)
And out into the air! Into the concrete yard!
Sixty minutes are already ticking away.
The clink of keys. And the sound of good-natured laughter:
'A bit of exercise'll do you good, girls!'
And my neighbour: 'Oh, I wish you'd all . . .'
The rest's not fit for print.
Five paces from wall to wall.
Netting above us – you won't fly away!
And just before she woke up this morning my neighbour
Dreamed of John the Baptist.
She dreamt he'd been brought to her cell.
As if he'd been on the march – so tired.
He was covered in grime, and his feet were caked with dust.
And how sorry for him she was!
She tore off a piece of her towel
So he could wash his feet.
He took it. And said to her: 'It's hard
To be alive, but your time is done.'
And he got ready to fly. Then a radiance
Began, and she cried:
'Let me see my daughter!
You can do it, see if you can't!'
But he gave her no sign
Either with a hand, or with a wing. He was silent.
She even thought he might be weeping.
That means – there will be sadness.
Or maybe a misfortune?
In the morning the dream came true . . .
And she – so unlucky! –
Wanted just this once to dream of something happy!
'Now then, that's enough of your gymnastics'
(This to me) 'Come on, you can't go on jumping up and down
For the whole hour! And don't spend

So much time writing in your exercise book – get some sleep!
Why, whenever I look at you, are you
Staring? Do you like me – or hate me?
It's just that this is the third year I've spent in here.
But I wish you well . . .'
I nod. And again – start running.
How many months – running on the spot.
How many dreams I run to you,
Tying them up, as in the sticky dough,
In the smell of chlorine, in my sheet,
The torn rags of the dirty walls . . .
Is there any place from which one can love more powerfully
Than from here? Not on the cross – but
In the torment of the Judas holes,
In the sophisticated boorishness of the interrogators,
In the agony of my neighbour's dreams,
In the blue smoke of her cigarette,
In the fierce pity I feel for her – ill,
Brought halfway to death,
Hysterical, kind and angry,
And cursing whoever it is who spins
This globe – in the nonsense
Of days without sun and tears without makeup –
More intensely, more sacredly – nowhere
Is it possible to love, my love!

IRINA RATUSHINSKAYA
(Translated by David McDuff.)

No, I'm Not Afraid

No, I'm not afraid: after a year
Of breathing these prison nights
I will survive into the sadness
To name which is escape.

The cockerel will weep freedom for me
And here – knee-deep in mire –
My gardens shed their water
And the northern air blows in draughts.

And how am I to carry to an alien planet
What are almost tears, as though towards home . . .
It isn't true, I *am* afraid, my darling!
But make it look as though you haven't noticed.

IRINA RATUSHINSKAYA

from *The Ballad of Reading Gaol*

I never saw a man who looked
   With such a wistful eye
Upon that little tent of blue
   Which prisoners call the sky,
And at every drifting cloud that went
   With sails of silver by.

I only knew what hunted thought
   Quickened his step, and why
He looked upon the garish day
   With such a wistful eye;
The man had killed the thing he loved,
   And so he had to die.

Yet each man kills the thing he loves,
   By each let this be heard,
Some do it with a bitter look,
   Some with a flattering word,
The coward does it with a kiss,
   The brave man with a sword!

Some kill their love when they are young,
   And some when they are old;
Some strangle with the hands of Lust,
   Some with the hands of Gold:
The kindest use a knife, because
   The dead so soon grow cold.

Some love too little, some too long,
   Some sell, and others buy;
Some do the deed with many tears,
   And some without a sigh:

For each man kills the thing he loves,
   Yet each man does not die.

He does not die a death of shame
   On a day of dark disgrace,
Nor have a noose about his neck,
   Nor a cloth upon his face,
Nor drop feet foremost through the floor
   Into an empty space.

He does not sit with silent men
   Who watch him night and day;
Who watch him when he tries to weep
   And when he tries to pray;
Who watch him lest himself should rob
   The prison of its prey.

He does not know that sickening thirst
   That sands one's throat, before
The hangman with his gardener's gloves
   Slips through the padded door,
And binds one with three leathern thongs,
   That the throat may thirst no more.

For oak and elm have pleasant leaves
   That in the spring-time shoot:
But grim to see is the gallows-tree,
   With its adder-bitten root,
And, green or dry, a man must die
   Before it bears its fruit!

The loftiest place is that seat of grace
   For which all worldlings try:
But who would stand in hempen band
   Upon a scaffold high,
And through a murderer's collar take
   His last look at the sky?

In Debtors' Yard the stones are hard,
   And the dripping wall is high,
So it was there he took the air
   Beneath the leaden sky,

And by each side a Warder walked,
    For fear the man might die.

Or else he sat with those who watched
    His anguish night and day;
Who watched him when he rose to weep,
    And when he crouched to pray;
Who watched him lest himself should rob
    Their scaffold of its prey.

That night the empty corridors
    Were full of forms of Fear,
And up and down the iron town
    Stole feet we could not hear,
And through the bars that hide the stars
    White faces seemed to peer.

He lay as one who lies and dreams
    In a pleasant meadow-land,
The watchers watched him as he slept,
    And could not understand
How one could sleep so sweet a sleep
    With a hangman close at hand.

But there is no sleep when men must weep
    Who never yet have wept:
So we – the fool, the fraud, the knave –
    That endless vigil kept,
And through each brain on hands of pain
    Another's terror crept.

Alas! it is a fearful thing
    To feel another's guilt!
For, right within, the sword of Sin
    Pierced to its poisoned hilt,
And as molten lead were the tears we shed
    For the blood we had not spilt.

We waited for the stroke of eight:
    Each tongue was thick with thirst:
For the stroke of eight is the stroke of Fate
    That makes a man accursed,

And Fate will use a running noose
    For the best man and the worst.

We had no other thing to do,
    Save to wait for the sign to come:
So, like things of stone in a valley lone,
    Quiet we sat and dumb:
But each man's heart beat thick and quick,
    Like a madman on a drum!

With sudden shock the prison-clock
    Smote on the shivering air,
And from all the gaol rose up a wail
    Of impotent despair,
Like the sound that frightened marshes hear
    From some leper in his lair.

There is no chapel on the day
    On which they hang a man:
The Chaplain's heart is far too sick,
    Or his face is far too wan,
Or there is that written in his eyes
    Which none should look upon.

The Chaplain would not kneel to pray
    By his dishonoured grave:
Nor mark it with that blessed Cross
    That Christ for sinners gave,
Because the man was one of those
    Whom Christ came down to save.

I know not whether Laws be right,
    Or whether Laws be wrong;
All that we know who lie in gaol
    Is that the wall is strong;
And that each day is like a year,
    A year whose days are long.

But this I know, that every Law
    That men have made for Man,
Since first Man took his brother's life,
    And the sad world began,

But straws the wheat and saves the chaff
   With a most evil fan.

The man in red who reads the Law
   Gave him three weeks of life,
Three little weeks in which to heal
   His soul of his soul's strife,
And cleanse from every blot of blood
   The hand that held the knife.

In Reading gaol by Reading town
   There is a pit of shame,
And in it lies a wretched man
   Eaten by teeth of flame,
In a burning winding-sheet he lies,
   And his grave has got no name.

And there, till Christ call forth the dead,
   In silence let him lie:
No need to waste the foolish tear,
   Or heave the windy sigh:
The man had killed the thing he loved,
   And so he had to die.

And all men kill the thing they love,
   By all let this be heard,
Some do it with a bitter look,
   Some with a flattering word,
The coward does it with a kiss,
   The brave man with a sword!

OSCAR WILDE

Oh Who is that Young Sinner

Oh who is that young sinner with the handcuffs on
   his wrists?
And what has he been after that they groan and shake
   their fists?
And wherefore is he wearing such a conscience-stricken
   air?

Oh they're taking him to prison for the colour of his
   hair.

A. E. HOUSMAN

18 June 1961

He will come out
Between two warders,
Lean and sunburnt,
A little bent,
As if apologising
For his strength,
His features tense,
But looking quite calm.

He will take off his jacket
And, with shirt torn open,
Stand up against the wall
To be executed.

He has not betrayed us.
He will meet his end.
Without weakness.
When I feel anxious,
It is not for him.
Do I fear a compulsion in me
To be so destroyed?
Or is there someone
In the depths of my being,
Waiting for permission
To pull the trigger?

DAG HAMMARSKJÖLD 1905–61
(Translated by Ley Sjöberg.)

Ode [We are the Music Makers]

We are the music-makers,
   And we are the dreamers of dreams,

Wandering by lone sea-breakers,
    And sitting by desolate streams;
World-losers and world forsakers,
    On whom the pale moon gleams:
Yet we are the movers and shakers
    Of the world for ever, it seems.

With wonderful deathless ditties
We build up the world's great cities.
    And out of a fabulous story
    We fashion an empire's glory:
One man with a dream, at pleasure,
    Shall go forth and conquer a crown;
And three with a new song's measure
    Can trample an empire down.

We, in the ages lying
    In the buried past of the earth,
Built Nineveh with our sighing,
    And Babel itself with our mirth;
And o'erthrew them with prophesying
    To the old of the new world's worth;
For each age is a dream that is dying,
    Or one that is coming to birth.

ARTHUR WILLIAM EDGAR O'SHAUGHNESSY 1844–81

Kubla Khan

In Xanadu did Kubla Khan
    A stately pleasure-dome decree:
Where Alph, the sacred river, ran
Through caverns measureless to man
    Down to a sunless sea.
So twice five miles of fertile ground
With walls and towers were girdled round:
And there were gardens bright with sinuous rills
Where blossom'd many an incense-bearing tree;
And here were forests ancient as the hills,
Enfolding sunny spots of greenery.

285

But O, that deep romantic chasm which slanted
Down the green hill athwart a cedarn cover!
A savage place! as holy and enchanted
As e'er beneath a waning moon was haunted
By woman wailing for her demon-lover!
And from this chasm, with ceaseless turmoil seething,
As if this earth in fast thick pants were breathing,
A mighty fountain momently was forced;
Amid whose swift half-intermitted burst
Huge fragments vaulted like rebounding hail,
Or chaffy grain beneath the thresher's flail:
And 'mid these dancing rocks at once and ever
It flung up momently the sacred river.
Five miles meandering with a mazy motion
Through wood and dale the sacred river ran,
Then reach'd the caverns measureless to man,
And sank in tumult to a lifeless ocean:
And 'mid this tumult Kubla heard from far
Ancestral voices prophesying war!

   The shadow of the dome of pleasure
      Floated midway on the waves;
   Where was heard the mingled measure
      From the fountain and the caves.
It was a miracle of rare device,
A sunny pleasure-dome with caves of ice!

   A damsel with a dulcimer
      In a vision once I saw:
   It was an Abyssinian maid,
      And on her dulcimer she play'd,
   Singing of Mount Abora.
   Could I revive within me,
      Her symphony and song,
To such a deep delight 'twould win me,
That with music loud and long,
I would build that dome in air,
That sunny dome! those caves of ice!
And all who heard should see them there,
And all should cry, Beware! Beware!
His flashing eyes, his floating hair!

Weave a circle round him thrice,
    And close your eyes with holy dread,
    For he on honey-dew hath fed,
And drunk the milk of Paradise.

SAMUEL TAYLOR COLERIDGE 1772–1834

(Addicted to drugs, Coleridge was twenty-five when he took an opiate, having just read a passage from Samuel Purchas's *Pilgrimage* (1614), a collection of travel stories: 'In Xanada did Cublai Can build a stately Pallace, encompassing sixteene miles of plaine ground with a wall, wherein are fertile Meddows, pleasant Springs, delightful Streames . . .' After a few hours' sleep, during which he felt he had composed two to three hundred lines, he awoke to find to his dismay that this was all he could recall.)

A Truthful Song

THE BRICKLAYER:
I tell this tale, which is strictly true,
Just by way of convincing you
How very little, since things were made,
Things have altered in the building trade.

A year ago, come the middle of March,
We was building flats near the Marble Arch,
When a thin young man with coal-black hair
Came up to watch us working there.

Now there wasn't a trick in brick or stone
Which this young man hadn't seen or known;
Nor there wasn't a tool from trowel to maul
But this young man could use 'em all!

Then up and spoke the plumbyers bold,
Which was laying the pipes for the hot and cold:
'Since you with us have made so free,
Will you kindly say what your name might be?'

The young man kindly answered them;
'It might be Lot or Methusalem,
Or it might be Moses (a man I hate)
Whereas it is Pharaoh surnamed the Great.

287

'Your glazing is new and your plumbing's strange,
But otherwise I perceive no change;
And in less than a month if you do as I bid
I'd learn you to build me a Pyramid!'

THE SAILOR:
I tell this tale, which is stricter true,
Just by way of convincing you
How very little, since things was made,
Things have altered in the shipwright's trade.

In Blackwall Basin yesterday
A China barque re-fitting lay;
When a fat old man with snow-white hair
Came up to watch us working there.

Now there wasn't a knot which the riggers knew
But the old man made it – and better too;
Nor there wasn't a sheet, or a lift, or a brace,
But the old man knew its lead and place.

Then up and spoke the caulkyers bold,
Which was packing the pump in the afterhold:
'Since you with us have made so free,
Will you kindly tell what your name might be?'

The old man kindly answered them:
'It might be Japheth, it might be Shem,
Or it might be Ham (though his skin was dark),
Whereas it is Noah, commanding the Ark.

'Your wheel is new and your pumps are strange,
But otherwise I perceive no change;
And in less than a week, if she did not ground,
I'd sail this hooker the wide world round!'

BOTH:
We tell these tales, which are strictest true,
Just by way of convincing you

How very little, since things was made,
Anything alters in any one's trade!
                    RUDYARD KIPLING

A Man's a Man for A' That

Is there, for honest poverty,
   That hangs his head, an' a' that?
The coward slave, we pass him by,
   We dare be poor for a' that!
     For a' that, an' a' that,
       Our toils obscure, an' a' that;
      The rank is but the guinea's stamp;
       The man's the gowd[1] for a' that.

What though on hamely fare we dine,
   Wear hodden-gray, an' a' that;
Gie fools their silks, and knaves their wine,
   A man's a man for a' that.
     For a' that, an' a' that,
       Their tinsel show, an' a' that;
      The honest man, though e'er sae poor,
       Is king o' men for a' that.

Ye see yon birkie,[2] ca'd a lord,
   Wha struts, an' stares, an' a' that;
Though hundreds worship at his word,
   He's but a coof[3] for a' that.
     For a' that, an' a' that,
       His riband, star, an' a' that,
      The man o' independent mind,
       He looks and laughs at a' that.

A prince can mak a belted knight,
   A marquis, duke an' a' that;
But an honest man's aboon[4] his might,
   Guid faith he mauna fa'[5] that!
     For a' that, an' a' that,
       Their dignities, an' a' that,

The pith o' sense, an' pride o' worth,
　　Are higher rank than a' that.

Then let us pray that come it may,
　　As come it will for a' that,
That sense and worth o'er a' the earth,
　　May bear the gree,⁶ an' a' that.
　　　　For a' that, an' a' that,
　　　　　　It's coming yet, for a' that,
　　　　That man to man, the warld o'er,
　　　　　　Shall brothers be for a' that.

ROBERT BURNS

The Song of the Shirt

With fingers weary and worn,
　　With eyelids heavy and red,
A woman sat, in unwomanly rags,
　　Plying her needle and thread, –
　　　　Stitch – stitch – stitch!
In poverty, hunger, and dirt;
　　And still with a voice of dolorous pitch
She sang the 'Song of the Shirt!'

'Work – work – work
　　While the cock is crowing aloof!
And work – work – work
　　Till the stars shine through the roof!
It's oh! to be a slave
　　Along with the barbarous Turk,
Where woman has never a soul to save.
　　If this is Christian work!

'Work – work –work
　　Till the brain begins to swim!
Work – work – work
　　Till the eyes are heavy and dim!

Seam, and gusset, and band,
    Band, and gusset, and seam, –
Till over the buttons I fall asleep,
    And sew them on in a dream!

'O men with sisters dear!
    O men with mothers and wives!
It is not linen you're wearing out,
    But human creatures' lives!
        Stitch – stitch – stitch,
    In poverty, hunger and dirt, –
Sewing at once, with a double thread,
    A shroud as well as a shirt!

'But why do I talk of death, –
    That phantom of grisly bone?
I hardly fear his terrible shape,
    It seems so like my own, –

It seems so like my own
    Because of the fasts I keep;
O God! that bread should be so dear,
    And flesh and blood so cheap!

'Work – work – work!
    My labor never flags;
And what are its wages? A bed of straw,
    A crust of bread – and rags.
That shattered roof – and this naked floor –
    A table – a broken chair –
And a wall so blank my shadow I thank
    For sometimes falling there!

'Work – work – work
    From weary chime to chime!
Work – work – work
    As prisoners work for crime!
Band, and gusset, and seam,
    Seam, and gusset, and band, –
Till the heart is sick and the brain benumbed,
    As well as the weary hand.

'Work – work – work
  In the dull December light!
And work – work – work
  When the weather is warm and bright!
While underneath the eaves
  The brooding swallows cling,
As if to show me their sunny backs,
  And twit me with the Spring.

'Oh but to breathe the breath
  Of the cowslip and primrose sweet, –
With the sky above my head,
  And the grass beneath my feet!
For only one short hour
  To feel as I used to feel,
Before I knew the woes of want
  And the walk that costs a meal!

'Oh but for one short hour, –
  A respite, however brief!
No blessèd leisure for love or hope,
  But only time for grief!
A little weeping would ease my heart;
  But in their briny bed
My tears must stop, for every drop
  Hinders needle and thread!'

With fingers weary and worn,
  With eyelids heavy and red,
A woman sat, in unwomanly rags,
  Plying her needle and thread, –
    Stitch – stitch – stitch!
  In poverty, hunger, and dirt;
And still with a voice of dolorous pitch –
Would that its tone could reach the rich! –
  She sang this 'Song of the Shirt!'

THOMAS HOOD

Vagabond

Dunno a heap about the what an' why,
    Can't say's I ever knowed.
Heaven to me's a fair blue stretch of sky,
    Earth's jest a dusty road.

Dunno the name o' things, nor what they are,
    Can't say's I ever will.
Dunno about God – He's jest the noddin' star
    Atop the windy hill.

Dunno about Life – it's jest a tramp alone
    From wakin'-time to doss.
Dunno about Death – it's jest a quiet stone
    All over-grey wi' moss.

An' why I live, an' why the old world spins,
    Are things I never knowed;
My mark's the gipsy fires, the lonely inns,
    An' jest the dusty road.

JOHN MASEFIELD 1878–1967

The Bleed'n' Sparrer

We 'ad a bleed'n' sparrer wot
Lived up a bleed'n' spaht,
One day the bleed'n' rain came dahn
An' washed the bleeder aht.

An' as 'e layed 'arf drahnded
Dahn in the bleed'n' street
'E begged that bleed'n' rainstorm
To bave 'is bleed'n' feet.

But then the bleed'n' sun came aht –
Dried up the bleed'n' rain –
So that bleed'n' little sparrer
'E climbed up 'is spaht again.

But, Oh! – the crewel sparrer'awk,
'E spies 'im in 'is snuggery,
'E sharpens up 'is bleed'n' claws
An' rips 'im aht by thuggery!

Jist then a bleed'n' sportin' type
Wot 'ad a bleed'n' gun
'E spots that bleed'n' sparrer'awk
An' blasts 'is bleed'n' fun.

★   ★   ★

The moral of this story
Is plain to everyone –
That them wot's up the bleed'n' spaht
Don't get no bleed'n' fun.

ANON.

Leisure

What is this life if, full of care,
We have no time to stand and stare.

No time to stand beneath the boughs
And stare as long as sheep or cows.

No time to see, when woods we pass,
Where squirrels hide their nuts in grass.

No time to see, in broad daylight,
Streams full of stars like skies at night.

No time to turn at Beauty's glance,
And watch her feet, how they can dance.

No time to wait till her mouth can
Enrich that smile her eyes began.

A poor life this if, full of care,
We have no time to stand and stare.

W. H. DAVIES 1871–1940

The Man With the Hoe

A REPLY

Let us a little permit Nature to take her own way: she better understands her own affairs than we. – MONTAIGNE

Nature reads not our labels, 'great' and 'small';
Accepts she one and all

Who, striving, win and hold the vacant place;
All are of royal race.

Him, there, rough-cast, with rigid arm and limb,
The Mother molded him,

Of his rude realm ruler and demigod,
Lord of the rock and clod.

With Nature is no 'better' and no 'worse,'
On this bared head no curse.

Humbled it is and bowed; so is he crowned
Whose kingdom is the ground.

Diverse the burdens on the one stern road
Where bears each back its load;

Varied the toil, but neither high nor low.
With pen or sword or hoe,

He that has put out strength, lo, he is strong;
Of him with spade or song

Nature but questions, – 'This one, shall he stay?'
She answers 'Yea,' or 'Nay,'

'Well, ill, he digs, he sings'; and he bides on,
Or shudders, and is gone.

Strength shall he have, the toiler, strength and grace,
So fitted to his place

As he leaned, there, an oak where sea winds blow,
Our brother with the hoe.

No blot, no monster, no unsightly thing,
The soil's long-lineaged king;

His changeless realm, he knows it and commands;
Erect enough he stands,

Tall as his toil. Nor does he bow unblest:
Labor he has, and rest.

Need was, need is, and need will ever be
For him and such as he;

Cast for the gap, with gnarlèd arm and limb,
The Mother molded him, –

Long wrought, and molded him with mother's care,
Before she set him there.

And aye she gives him, mindful of her own,
Peace of the plant, the stone;

Yea, since above his work he may not rise,
She makes the field his skies.

See! she that bore him, and metes out the lot,
He serves her. Vex him not

To scorn the rock whence he was hewn, the pit
And what was digged from it;

Lest he no more in native virtue stand,
The earth-sword in his hand,

But follow sorry phantoms to and fro,
And let a kingdom go.

JOHN VANCE CHENEY 1848–1922

Song

We only ask for sunshine,
We did not want the rain;
But see the flowers that spring from showers
All up and down the plain.

We beg the gods for laughter,
We shrink, we dread the tears;
But grief's redress is happiness,
Alternate through the years.

HELEN HAY WHITNEY

The Village Blacksmith

Under a spreading chestnut-tree
   The village smithy stands;
The smith, a mighty man is he,
   With large and sinewy hands;
And the muscles of his brawny arms
   Are strong as iron bands.

His hair is crisp, and black, and long,
   His face is like the tan;
His brow is wet with honest sweat,
   He earns whate'er he can,
And looks the whole world in the face,
   For he owes not any man.

Week in, week out, from morn till night,
   You can hear his bellows blow;
You can hear him swing his heavy sledge,
   With measured beat and slow,
Like a sexton ringing the village bell,
   When the evening sun is low.

And children coming home from school
   Look in at the open door;

They love to see the flaming forge,
　　And hear the bellows roar,
And catch the burning sparks that fly
　　Like chaff from a threshing-floor.

He goes on Sunday to the church,
　　And sits among his boys;
He hears the parson pray and preach,
　　He hears his daughter's voice,
Singing in the village choir,
　　And it makes his heart rejoice.

It sounds to him like her mother's voice,
　　Singing in Paradise!
He needs must think of her once more,
　　How in the grave she lies;
And with his hard, rough hand he wipes
　　A tear out of his eyes.

Toiling – rejoicing – sorrowing,
　　Onward through life he goes;
Each morning sees some task begin,
　　Each evening sees it close;
Something attempted, something done,
　　Has earned a night's repose.

Thanks, thanks to thee, my worthy friend,
　　For the lesson thou hast taught!
Thus at the flaming forge of life
　　Our fortunes must be wrought;
Thus on its sounding anvil shaped
　　Each burning deed and thought.
　　　　HENRY WADSWORTH LONGFELLOW

Psalm 146

Verses 3–9

Put not your trust in princes,
nor in the son of man, in whom
there is no help.

His breath goeth forth, he
returneth to his earth; in that
very day his thoughts perish.

Happy *is he* that *hath* the
God of Jacob for his help, whose
hope *is* in the LORD his God:

Which made heaven, and
earth, the sea, and all that there-
in *is:* which keepeth truth for
ever:

Which executeth judgment
for the oppressed: which giveth
food to the hungry. The LORD
looseth the prisoners:

The LORD openeth *the eyes of*
the blind: the LORD raiseth them
that are bowed down: the LORD
loveth the righteous:

The LORD preserveth the
strangers; he relieveth the
fatherless and widow: but the
way of the wicked he turneth
upside down.

Impromptu on Charles II

God bless our good and gracious King,
　　Whose promise none relies on;
Who never said a foolish thing,
　　Nor ever did a wise one.

JOHN WILMOT, EARL OF ROCHESTER 1647–80

The Vicar of Bray

In good King Charles's golden days,
   When loyalty no harm meant,
A zealous High-Churchman I was,
   And so I got preferment;
Unto my flock I daily preached
   Kings were by God appointed,
And damned was he that durst resist
   Or touch the Lord's anointed.
And this is law, I will maintain,
   Until my dying day, Sir,
That whatsoever king shall reign,
   I'll be the Vicar of Bray, Sir.

When royal James obtained the crown,
   And Popery came in fashion,
The penal laws I hooted down,
   And read the declaration:
The Church of Rome I found would fit
   Full well my constitution,
And had become a Jesuit,
   But for the Revolution.
When William was our king declared
   To ease the nation's grievance,
With this new wind about I steered,
   And swore to him allegiance;
Old principles I did revoke,
   Set conscience at a distance;
Passive obedience was a joke,
   A jest was non-resistance.
When gracious Anne became our queen,
   The Church of England's glory,
Another face of things was seen –
   And I became a Tory:
Occasional Conformists base,
   I scorned their moderation,
And swore the church in danger was
   By such prevarication.
When George in pudding-time came o'er,
   And moderate men looked big, Sir,

I turned a cat-in-pan once more –
    And so became a Whig, Sir:
And this preferment I procured
    From our new faith's defender,
And almost every day abjured
    The Pope and the Pretender.
The illustrious house of Hanover,
    And Protestant succession,
To these I do allegiance swear –
    While they can keep possession:
For in my faith and loyalty
    I never more will falter,
And George my lawful King shall be –
    Until the times do alter.
And this is law, I will maintain,
    Until my dying day, Sir,
That whatsoever king shall reign,
    I'll be the Vicar of Bray, Sir.

ANON.

The Touch

from *My Dear and Only Love*

He either fears his fate too much,
    Or his deserts are small,
That puts it not unto the touch
    To win or lose it all.

JAMES GRAHAM, MARQUIS OF MONTROSE 1612–50

The Road Not Taken

Two roads diverged in a yellow wood,
And sorry I could not travel both
And be one traveler, long I stood
And looked down one as far as I could
To where it bent in the undergrowth;

Then took the other, as just as fair,
And having perhaps the better claim,
Because it was grassy and wanted wear;
Though as for that, the passing there
Had worn them really about the same,

And both that morning equally lay
In leaves no step had trodden black.
Oh, I kept the first for another day!
Yet knowing how way leads on to way,
I doubted if I should ever come back.

I shall be telling this with a sigh
Somewhere ages and ages hence:
Two roads diverged in a wood, and I —
I took the one less traveled by,
And that has made all the difference.

ROBERT FROST

Is this a Dagger?

from *Macbeth*, Act II, Scene ii

Is this a dagger which I see before me,
The handle toward my hand? Come, let
    me clutch thee.
I have thee not, and yet I see thee still.
Art thou not, fatal vision, sensible
To feeling as to sight? or art thou but
A dagger of the mind, a false creation,
Proceeding from the heat-oppressed brain?
I see thee yet, in form as palpable
As this which now I draw.

WILLIAM SHAKESPEARE

To Be, or Not to Be

from *Hamlet*, Act III, Scene i

To be, or not to be – that is the question;
Whether 'tis nobler in the mind to suffer
The slings and arrows of outrageous fortune,
Or to take arms against a sea of troubles,
And by opposing end them? To die, to sleep –
No more; and by a sleep to say we end
The heart-ache and the thousand natural shocks
That flesh is heir to. 'Tis a consummation
Devoutly to be wish'd. To die, to sleep;
To sleep, perchance to dream. Ay, there's the rub;
For in that sleep of death what dreams may come,
When we have shuffled off this mortal coil,
Must give us pause. There's the respect
That makes calamity of so long life;
For who would bear the whips and scorns of time,
Th' oppressor's wrong, the proud man's contumely,
The pangs of despis'd love, the law's delay,
The insolence of office, and the spurns
That patient merit of th' unworthy takes,
When he himself might his quietus make
With a bare bodkin? Who would these fardels bear,
To grunt and sweat under a weary life,
But that the dread of something after death –
The undiscover'd country, from whose bourn
No traveller returns – puzzles the will,
And makes us rather bear those ills we have
Than fly to others that we know not of?
Thus conscience does make cowards of us all;
And thus the native hue of resolution
Is sicklied o'er with the pale cast of thought.
And enterprises of great pitch and moment,
With this regard, their currents turn awry
And lost the name of action.

WILLIAM SHAKESPEARE

The King of Brentford

There was a King in Brentford – of whom no legends tell,
But who, without his glory, – could eat and sleep right well.
His Polly's cotton nightcap, – it was his crown of state,
He slept of evenings early, – and rose of mornings late.

All in a fine mud palace, – each day he took four meals,
And for a guard of honour, – a dog ran at his heels.
Sometimes to view his kingdoms, – rode forth this monarch good.
And then a prancing jackass – he royally bestrode.

There were no costly habits – with which this King was curst,
Except (and where's the harm on't?) – a somewhat lively thirst;
But people must pay taxes, – and Kings must have their sport;
So out of every gallon – his Grace he took a quart.

He pleased the ladies round him, – with manners soft and bland
With reason good, they named him – the father of his land.
Each year his mighty armies – marched forth in gallant show;
Their enemies were targets, – their bullets they were tow.

He vexed no quiet neighbour, – no useless conquest made,
But by the laws of pleasure, – his peaceful realm he swayed.
And in the years he reignèd, – through all this country wide,
There was no cause for weeping, – save when the good man died.

The faithful men of Brentford, – do still their King deplore,
His portrait yet is swinging, – beside an alehouse door.
And topers, tender-hearted, – regard his honest phiz,
And envy times departed, – that knew a reign like his.

WILLIAM MAKEPEACE THACKERAY 1811–63

London, 1802

Milton! thou should'st be living at this hour:
England hath need of thee: she is a fen
Of stagnant waters: altar, sword, and pen,
Fireside, the heroic wealth of hall and bower,
Have forfeited their ancient English dower
Of inward happiness. We are selfish men;
Oh! raise us up, return to us again;
And give us manners, virtue, freedom, power,
Thy soul was like a Star, and dwelt apart:
Thou hadst a voice whose sound was like the sea:
Pure as the naked heavens, majestic, free,
So didst thou travel on life's common way,
In cheerful godliness; and yet thy heart
The lowliest duties on herself did lay.

WILLIAM WORDSWORTH

The Lost Leader

I

Just for a handful of silver he left us,
  Just for a riband to stick in his coat –
Found the one gift of which fortune bereft us,
  Lost all the others she lets us devote;
They, with the gold to give, doled him out silver,
  So much was theirs who so little allowed:
How all our copper had gone for his service!
  Rags – were they purple, his heart had been proud!.
We that had loved him so, followed him, honoured him,
  Lived in his mild and magnificent eye,
Learned his great language, caught his clear accents,
  Made him our pattern to live and to die!
Shakespeare was of us, Milton was for us,
  Burns, Shelley, were with us, – they watch from their
    graves!
He alone breaks from the van and the freemen,
  – He alone sinks to the rear and the slaves!

305

We shall march prospering, – not thro' his presence;
  Songs may inspirit us, – not from his lyre;
Deeds will be done, – while he boasts his quiescence,
  Still bidding crouch whom the rest bade aspire:
Blot out his name, then, record one lost soul more,
  One task more declined, one more footpath untrod,
One more devils'-triumph and sorrow for angels,
  One wrong more to man, one more insult to God!
Life's night begins: let him never come back to us!
  There would be doubt, hesitation and pain,
Forced praise on our part – the glimmer of twilight,
  Never glad confident morning again!
Best fight on well, for we taught him – strike gallantly,
  Menace our heart ere we master his own;
Then let him receive the new knowledge and wait us,
  Pardoned in heaven, the first by the throne!

ROBERT BROWNING

(This was written in anguish after William Wordsworth, once a radical, had agreed to become Poet Laureate.)

This England

from *King Richard II*, Act II, Scene i

This royal throne of kings, this sceptered isle,
This earth of majesty, this seat of Mars,
This other Eden, demi-Paradise;
This fortress built by Nature for herself
Against infection and the hand of war;
This happy breed of men, this little world;
This precious stone set in the silver sea,
Which serves it in the office of a wall,
Or as a moat defensive to a house,
Against the envy of less happier lands;
This blessed plot, this earth, this realm, this England,
This nurse, this teeming womb of royal kings,
Feared by their breed, and famous by their birth,

Renowned for their deeds as far from home,
For Christian service and true chivalry,
As is the sepulchre, in stubborn Jewry,
Of the world's ransom, blessed Mary's Son;
This land of such dear souls, this dear dear land,
Dear for her reputation through the world,
Is now leased out – I die pronouncing it –
Like to a tenement or pelting farm:
England, bound in with the triumphant sea,
Whose rocky shore beats back the envious siege
Of watery Neptune, is now bound in with shame,
With inky blots, and rotten parchment bonds:
That England, that was wont to conquer others,
Hath made a shameful conquest of itself.

WILLIAM SHAKESPEARE

Home-Thoughts, from Abroad

Oh, to be in England
Now that April's there,
And whoever wakes in England
Sees, some morning, unaware,
That the lowest boughs and the brush-wood sheaf
Round the elm-tree bole are in tiny leaf,
While the chaffinch sings on the orchard bough
In England – now!

And after April, when May follows,
And the whitethroat builds, and all the swallows!
Hark, where my blossomed pear-tree in the hedge
Leans to the field and scatters on the clover
Blossoms and dewdrops – at the bent-spray's edge –
That's the wise thrush; he sings each song twice over,
Lest you should think he never could recapture
The first fine careless rapture!
And though the fields look rough with hoary dew,
All will be gay when noontide wakes anew
The buttercups, the little children's dower,
– Far brighter than this gaudy melon-flower!

ROBERT BROWNING

The Old Stone Cross

A statesman is an easy man,
He tells his lies by rote;
A journalist makes up his lies
And takes you by the throat;
So stay at home and drink your beer
And let the neighbours vote,
    Said the man in the golden breastplate
    Under the old stone Cross.

Because this age and the next age
Engender in the ditch,
No man can know a happy man
From any passing wretch,
If Folly link with Elegance
No man knows which is which,
    Said the man in the golden breastplate
    Under the old stone Cross.

But actors lacking music
Do most excite my spleen,
They say it is more human
To shuffle, grunt and groan,
Not knowing what unearthly stuff
Rounds a mighty scene.
    Said the man in the golden breastplate
    Under the old stone Cross.

W. B. YEATS

The British Journalist

You cannot hope
    to bribe or twist,
thank God! the
    British journalist.

But, seeing what
    the man will do

unbribed, there's
no occasion to.
HUMBERT WOLFE 1885–1940

England Expects

Let us pause to consider the English,
Who when they pause to consider themselves they get all reticently
    thrilled and tinglish,
Because every Englishman is convinced of one thing, viz:
That to be an Englishman is to belong to the most exclusive club
    there is:
A club to which benighted bounders of Frenchmen and Germans
    and Italians et cetera cannot even aspire to belong,
Because they don't even speak English, and the Americans are
    worst of all because they speak it wrong.
Englishmen are distinguished by their traditions and ceremonials,
And also by their affection for their colonies and their contempt for
    the colonials.
When foreigners ponder world affairs, why sometimes by doubts
    they are smitten,
But Englishmen know instinctively that what the world needs most
    is whatever is best for Great Britain.
They have a splendid navy and they conscientiously admire it,
And every English schoolboy know that John Paul Jones was only
    an unfair American pirate.
English people disclaim sparkle and verve,
But speak without reservations of their Anglo-Saxon reserve.
After listening to little groups of English ladies and gentlemen at
    cocktail parties and in hotels and Pullmans, of defining
    Anglo-Saxon reserve I despair,
But I think it consists of assuming that nobody else is there,
And I shudder to think where Anglo-Saxon reserve ends when I
    consider where it begins,
Which is in a few high-pitched statements of what one's income is
    and just what foods give one a rash and whether one and
    one's husband or wife sleep in a double bed or twins.
All good Englishmen go to Oxford or Cambridge and they all
    write and publish books before their graduation,

309

And I often wondered how they did it until I realized that they
have to do it because their genteel accents are so developed
that they can no longer understand each other's spoken
words so the written word is their only means of inter-
communication.
England is the last home of the aristocracy, and the art of protecting
the aristocracy from the encroachments of commerce has been
raised to quite an art.
Because in America a rich butter-and-egg man is only a rich butter-
and-egg man or at most an honorary LLD of some hungry
university, but in England he is Sir Benjamin Buttery, Bart.
Anyhow, I think the English people are sweet,
And we might as well get used to them because when they slip and
fall they always land on their own or somebody else's feet.

OGDEN NASH

from *The Old Vicarage, Grantchester*

In Grantchester, in Grantchester! –
Some, it may be, can get in touch
With Nature there, or Earth, or such.
And clever modern men have seen
A Faun a-peeping through the green,
And felt the Classics were not dead,
To glimpse a Naiad's reedy head,
Or hear the Goat-foot piping low: . . .
But these are things I do not know.
I only know that you may lie
Day-long and watch the Cambridge sky,
And, flower-lulled in sleepy grass,
Hear the cool lapse of hours pass,
Until the centuries blend and blur
In Grantchester, in Grantchester . . .
Still in the dawnlit waters cool
His ghostly Lordship swims his pool,
And tries the strokes, essays the tricks,
Long learnt on Hellespont, or Styx.
Dan Chaucer hears his river still
Chatter beneath a phantom mill.

Tennyson notes, with studious eye,
How Cambridge waters hurry by . . .
And in that garden, black and white,
Creep whispers through the grass all night;
And spectral dance, before the dawn,
A hundred Vicars down the lawn;
Curates, long dust, will come and go
On lissom, clerical, printless toe;
And oft between the boughs is seen
The sly shade of a Rural Dean . . .
Till, at a shiver in the skies,
Vanishing with Satanic cries,
The prim ecclesiastic rout
Leaves but a startled sleeper-out,
Grey heavens, the first bird's drowsy calls,
The falling house that never falls.

God! I will pack, and take a train,
And get me to England once again!

RUPERT BROOKE

SIXTH AGE

               The sixth age shifts
Into the lean and slippered pantaloon,
With spectacles on nose and pouch on side;
His youthful hose, well saved, a world too wide
For his shrunk shank; and his big manly voice,
Turning again toward childish treble, pipes
And whistles in his sound.

The View

The view is fine from fifty,
    Experienced climbers say;
So, overweight and shifty,
    I turn to face the way
    That led me to this day.

Instead of fields and snowcaps
    And flowered lanes that twist,
The track breaks at my toe-caps
    And drops away in mist.
    The view does not exist.

Where has it gone, the lifetime?
    Search me. What's left is drear.
Unchilded and unwifed, I'm
    Able to view that clear:
    So final. And so near.

                    PHILIP LARKIN

Peekaboo, I Almost See You

Middle-aged life is merry, and I love to lead it
But there comes a day when your eyes are all right, but your arm
    isn't long enough to hold the telephone book where you can
    read it,
And your friends get jocular, so you go to the oculist,
And of all your friends he is the joculist,
So over his facetiousness let us skim,
Only noting that he has been waiting for you ever since you said
    Good Evening to his grandfather clock under the impression
    that it was him.
And you look at his chart and it says SHRDLU QWERTYOP, and
    you say Well, why SHRDNTLU QWERTYOP? and he says one
    set of glasses won't do.
You need two,

One for reading Erle Stanley Gardner's Perry Mason and Keats's
  'Endymion' with,
And the other for walking around without saying Hallo to strange
  wymion with.
So you spend your time taking off your seeing glasses to put on
  your reading glasses, and then remembering that your reading
  glasses are upstairs or in the car,
And then you can't find your seeing glasses again because without
  them you can't see where they are.
Enough of such mishaps, they would try the patience of an ox,
I prefer to forget both pairs of glasses and pass my declining years
  saluting strange women and grandfather clocks.

OGDEN NASH

Politics

'In our time the destiny of man presents
its meanings in political terms.' –
THOMAS MANN

How can I, that girl standing there,
My attention fix
On Roman or on Russian
Or on Spanish politics?
Yet here's a travelled man that knows
What he talks about,
And there's a politician
That has read and thought,
And maybe what they say is true
Of war and war's alarms,
But O that I were young again
And held her in my arms!

W. B. YEATS

Late-Flowering Lust

My head is bald, my breath is bad,
   Unshaven is my chin,
I have not now the joys I had
   When I was young in sin.

I run my fingers down your dress
   With brandy-certain aim
And you respond to my caress
   And maybe feel the same.

But I've a picture of my own
   On this reunion night,
Wherein two skeletons are shewn
   To hold each other tight;

Dark sockets look on emptiness
   Which once was loving-eyed,
The mouth that opens for a kiss
   Has got no tongue inside.

I cling to you inflamed with fear
   As now you cling to me,
I feel how frail you are my dear
   And wonder what will be –

A week? or twenty years remain?
   And then – what kind of death?
A losing fight with frightful pain
   Or a gasping fight for breath?

Too long we let our bodies cling,
   We cannot hide disgust
At all the thoughts that in us spring
   From this late-flowering lust.

JOHN BETJEMAN

He Loved Three Things

He loved three things in this world:
evensong, white peacocks,
and faded maps of America.
He didn't like crying children,
he didn't like raspberry jam with his tea –
and womanish hysterics.
. . . And I was his wife.

ANNA AKHMATOVA
(Translated by Richard McKane.)

Sad Steps

Groping back to bed after a piss
I part thick curtains, and am startled by
The rapid clouds, the moon's cleanliness.

Four o'clock: wedge-shadowed gardens lie
Under a cavernous, a wind-picked sky.
There's something laughable about this,

The way the moon dashes through clouds that blow
Loosely as cannon-smoke to stand apart
(Stone-coloured light sharpening the roofs below)

High and preposterous and separate –
Lozenge of love! Medallion of art!
O wolves of memory! Immensements! No,

One shivers slightly, looking up there.
The hardness and the brightness and the plain
Far-reaching singleness of that wide stare

Is a reminder of the strength and pain
Of being young; that it can't come again,
But is for others undiminished somewhere.

PHILIP LARKIN

Talking in Bed

Talking in bed ought to be easiest,
Lying together there goes back so far,
An emblem of two people being honest.

Yet more and more time passes silently.
Outside, the wind's incomplete unrest
Builds and disperses clouds about the sky,

And dark towns heap up on the horizon.
None of this cares for us. Nothing shows why
At this unique distance from isolation

It becomes still more difficult to find
Words at once true and kind,
Or not untrue and not unkind.

PHILIP LARKIN

Samson Agonistes

I test my bath before I sit,
And I'm always moved to wonderment
That what chills the finger not a bit
Is so frigid upon the fundament.

OGDEN NASH

'Twas at the Pictures, Child, We Met

'Twas at the pictures, child, we met,
    Your father and your mother;
The drama's name I now forget,
    But it was like another.

The Viscount had too much to drink,
    And so his plot miscarried,

And at the end I rather think
   Two citizens were married.

But at the opening of the play
   By Fortune's wise design –
It was an accident, I say –
   A little hand met mine.

My fingers round that little hand
   Unconsciously were twisted;
I do not say that it was planned,
   But it was not resisted.

I held the hand. The hand was hot.
   I could not see her face,
But in the dark I gazed at what
   I took to be the place.

From shock to shock, from sin to sin
   The fatal film proceeded;
I cannot say I drank it in,
   I rather doubt if she did.

In vain did pure domestics flout
   The base but high-born brute;
Their honour might be up the spout,
   We did not care a hoot.

For, while those clammy palms were clutched,
   By stealthy slow degrees
We moved an inch or two and touched
   Each other with our knees.

No poet makes a special point
   Of any human knee,
But in that plain prosaic joint
   Was high romance for me.

Thus hand in hand and toe to toe,
   Reel after reel we sat;

You are not old enough to know
    The ecstasy of that.

A touch of cramp about the shins
    Was all that troubled me;
Your mother tells me she had pins
    And needles in the knee.

But our twin spirits rose above
    Mere bodily distress;
And if you ask me 'Is this Love?'
    The answer, child, is 'Yes.'

And when the film was finished quite
    It made my bosom swell
To find that by electric light
    I loved her just as well.

For women, son, are seldom quite
    As worthy of remark
Beneath a strong electric light
    As they are in the dark.

But this was not the present case,
    And it was joy to see
A form as fetching and a face
    Magnetic as her knee.

And still twice weekly we enjoy
    The pictures, grave and gross;
We don't hold hands so much, my boy,
    Our knees are not so close;

But now and then, for Auld Lang Syne,
    Or frenzied by the play,
Your mother slips her hand in mine
    To my intense dismay;

And then, though at my time of life
    It seems a trifle odd,
I move my knee and give my wife
    A sentimental prod.

Well, such is Love and such is Fate,
    And such is Marriage too;
And such will happen, soon or late,
    Unhappy youth, to you.

And, though most learned men have strained
    To work the matter out,
No mortal man has yet explained
    What it is all about.

And I don't know why mortals try
    But if with vulgar chaff
You hear some Philistine decry
    The cinematograph,

Think then, my son, of your papa,
    And take the kindly view,
For had there been no cinema
    There might have been no you.

A. P. HERBERT 1890–1971

Young Men

Young men who frequent pictures palaces
Haven't heard of our psycho-analysis,
They've never read Freud
But they feel overjoyed
As they cling to their long-standing fallacies.

ANON.

Mary's Lamb

Mary had a little lamb,
But her sister came to grief
She lived in 1951
And only got Corned Beef.

ANON.

(On a poster carried by protesting housewives demonstrating near the House of Commons during the debate on Winston Churchill's Censure Motion against the Labour Government for its mishandling of the reduction of the meat ration: February 1951.)

The Thin People

They are always with us, the thin people
Meager of dimension as the gray people

On a movie-screen. They
Are unreal, we say:

It was only in a movie, it was only
In a war making evil headlines when we

Were small that they famished and
Grew so lean and would not round

Out their stalky limbs again though peace
Plumped the bellies of the mice

Under the meanest table.
It was during the long hunger-battle

They found their talent to persevere
In thinness, to come, later,

Into our bad dreams, their menace
Not guns, not abuses,

But a thin silence.
Wrapped in flea-ridden donkey skins,

Empty of complaint, forever
Drinking vinegar from tin cups: they wore

The insufferable nimbus of the lot-drawn
Scapegoat. But so thin,

So weedy a race could not remain in dreams,
Could not remain outlandish victims

In the contracted country of the head
Any more than the old woman in her mud hut could

Keep from cutting fat meat
Out of the side of the generous moon when it

Set foot nightly in her yard
Until her knife had pared

The moon to a rind of little light.
Now the thin people do not obliterate

Themselves as the dawn
Grayness blues, reddens, and the outline

Of the world comes clear and fills with color.
They persist in the sunlit room: the wallpaper

Frieze of cabbage-roses and cornflowers pales
Under their thin-lipped smiles,

Their withering kingship.
How they prop each other up!

We own no wildernesses rich and deep enough
For stronghold against their stiff

Battalions. See, how the tree boles flatten
And lose their good browns

If the thin people simply stand in the forest,
Making the world go thin as a wasp's nest

And grayer; not even moving their bones.

SYLVIA PLATH 1932–63

Peas

I always eat peas with honey,
I've done it all my life,

They do taste kind of funny,
But it keeps them on the knife.
ANON.

Burns Grace at Kirkcudbright

Some have meat and cannot eat,
Some cannot eat that want it:
But we have meat and we can eat,
Sae let the Lord be thankit.
ANON.

Plymouth

A box of teak, a box of sandalwood,
A brass-ringed spyglass in a case,
A coin, leaf-thin with many polishings,
Last kingdom of a gold forgotten face,
These lie about the room, and daily shine
When new-built ships set out towards the sun.

If they had any roughness, any flaw,
An unfamiliar scent, all this has gone;
They are no more than ornaments, or eyes,
No longer knowing what they looked upon,
Turned sightless; rivers of Eden, rivers of blood
Once blinded them, and were not understood.

The hands that chose them rust upon a stick.
Let my hands find such symbols, that can be
Unnoticed in the casual light of day,
Lying in wait for half a century
To split chance lives across, that had not dreamed
Such coasts had echoed, or such seabirds screamed.
PHILIP LARKIN

Sea-Fever

I must down to the seas again, to the lonely sea and the sky,
And all I ask is a tall ship and a star to steer her by,
And the wheel's kick and the wind's song and the white sail's
    shaking,
And a grey mist on the sea's face and a grey dawn breaking.

I must down to the seas again, for the call of the running tide
Is a wild call and a clear call that may not be denied;
And all I ask is a windy day with the white clouds flying,
And the flung spray and the blown spume, and the sea-gulls
    crying.

I must down to the seas again, to the vagrant gypsy life,
To the gull's way and the whale's way where the wind's like a
    whetted knife;
And all I ask is a merry yarn from a laughing fellow-rover,
And quiet sleep and a sweet dream when the long trick's over.

JOHN MASEFIELD

76. Exultation

Exultation is the going
Of an inland soul to sea,
Past the houses – past the headlands –
Into deep Eternity –

Bred as we, among the mountains,
Can the sailor understand

The divine intoxication
Of the first league out from land?

EMILY DICKINSON

The Mountaineers

Despite the drums we were ready to go.
The natives warned us shaking their spears.
Soon we'd look down on them a mile below
rather as Icarus, so many poets ago,
waved to those shy, forlorn ones, dumb on a thumbnail field.
We started easily but oh the climb was slow.

Above us, the grey perilous rocks like our pride
rose higher and higher – broken teeth of the mountain –
while below the dizzy cliffs, the tipsy angles signified
breathless vertigo and falling possible suicide.
So we climbed on, roped together. At the night camps
our voices babel yet our journey glorified.

The soul too has altitudes and the great birds fly
over. All the summer long we climbed higher,
crag above crag under a copper sulphate sky,
peak above peak singing of the deserted, shy,
inconsolable ones. Still we climb to the chandelier stars
and the more we sing the more we die.

So ascending in that high Sinai of the air,
in space and canyons of the spirit, we lost ourselves
amongst the animals of the mountain – the terrible stare
of self meeting itself – and no one would dare
return, descend to that most flat and average world.
Rather, we made a small faith out of a tall despair.

Shakespeare, Milton, Wordsworth, came this way
near the lonely precipice, their faces gold
in the marigold sunset. But they could never stay
under the hurricane tree so climbed to allay
that voice which cried: 'You may never climb again.'
Our faces too are gold but our feet are clay.

We discovered more than footprints in the snow,
more than mountain ghost, more than desolate glory,
yet now, looking down, we see nothing below
except wind, steaming ice, floating mist – and so

silently, sadly, we follow higher the rare songs of oxygen.
The more we climb the further we have to go.

DANNIE ABSE 1923–

We Have Been Here Before

I think I remember this moorland,
    The tower on the tip of the tor;
I feel in the distance another existence;
    I think I have been here before.

And I think you were sitting beside me
    In a fold in the face of the fell;
For Time at its work'll go round in a circle,
    And what is befalling, befell.

'I have been here before!' I asserted,
    In a nook on a neck of the Nile.
I once in a crisis was punished by Isis,
    And you smiled, I remember your smile.

I had the same sense of persistence
    On the site of the seat of the Sioux;
I heard in the tepee the sound of a sleepy
    Pleistocene grunt. It was you.

The past made a promise, before it
    Began to begin to begone.
This limited gamut brings you again . . . Damn it,
    How long has this got to go on?

MORRIS BISHOP

The Great Carbuncle

We came over the moor-top
Through air streaming and green-lit,
Stone farms foundering in it,

328

Valleys of grass altering
In a light neither of dawn

Nor nightfall, our hands, faces
Lucent as porcelain, the earth's
Claim and weight gone out of them.
Some such transfiguring moved
The eight pilgrims towards its source –

Toward that great jewel: shown often,
Never given; hidden, yet
Simultaneously seen
On moor-top, at sea-bottom,
Knowable only by light

Other than noon, than moon, stars –
The once-known way becoming
Wholly other, and ourselves
Estranged, changed, suspended where
Angels are rumored, clearly

Floating, among the floating
Tables and chairs. Gravity's
Lost in the lift and drift of
An easier element
Than earth, and there is nothing

So fine we cannot do it.
But nearing means distancing:
At the common homecoming
Light withdraws. Chairs, tables drop
Down: the body weighs like stone.

SYLVIA PLATH

from *The Brook*

I come from haunts of coot and hern,
    I make a sudden sally

329

And sparkle out among the fern,
    To bicker down a valley.

By thirty hills I hurry down,
    Or slip between the ridges,
By twenty thorps, a little town,
    And half a hundred bridges.

Till last by Philip's farm I flow
    To join the brimming river,
For men may come and men may go,
    But I go on for ever.

I chatter over stony ways,
    In little sharps and trebles,
I bubble into eddying bays,
    I babble on the pebbles.

With many a curve my banks I fret
    By many a field and fallow,
And many a fairy foreland set
    With willow-weed and mallow.

I chatter, chatter, as I flow
    To join the brimming river,
For men may come and men may go,
    But I go on for ever.

I wind about, and in and out,
    With here a blossom sailing,
And here and there a lusty trout,
    And here and there a grayling.

And here and there a foamy flake
    Upon me, as I travel
With many a silvery waterbreak
    Above the golden gravel.

And draw them all along, and flow
    To join the brimming river,

For men may come and men may go,
    But I go on for ever.

I steal by lawns and grassy plots,
    I slide by hazel covers;
I move the sweet forget-me-nots
    That grow for happy lovers.

I slip, I slide, I gloom, I glance,
    Among my skimming swallows;
I make the netted sunbeam dance
    Against my sandy shallows.

ALFRED, LORD TENNYSON

Night Mail
(Commentary for a G.P.O. Film)

I

This is the Night Mail crossing the Border,
Bringing the cheque and the postal order,

Letters for the rich, letters for the poor,
The shop at the corner, the girl next door.

Pulling up Beattock, a steady climb:
The gradient's against her, but she's on time.

Past cotton-grass and moorland boulder,
Shovelling white steam over her shoulder,

Snorting noisily, she passes
Silent miles of wind-bent grasses.

Birds turn their heads as she approaches,
Stare from bushes at her blank-faced coaches.

Sheep-dogs cannot turn her course;
They slumber on with paws across.

In the farm she passes no one wakes,
But a jug in a bedroom gently shakes.

II

Dawn freshens. Her climb is done.
Down towards Glasgow she descends,
Towards the steam tugs yelping down a glade of cranes,
Towards the fields of apparatus, the furnaces
Set on the dark plain like gigantic chessmen.
All Scotland waits for her:
In dark glens, beside pale-green lochs,
Men long for news.

III

Letters of thanks, letters from banks,
Letters of joy from girl and boy,
Receipted bills and invitations
To inspect new stock or to visit relations,
And applications for situations,
And timid lovers' declarations,
And gossip, gossip from all the nations,
News circumstantial, news financial,
Letters with holiday snaps to enlarge in,
Letters with faces scrawled on the margin,
Letters from uncles, cousins and aunts,
Letters to Scotland from the South of France,
Letters of condolence to Highlands and Lowlands,
Written on paper of every hue,
The pink, the violet, the white and the blue,
The chatty, the catty, the boring, the adoring,
The cold and official and the heart's outpouring,
Clever, stupid, short and long,
The typed and the printed and the spelt all wrong.

IV

Thousands are still asleep,
Dreaming of terrifying monsters
Or a friendly tea beside the band in Cranston's or Crawford's.
Asleep in working Glasgow, asleep in well-set Edinburgh,
Asleep in granite Aberdeen,

They continue their dreams,
But shall wake soon and hope for letters,
And none will hear the postman's knock
Without a quickening of the heart.
For who can bear to feel himself forgotten?

W. H. AUDEN

The Urals for the First Time

Without an accoucheuse, in darkness, pushing her
Blind hands against the night, the Ural fastness, torn and
Half-dead with agony, was screaming in a blur
Of mindless pain, as she was giving birth to morning.

And brushed by chance, tall ranges far and wide
Loosed toppling bronze pell-mell in thunder-coloured rumbling.
The train panted and coughed, clutching the mountain-side,
And at that sound the ghosts of far trees shied and stumbled.

The smoky dawn was a narcotic for the peaks,
A drug with which the fire-breathing dragon plied them
As when a specious thief upon a journey seeks
To lull his fellow travelers with opium slipped them slyly.

They woke on fire. The skies were poppy-colored flame,
Whence Asiatics skied like hunters after quarry;
To kiss the forests' feet the eager strangers came
And thrust upon the firs the regal crowns they carried.

Arrayed in majesty, by rank the firs arose,
Those shaggy dynasts, their grave glory clamant,
And trod the orange velvet of the frozen snows
Spread on a tinseled cloth and richly demarked.

BORIS PASTERNAK
(Translated by Babette Deutsch.)

Sunday Morning, King's Cambridge

File into yellow candle light, fair choristers of King's
    Lost in the shadowy silence of canopied Renaissance stalls
In blazing glass above the dark glow skies and thrones and wings
    Blue, ruby, gold and green between the whiteness of the walls
And with what rich precision the stonework soars and springs
    To fountain out a spreading vault – a shower that never falls.

The white of windy Cambridge courts, the cobbles brown and dry,
    The gold of plaster Gothic with ivy overgrown,
The apple-red, the silver fronts, the wide green flats and high,
    The yellowing elm-trees circled out on islands of their own –
Oh, here behold all colours change that catch the flying sky
    To waves of pearly light that heave along the shafted stone.

In far East Anglian churches, the clasped hands lying long
    Recumbent on sepulchral slabs or effigied in brass
Buttress with prayer this vaulted roof so white and light and strong
    And countless congregations as the generations pass
Join choir and great crowned organ case, in centuries of song
    To praise Eternity contained in Time and coloured glass.

JOHN BETJEMAN

Note on Intellectuals

To the man-in-the-street, who, I'm sorry to say
    Is a keen observer of life,
The word Intellectual suggests straight away
    A man who's untrue to his wife.

W. H. AUDEN

Lines to a Don

Remote and ineffectual Don
That dared attack my Chesterton,
With that poor weapon, half-impelled,
Unlearnt, unsteady, hardly held,
Unworthy for a tilt with men –

Your quavering and corroded pen;
Don poor at Bed and worse at Table,
Don pinched, Don starved, Don miserable;
Don stuttering, Don with roving eyes,
Don nervous, Don of crudities;
Don clerical, Don ordinary,
Don self-absorbed and solitary;
Don here-and-there, Don epileptic;
Don puffed and empty, Don dyspeptic;
Don middle-class, Don sycophantic,
Don dull, Don brutish, Don pedantic;
Don hypocritical, Don bad,
Don furtive, Don three-quarters mad;
Don (since a man must make an end),
Don that shall never be my friend.

Don different from those regal Dons!
With hearts of gold and lungs of bronze,
Who shout and bang and roar and bawl
The Absolute across the hall,
Or sail in amply bellying gown
Enormous through the Sacred Town,
Bearing from College to their homes
Deep cargoes of gigantic tomes;
Dons admirable! Dons of Might!
Uprising on my inward sight
Compact of ancient tales, and port,
And sleep – and learning of a sort.
Dons English, worthy of the land;
Dons rooted; Dons that understand.
Good Dons perpetual that remain
A landmark, walling in the plain –
The horizon of my memories –
Like large and comfortable trees.

Don very much apart from these,
Thou scapegoat Don, thou Don devoted,
Don to thine own damnation quoted,
Perplexed to find thy trivial name
Reared in my verse to lasting shame.
Don dreadful, rasping Don and wearing,

Repulsive Don – Don past all bearing.
Don of the cold and doubtful breath,
Don despicable, Don of death;
Don nasty, skimpy, silent, level;
Don evil; Don that serves the devil.
Don ugly – that makes fifty lines.
There is a Canon which confines
A Rhymed Octosyllabic Curse
If written in Iambic Verse
To fifty lines. I never cut;
I far prefer to end it – but
Believe me I shall soon return.
My fires are banked, but still they burn
To write some more about the Don
That dared attack my Chesterton.

HILAIRE BELLOC

Satire upon the Heads;
or, Never a Barrel the Better Herring

O Cambridge, attend
To the Satire I've pen'd
On the Heads of thy Houses,
Thou Seat of the Muses!

Know the Master of Jesus
Does hugely displease us;
The Master of Maudlin
In the same dirt is dawdling;
The Master of Sidney
Is of the same kidney;
The Master of Trinity
To him bears affinity;
As the Master of Keys
Is as like as two pease,
So the Master of Queens'
Is as like as two beans;
The Master of King's

Copies them in all things;
The Master of Catherine
Takes them all for his pattern;
The Master of Clare
Hits them all to a hair;
The Master of Christ
By the rest is enticed;
But the Master of Emmanuel
Follows them like a spaniel;
The Master of Benet
Is of the like tenet;
The Master of Pembroke
Has from them his system took;
The Master of Peter's
Has all the same features;
The Master of St John's
Like the rest of the Dons.

P.S. – As to Trinity Hall
We say nothing at all.
                    THOMAS GRAY 1716–71

Why are the Clergy . . .?

Why are the clergy of the Church of England
Always altering the words of the prayers in the Prayer Book?
Cranmer's touch was surer than theirs, do they not respect him?
For instance last night in church I heard
(I italicize the interpolation)
'The Lord bless you and keep you *and all who are dear unto you.*'
As the blessing is a congregational blessing and meant to be
This is questionable on theological grounds
But is it not offensive to the ear and also ludicrous?
That 'unto' is a particularly ripe piece of idiocy
Oh how offensive it is. I suppose we shall have next
'Lighten our darkness we beseech thee oh Lord *and the darkness of
    all who are dear unto us.*'
It seems a pity. Does Charity object to the objection?

Then I cry, and not for the first time to that smooth face
Charity, have pity.

STEVIE SMITH 1902–71

Pseudo-hymn

If I were a Cassowary
On the plains of Timbuctoo,
I would eat a missionary,
Coat and band and hymn-book too.

ATTRIBUTED TO BISHOP SAMUEL WILBERFORCE

Mystery

They said this mystery shall never cease:
The priest promotes war and the soldier peace.

WILLIAM BLAKE

A Priest in the Sabbath Dawn
Addresses His Somnolent Mistress

Wake up, my heart, get out of bed
and put your scarlet shirt back on and leave,
for Sunday is coming down the chimney
with its feet in little socks,
and I need a space in which to write my sermon.
Although the hour's already late
it can still be done, if only you'll depart!
Down the pipe and out across the lawn
would take you to the station yard
in which you left your bicycle last week
and give me time to clothe in flesh the text
I have in mind for the instruction of my flock.
Please hurry dear. The earliest note of the matin bell

has left its tower like an urgent dove
and is beating its way to woods outside the town.
The sun is up, the parish breakfasted,
the ghosts are all returned into the flint
yet still you lie here, shaming me with sleep.
Wake up, I say, for Sabbath legs
are landing in the grate. Go naked if you must
but grant me these few minutes with my pen
to write of how I cut myself while shaving.
Be useful, at least, and fetch my very razor,
for the faithful have set their feet upon the road
and are hurrying here with claims on the kind of story
which I cannot fittingly make from your sudden grin.

PETER DIDSBURY 1946–

The Suburban Classes

There is far too much of the suburban classes
Spiritually not geographically speaking. They're asses.
Menacing the greatness of our beloved England, they lie
Propagating their kind in an eightroomed stye.
Now I have a plan which I will enfold
(There's this to be said for them, they do as they're told)
Then tell them their country's in mortal peril
They believed it before and again will not cavil
Put it in caption form firm and slick:
If they see it in print it is bound to stick:
'Your King and your Country need you Dead'
You see the idea? Well, let it spread.
Have a suitable drug under string and label
Free from every Registered Reader's table.
For the rest of the gang who are not patriotic
I've another appeal they'll discover hypnotic:
Tell them it's smart to be dead and won't hurt
And they'll gobble up drug as they gobble up dirt.

STEVIE SMITH

Hymn and Prayer for Civil Servants

O, Lord, Grant that this day we come to no decisions, neither run we into any kind of responsibility, but that all our doings may be ordered to establish new departments, for ever and ever. Amen.

O Thou who seest all things below,
Grant that Thy servants may go slow,
That they may study to comply
With regulations till they die.

Teach us, O Lord, to reverence
Committees more than common sense;
To train our minds to make no plan
And pass the baby when we can.

So when the tempter seeks to give
Us feelings of initiative,
Or when alone we go too far,
Chastise us with a circular.

Mid war and tumult, fire and storms,
Give strength O Lord, to deal out forms.
Thus may Thy servants ever be
A flock of perfect sheep for Thee.

ANON.

Limerick

There once was a man who said, 'Damn!
It is borne in upon me I am
    An engine that moves
    In predestinate grooves:
I'm not even a bus I'm a tram.'

M. E. HARE 1886—

Gehazi

1915

Whence comest thou, Gehazi,
  So reverend to behold,
In scarlet and in ermines
  And chain of England's gold?
'From following after Naaman
  To tell him all is well,
Whereby my zeal hath made me
  A Judge in Israel.'

Well done, well done, Gehazi!
  Stretch forth thy ready hand.
Thou barely 'scaped from judgment,
  Take oath to judge the land
Unswayed by gift of money
  Or privy bribe, more base,
Of knowledge which is profit
  In any market-place.

Search out and probe, Gehazi,
  As thou of all canst try,
The truthful, well-weighed answer
  That tells the blacker lie –
The loud, uneasy virtue,
  The anger feigned at will,
To overbear a witness

  And make the Court keep still.
Take order now, Gehazi,
  That no man talk aside
In secret with his judges
  The while his case is tried.
Lest he should show them – reason
  To keep a matter hid,
And subtly lead the questions
  Away from what he did.

Thou mirror of uprightness,
  What ails thee at thy vows?

What means the risen whiteness
  Of the skin between thy brows?
The boils that shine and burrow,
  The sores that slough and bleed –
The leprosy of Naaman
  On thee and all thy seed?
  Stand up, stand up, Gehazi,
    Draw close thy robe and go,
  Gehazi, Judge in Israel,
    A leper white as snow!

RUDYARD KIPLING
(Written about the Marconi scandal of 1912–13.)

I Had a Duck-Billed Platypus

from *Songs of a Sub-man*

I had a duck-billed platypus when I was up at Trinity,
With whom I soon discovered a remarkable affinity.
He used to live in lodgings with myself and Arthur Purvis,
And we all went up together for the Diplomatic Service.
I had a certain confidence, I own, in his ability;
He mastered all the subjects with remarkable facility;
The wisdom of the choice, it soon appeared, was undeniable,
There never was a diplomat more thoroughly reliable.
The creature never acted with undue precipitation O,
But gave to every question his mature consideration O.
He never made rash statements that his enemies might hold
    him to;
He never stated anything, for no one ever told him to;
And soon he was appointed, so correct with his behaviour,
Our Minister (without portfolio) in Trans Moravia.

My friend was loved and honoured from the Andes to Esthonia;
He soon achieved a pact between Peru and Patagonia;
He never vexed the Russians nor offended the Rumanians;
He pacified the Letts and he appeased the Lithuanians.

No Minister has ever worked more cautiously or slowly O;
In fact they had decided to award him a portfolio,
When, on the anniversary of Greek Emancipation,
Alas! He laid an egg in the Bulgarian Legation.

This unexpected action caused unheard-of inconvenience,
A breach at once occurred between the Turks and the
   Armenians;
The Greeks poured ultimata, quite unhinged by the mishap,
   at him;
The Poles began to threaten and the Finns began to flap at him;
The Swedes withdrew entirely from the Anglo-Saxon dailies
The right of photographing the Aurora Borealis;
And, all attempts to come to a *rapprochement* proving barren,
The Japanese in self-defence annexed the Isle of Arran.

My platypus, once thought to be more cautious and more
   tentative
Than any other living diplomatic representative,
Was now a sort of warning to all diplomatic students –
The perfect incarnation of the perils of imprudence.
Beset and persecuted by the forces of reaction O,
He reaped the consequences of his ill-considered action O;
And, branded in the Honours List as Platypus, Dame Vera,
Retired, a lonely figure, to lay eggs at Bordighera.

PATRICK BARRINGTON

Upon Westminster Bridge

3 September 1802

Earth has not anything to show more fair:
Dull would he be of soul who could pass by
A sight so touching in its majesty:
This City now doth like a garment wear

The beauty of the morning: silent, bare,
Ships, towers, domes, theatres, and temples lie
Open unto the fields, and to the sky,
All bright and glittering in the smokeless air.

343

Never did sun more beautifully steep
In his first splendour valley, rock, or hill;
Ne'er saw I, never felt, a calm so deep!

The river glideth at his own sweet will:
Dear God! the very houses seem asleep;
And all that mighty heart is lying still!

WILLIAM WORDSWORTH

The City

Business men with awkward hips
And dirty jokes upon their lips,
And large behinds and jingling chains,
And riddled teeth and riddling brains,
And plump white fingers made to curl
Round some anaemic city girl,
And so lend colour to the lives
And old suspicions of their wives.

Young men who wear on office stools
The ties of minor public schools,
Each learning how to be a sinner
And tell 'a good one' after dinner,
And so discover it is rather
Fun to go one more than father.
But father, son and clerk join up
To talk about the Football Cup.

JOHN BETJEMAN

Not Waving but Drowning

Nobody heard him, the dead man,
But still he lay moaning:
I was much further out than you thought
And not waving but drowning.

Poor chap, he always loved larking
And now he's dead
It must have been too cold for him his heart gave way,
They said.

Oh, no no no, it was too cold always
(Still the dead one lay moaning)
I was much too far out all my life
and not waving but drowning.

STEVIE SMITH

Oedipus

Oedipus said to the Sphinx:
'My name's been perverted by shrinks.
  Who'd think Jocasta'd
  Call me a bastard?
I think psychiatry stinks.'

VICTOR GRAY

Snow Joke

Heard the one about the guy from Heaton Mersey?
Wife at home, lover in Hyde, mistress
in Newton-le-Willows and two pretty girls
in the top grade at Werneth prep. Well,

he was late and he had a good car so he snubbed
the police warning-light and tried to finesse
the last six miles of moorland blizzard,
and the story goes he was stuck within minutes.

So he sat there thinking about life and things;
what the dog does when it catches its tail
and about the snake that ate itself to death.
And he watched the windscreen filling up

with snow, and it felt good and the whisky
from his hip-flask was warm and smooth.
And of course, there isn't a punchline
but the ending goes something like this.

They found him slumped against the steering wheel
with VOLVO printed backwards in his frozen brow.
And they fought in the pub over hot toddies
as to who was to take the most credit.

Him who took the aerial to be a hawthorn twig?
Him who figured out the contour of his car?
Or him who said he heard the horn, moaning
softly like an alarm clock under an eiderdown?

SIMON ARMITAGE 1963—

This Be the Verse

They fuck you up, your mum and dad.
   They may not mean to, but they do.
They fill you with the faults they had
   And add some extra, just for you.

But they were fucked up in their turn
   By fools in old-style hats and coats,
Who half the time were soppy-stern
   And half at one another's throats.

Man hands on misery to man.
   It deepens like a coastal shelf.
Get out as early as you can,
   And don't have any kids yourself.

PHILIP LARKIN

Wishes of an Elderly Man

I wish I loved the Human Race;
I wish I loved its silly face;
I wish I liked the way it walks;
I wish I liked the way it talks;
And when I'm introduced to one
I wish I thought *What Jolly Fun!*

WALTER RALEIGH 1861—1922

Report on Experience

I have been young, and now am not too old;
And I have seen the righteous forsaken,
His health, his honour and his quality taken.
   This is not what we were formerly told.

I have seen a green country, useful to the race,
Knocked silly with guns and mines, its villages vanished,
Even the last rat and the last kestrel banished –
   God bless us all, this was peculiar grace.

EDMUND BLUNDEN 1896–1974

Resolutions
When I Come to be Old

Not to marry a young Woman.
Not to keep young Company unless they really
   desire it.
Not to be peevish or morose, or suspicious.
Not to scorn present Ways, or Wits, or Fashions,
   or Men, or War, &c.
Not to be fond of Children, or let them come
   near me hardly.
Not to tell the same Story over and over to the
   same People.
Not to be covetous.
Not to neglect decency, or cleenliness, for fear
   of falling into Nastyness.
Not to be over severe with young People, but
   give Allowances for their Youthfull Follyes,
   and Weeknesses.
Not to be influenced by, or give ear to knavish
   tatling servants or others.
Not to be too free of advise nor trouble any but
   those that desire it.
To desire some good Friends to inform me wch
   of these Resolutions I break, or neglect, and
   wherein; and reform accordingly.

Not to talk much, nor of my self.
Not to boast of my former beauty, or strength,
or favour with Ladyes, &c.
Not to hearken to Flatteryes, nor conceive I can
be beloved by a Young Woman. Et eos qui
hereditatem captant odisse ac vitare.
Not to be positive or opiniative.
Not to sett up for observing all these Rules, for
fear I should observe none.

JONATHAN SWIFT 1667–1745

A Song of a Young Lady to her Ancient Lover

Ancient person, for whom I
All the flattering youth defy,
Long be it ere thou grow old,
Aching, shaking, crazy, cold;
   But still continue as thou art,
   Ancient person of my heart.

On thy withered lips and dry,
Which like barren furrows lie,
Brooding kisses I will pour
Shall thy youthful heat restore
(Such kind showers in autumn fall,
And a second spring recall);
   Nor from thee will ever part,
   Ancient person of my heart.

The nobler part, which but to name
In our sex would be counted shame,
By age's frozen grasp possessed,
From his ice shall be released,
And soothed by my reviving hand,
In former warmth and vigour stand.
All a lover's wish can reach
For thy joy my love shall teach,
And for thy pleasure shall improve

348

All that art can add to love.
　　Yet still I love thee without art,
　　Ancient person of my heart.
JOHN WILMOT, EARL OF ROCHESTER

John Anderson, My Jo

John Anderson, my jo, John,
　　I wonder what ye mean
To lie sae lang i' the mornin'
　　And sit sae late at e'en?
Ye'll blear a' your een, John,
　　And why do ye so?
Come sooner to your bed at e'en,
　　John Anderson, my jo.

John Anderson, my jo, John,
　　When first that ye began,
Ye had as good a tail-tree
　　As ony ither man;
But now it's waxen wan, John,
　　And wrinkles to and fro,
And aft requires my helping hand,
　　John Anderson, my jo.

When we were young and yauld,[1] John,
　　We've lain out-owre the dyke,
And O! it was a fine thing
　　To see your hurdies[2] fyke; –
To see your hurdies fyke, John,
　　And strike the rising blow;
'Twas then I lik'd your chanter-pipe,[3]
　　John Anderson, my jo.

John Anderson, my jo, John,
　　You're welcome when you please;
It's either in the warm bed,
　　Or else aboon the claes.
Do ye your part aboon, John,

And trust to me below;
I've twa gae-ups for your gae-down,
   John Anderson, my jo.

When ye come on before, John
   See that ye do your best;
When I begin to haud ye,
   See that ye grip me fast;
See that ye grip me fast, John,
   Until that I cry 'Oh!'
Your back shall crack, or I do that,
   John Anderson, my jo.

I'm backet like a salmon,
   I'm breastit like a swan,
My wyme is like a down-cod,
   My waist ye weel may span;
My skin fra tap to tae, John,
   Is like the new fa'n snow
And it's a' for your conveniency,
   John Anderson, my jo.
                   ROBERT BURNS

1. Yauld: sprightly   2. Hurdies: buttocks   3. Chanter-pipe: the flute of the bagpipe

Bill and Joe

Come, dear old comrade, you and I
Will steal an hour from days gone by,
The shining days when life was new,
And all was bright with morning dew,
The lusty days of long ago,
When you were Bill and I was Joe:

Your name may flaunt a titled trail,
Proud as a cockerel's rainbow tail;
And mine as brief appendix wear
As Tam O'Shanter's luckless mare;

350

To-day, old friend, remember still
That I am Joe and you are Bill.

You've won the great world's envied prize,
And grand you look in people's eyes,
With HON. and LL. D.
In big brave letters, fair to see, –
Your fist, old fellow! off they go! –
How are you, Bill? How are you, Joe?

You've worn the judge's ermined robe;
You've taught your name to half the globe;
You've sung mankind a deathless strain;
You've made the dead past live again:
The world may call you what it will,
But you and I are Joe and Bill.

The chaffing young folks stare and say,
'See those old buffers, bent and gray, –
They talk like fellows in their teens!
Mad, poor old boys! That's what it means,' –
And shake their heads; they little know
The throbbing hearts of Bill and Joe! –

How Bill forgets his hour of pride,
While Joe sits smiling at his side;
How Joe, in spite of time's disguise,
Finds the old schoolmate in his eyes, –
Those calm, stern eyes that melt and fill
As Joe looks fondly up at Bill.

Ah, pensive scholar, what is fame?
A fitful tongue of leaping flame;
A giddy whirlwind's fickle gust,
That lifts a pinch of mortal dust;
A few swift years, and who can show
Which dust was Bill and which was Joe?

The weary idol takes his stand,
Holds out his bruised and aching hand,
While gaping thousands come and go, –

How vain it seems, this empty show!
Till all at once his pulses thrill; –
'Tis poor old Joe's 'God bless you, Bill!'

And shall we breathe in happier spheres
The names that pleased our mortal ears;
In some sweet lull of harp and song,
For earth-born spirits none too long,
Just whispering of the world below
Where this was Bill and that was Joe?

No matter; while our home is here
No sounding name is half so dear;
When fades at length our lingering day,
Who cares what pompous tombstones say?
Read on the hearts that love us still,
Hic jacet Joe. *Hic jacet* Bill.

OLIVER WENDELL HOLMES

The Bridge

I stood on the bridge at midnight,
  As the clocks were striking the hour,
And the moon rose o'er the city,
  Behind the dark church-tower.

I saw her bright reflection
  In the waters under me,
Like a golden goblet falling
  And sinking into the sea.

And far in the hazy distance
  Of that lovely night in June,
The blaze of the flaming furnace
  Gleamed redder than the moon.

Among the long, black rafters
  The wavering shadows lay,

And the current that came from the ocean
   Seemed to lift and bear them away;

As, sweeping and eddying through them,
   Rose the belated tide,
And, streaming into the moonlight,
   The sea-weed floated wide.

And like those waters rushing
   Among the wooden piers,
A flood of thoughts came o'er me
   That filled my eyes with tears.

How often, oh, how often,
   In the days that had gone by,
I had stood on that bridge at midnight,
   And gazed on that wave and sky!

How often, oh, how often,
   I had wished that the ebbing tide
Would bear me away on its bosom
   O'er the ocean wild and wide!

For my heart was hot and restless,
   And my life was full of care,
And the burden laid upon me
   Seemed greater than I could bear.

But now it has fallen from me,
   It is buried in the sea;
And only the sorrow of others
   Throws its shadow over me.

Yet whenever I cross the river,
   On its bridge with wooden piers,
Like the odour of brine from the ocean
   Comes the thought of other years.

And I think how many thousands
   Of care-encumbered men,

Each bearing his burden of sorrow,
   Have crossed the bridge since then!

I see the long procession
   Still passing to and fro,
The young heart hot and restless,
   And the old subdued and slow.

And for ever and for ever,
   As long as the river flows,
As long as the heart has passions,
   As long as life has woes;

The moon and its broken reflection
   And its shadows shall appear,
As the symbol of love in heaven,
   And its wavering image here.

HENRY WADSWORTH LONGFELLOW

Upper Lambourne

Up the ash tree climbs the ivy,
   Up the ivy climbs the sun.
With a twenty thousand pattering
   Has a valley breeze begun,
Feathery ash, neglected elder,
   Shift the shade and make it run –

Shift the shade towards the nettles,
   And the nettles set it free
To streak the stained Cararra headstone
   Where, in nineteen-twenty-three,
He who trained a hundred winners
   Paid the Final Entrance Fee.

Leathery limbs of Upper Lambourne,
   Leathery skin from sun and wind,
Leathery breeches, spreading stables,
   Shining saddles left behind,

To the down the string of horses
   Moving out of sight and mind.   .

Feathery ash in leathery Lambourne
   Waves above the sarsen stone,
And Edwardian plantations
   So coniferously moan
As to make the swelling downland,
   Far surrounding, seem their own.

JOHN BETJEMAN

from *Uphill*

Does the road wind uphill all the way?
   Yes, to the very end.
Will the day's journey take the whole long day?
   From morn to night, my friend.

CHRISTINA ROSSETTI

Song

When I am dead, my dearest,
   Sing no sad songs for me;
Plant thou no roses at my head,
   Nor shady cypress tree:
Be the green grass above me
   With showers and dewdrops wet;
And if thou wilt, remember,
   And if thou wilt, forget.

I shall not see the shadows,
   I shall not feel the rain;
I shall not hear the nightingale
   Sing on, as if in pain;
And dreaming through the twilight
   That doth not rise nor set,

Haply I may remember,
And haply may forget.
CHRISTINA ROSSETTI

Days of 1903

I never found them again – those things so speedily lost . . .
the poetic eyes, the pallid face . . .
in the dusk of the road . . .

I never found them again – those quite haphazardly acquired,
that I gave up so lightly;
and that later in agony I craved.
The poetic eyes, the pallid face,
I never found those lips again.

C. P. CAVAFY
(Translated by Rae Dalven.)

Candles

The days of our future stand before us
like a row of little lighted candles –
golden, warm, and lively little candles.

The days gone by remain behind us,
a mournful line of burnt-out candles;
the nearest ones are still smoking,
cold candles, melted and bent.

I do not want to look at them; their form saddens me,
and it saddens me to recall their first light.
I look ahead at my lighted candles.

I do not want to turn back, lest I see and shudder –
how quickly the somber line lengthens,
how quickly the burnt-out candles multiply.

C. P. CAVAFY
(Translated by Rae Dalven.)

356

I Remember

It was my bridal night I remember,
An old man of seventy-three
I lay with my young bride in my arms,
A girl with t.b.
It was wartime, and overhead
The Germans were making a particularly heavy raid on
    Hampstead.
What rendered the confusion worse, perversely
Our bombers had chosen that moment to set out for Germany.
Harry, do they ever collide?
I do not think it has ever happened,
Oh my bride, my bride.

STEVIE SMITH

Turn the Key Deftly

We turn out the light to undress by,
can no longer bear the witness
of bodies that have shivered through
too many winters. We are more coy now
than ten or fifteen years ago, do not show
ourselves proudly. Sometimes when you catch my eye
I do a comedian shuffle, acknowledging the joke
about my loud paunch, the profile of my buttocks.

Side by side under kind covers we try
to push the heavy years away, resurrecting
for a moment an afternoon beside a pond.
Yet, sophisticated, prefer to joke,
allowing sleep to do our dreaming for us.

EDWIN BROCK 1927–

Body, Remember . . .

Body, remember not only how much you were loved,
not only the beds on which you lay,
but also those desires for you
that glowed plainly in the eyes,
and trembled in the voice – and some
chance obstacle made futile.
Now that all of them belong to the past,
it almost seems as if you had yielded
to those desires – how they glowed,
remember, in the eyes gazing at you;
how they trembled in the voice, for you, remember, body.

C. P. CAVAFY
(Translated by Rae Dalven.)

What the Bones Know

Remembering the past
And gloating at it now,
I know the frozen brow
And shaking sides of lust
Will dog me at my death
To catch my ghostly breath.

I think that Yeats was right,
That lust and love are one.
The body of this night
May beggar me to death,
But we are not undone
Who love with all our breath.

I know that Proust was wrong,
His wheeze: love, to survive,
Needs jealousy, and death
And lust, to make it strong
Or goose it back alive.
Proust took away my breath.

The later Yeats was right
To think of sex and death
And nothing else. Why wait
Till we are turning old?
My thoughts are hot and cold.
I do not waste my breath.
CAROLYN KIZER 1925–

The Way Through the Woods

They shut the road through the woods
Seventy years ago.
Weather and rain have undone it again,
And now you would never know
There was once a road through the woods
Before they planted the trees.
It is underneath the coppice and heath
And the thin anemones.
Only the keeper sees
That, where the ring-dove broods,
And the badgers roll at ease,
There was once a road through the woods.

Yet, if you enter the woods
Of a summer evening late,
When the night-air cools on the trout-ringed pools
Where the otter whistles his mate,
(They fear not men in the woods,
Because they see so few.)
You will hear the beat of a horse's feet,
And the swish of a skirt in the dew,
Steadily cantering through
The misty solitudes,
As though they perfectly knew
The old lost road through the woods . . .
But there is no road through the woods.
RUDYARD KIPLING

Roads Go Ever Ever On

from *The Hobbit*

Roads go ever ever on,
   Over rock and under tree,
By caves where sun has never shone,
   By streams that never find the sea;
Over snow by winter sown,
   And through the merry flowers of June,
Over grass and over stone,
   And under mountains in the moon.

Roads go eve ever on
   Under cloud and under star,
Yet feet that wandering have gone
   Turn at last to home afar.
Eyes that fire and sword have seen
   And horror in the halls of stone
Look at last on meadows green
   And trees and hills they long have known.

J. R. R. TOLKIEN 1892–1973

LAST SCENE

Last scene of all,
That ends this strange eventful history,
Is second childishness and mere oblivion,
Sans teeth, sans eyes, sans taste, sans everything.

from *The Rubá 'iyat of Omar Khayyám*

Ah, my Beloved, fill the Cup that clears
To-day of past Regret and future Fears:
    To-morrow! – Why, To-morrow, I may be
Myself with Yesterday's Seven thousand Years.

For some we loved, the loveliest and the best
That from his Vintage rolling Time hath pressed,
    Have drunk their Cup a Round or two before,
And one by one crept silently to rest.

And we that now make merry in the Room
They left, and Summer dresses in new bloom,
    Ourselves must we beneath the Couch of Earth
Descend – ourselves to make a Couch – for whom?

Ah, make the most of what we yet may spend,
Before we too into the Dust descend;
    Dust into Dust, and under Dust, to lie,
Sans Wine, sans Song, sans Singer, and – sans End!

Alike for those who for To-day prepare,
And those that after some To-morrow stare,
    A Muezzin from the Tower of Darkness cries,
'Fools! your Reward is neither Here nor There!'

Why, all the Saints and Sages who discussed
Of the two Worlds so wisely – they are thrust
    Like foolish Prophets forth; their Words to Scorn
Are scattered, and their Mouths are stopped with Dust.

Myself when young did eagerly frequent
Doctor and Saint, and heard great argument
    About it and about: but evermore
Came out by the same door where in I went.

With them the seed of Wisdom did I sow,
And with mine own hand wrought to make it grow;
    And this was all the Harvest that I reaped –
'I came like Water, and like Wind I go.'

Into this Universe, and *Why* not Knowing
Nor *Whence*, like Water willy-nilly flowing;
   And out of it, as Wind along the Waste,
I know not *Whither*, willy-nilly blowing.

What, without asking, hither hurried *Whence?*
And, without asking, *Whither* hurried hence!
   Oh, many a Cup of this forbidden Wine
Must drown the memory of that insolence!

Up from Earth's Center through the Seventh Gate
I rose, and on the Throne of Saturn sate,
   And many a Knot unraveled by the Road;
But not the Master-knot of Human Fate.

There was the Door to which I found no Key;
There was the Veil through which I might not see;
   Some little talk awhile of ME and THEE
There was – and then no more of THEE and ME.

Earth could not answer; nor the Seas that mourn
In flowing Purple, of their Lord forlorn;
   Nor rolling Heaven, with all his Signs revealed
And hidden by the sleeve of Night and Morn.

Then of the THEE IN ME who works behind
The Veil, I lifted up my hands to find
   A Lamp amid the Darkness; and I heard,
As from Without – 'THE ME WITHIN THEE BLIND!'

Then to the Lip of this poor earthen Urn
I leaned the Secret of my Life to learn:
   And Lip to Lip it murmured – 'While you live,
Drink! – for, once dead, you never shall return.'

EDWARD FITZGERALD 1809–83

Demogorgon

from *Prometheus Unbound*

To suffer woes which Hope thinks infinite;
To forgive wrongs darker than death or night;
   To defy Power, which seems omnipotent;

To love, and bear; to hope till Hope creates
From its own wreck the thing it contemplates;
    Neither to change, nor falter, nor repent;
This, like thy glory, Titan, is to be
Good, great and joyous, beautiful and free;
This is alone Life, Joy, Empire, and Victory.

PERCY BYSSHE SHELLEY

Tomorrow

from *Macbeth*, Act V, Scene v

Tomorrow, and tomorrow, and tomorrow,
Creeps in this petty pace from day to day,
To the last syllable of recorded time;
And all our yesterdays have lighted fools
The way to dusty death. Out, out, brief candle!
Life's but a walking shadow, a poor player
That struts and frets his hour upon the stage
And then is heard no more: it is a tale
Told by an idiot, full of sound and fury,
Signifying nothing.

WILLIAM SHAKESPEARE

from *Ceremony After a Fire Raid*

Into the organpipes and steeples
Of the luminous cathedrals,
Into the weathercocks' molten mouths
Rippling in twelve-winded circles,
Into the dead clock burning the hour
Over the urn of sabbaths
Over the whirling ditch of daybreak
Over the sun's hovel and the slum of fire
And the golden pavements laid in requiems,

365

Into the bread in a wheatfield of flames,
Into the wine burning like brandy,
The masses of the sea
The masses of the sea under
The masses of the infant-bearing sea
Erupt, fountain, and enter to utter for ever
Glory glory glory
The sundering ultimate kingdom of genesis' thunder.

DYLAN THOMAS

Come Away

His name
filled my scream
I ran barefoot down the stairs
fast as the childhood dream

when lions follow;
up again I ran,
the stairs a current of air
blew me like thistledown.

I laid my palm on his calf
and it was warm and muscled
and like life.

Come away said the kind doctor.
I left the body there
lying straight, our wide bed
a single bier.

All night I watched
tree branches scratch the sky,
printed another window-frame
for ever on my eye.

When I came home in the morning
all the warmth had gone.
I touched his useless hand.

Where his eyes had shone
behind half-lifted lids were grown
cataracts of stone.

PAMELA GILLILAN

When You Died

1.
When you died
I went through the rain
Carrying my nightmare
To register the death.

A well-groomed healthy gentleman
Safe within his office
Said – Are you the widow?

Couldn't he have said
Were you his wife?

2.
After the first shock
I found I was
Solidly set in my flesh.
I was an upright central pillar,
The soft flesh melted round me.
My eyes melted
Spilling the inexhaustible essence of sorrow.
The soft flesh of the body
Melted onto chairs and into beds
Dragging its emptiness and pain.

I lodged inside holding myself upright,
Warding off the dreadful deliquescence.

3.
November.
Stooping under muslins
Of grey rain I fingered
Through ribbons of wet grass,
Traced stiff stems down to the wormy earth

And one by one snapped off
The pale surviving flowers; they would ride

With him, lie on the polished plank
Above his breast.

People said – Why do you not
Follow the coffin?
Why do you not
Have any funeral words spoken?
Why not
Send flowers from a shop?

4.
When you died
They burnt you.
They brought home to me
A vase of thin metal;
Inside, a plasty bag
Crammed, full of gritty pieces.
Ground bones, not silky ash.

Where shall I put this substance?
Shall I scatter it
With customary thoughts
Of nature's mystical balance
Among the roses?

Shall I disperse it into the winds
That blow across Cambeake Cliff
Or drop it onto places where you
Lived, worked, were happy?

Finally shall I perhaps keep it
Which after all was you
Quietly on a shelf
And when I follow
My old grit can lie
No matter where with yours
Slowly sinking into the earth together.

5.
When you died
I did not for the moment
Think about myself;
I grieved deeply and purely for your loss,
That you had lost your life.
I grieved bitterly for your mind destroyed,
Your courage thrown away,
Your senses aborted under the amazing skin
No one would ever touch again.

I grieve still
That we'd have grown
Even more deeply close and old together
And now shall not.

PAMELA GILLILAN

Time

Time does not bring relief; you all have lied
Who told me time would ease me of my pain!
I miss him in the weeping of the rain;
I want him at the shrinking of the tide;
The old snows melt from every mountain-side,
And last year's leaves are smoke in every lane;
But last year's bitter loving must remain
Heaped on my heart, and my old thoughts abide.
There are a hundred places where I fear
To go, – so with his memory they brim.
And entering with relief some quiet place
Where never fell his foot or shone his face
I say, 'There is no memory of him here!'
And so stand stricken, so remembering him.

EDNA ST VINCENT MILLAY

In Death Divided

I shall rot here, with those whom in their day
    You never knew,

And alien ones who, ere they chilled to clay,
 Met not my view,
Will in your distant grave-place ever neighbour you.

No shade of pinnacle or tree or tower,
 While earth endures,
Will fall on my mound and within the hour
 Steal on to yours;
One robin never haunt our two green covertures.

Some organ may resound on Sunday noons
 By where you lie,
Some other thrill the panes with other tunes
 Where moulder I;
No selfsame chords compose our common lullaby.

The simply-cut memorial at my head
 Perhaps may take
A rustic form, and that above your bed
 A stately make;
No linking symbol show thereon for our tale's sake.

And in the monotonous moils of strained, hard-run
 Humanity,
The eternal tie which binds us twain in one
 No eye will see
Stretching across the miles that sever you from me.

THOMAS HARDY

On Prince Frederick

Here lies Fred,
Who was alive and is dead:
Had it been his father,
I had much rather;
Had it been his brother,
Still better than another;
Had it been his sister,
No one would have missed her;

Had it been the whole generation,
So much the better for the nation:
But since 'tis only Fred,
Who was alive and is dead,
There's no more to be said.

ANON.

The Mary Gloster
1894

I've paid for your sickest fancies; I've humoured your
　　crackedest whim –
Dick, it's your daddy, dying; you've got to listen to him!
Good for a fortnight, am I? The doctor told you? He
　　lied.
I shall go under by morning and – Put that nurse outside.
'Never seen death yet, Dickie? Well, now is your time to
　　learn,
And you'll wish you held my record before it comes to your
　　turn.
Not counting the Line and the Foundry, the Yards and the
　　village, too,
I've made myself and a million; but I'm damned if I made
　　you.
Master at two-and-twenty, and married at twenty-three –
Ten thousand men on the pay-roll, and forty freighters at
　　sea!

Fifty years between 'em, and every year of it fight,
And now I'm Sir Anthony Gloster, dying, a baronite:
For I lunched with his Royal 'Ighness – what was it the
　　papers had?
'Not least of our merchant-princes.' Dickie, that's me,
　　your dad!
I didn't begin with askings. I took my job and I stuck;
I took the chances they wouldn't, an' now they're calling it
　　luck.
Lord, what boats I've handled – rotten and leaky and old –
Ran 'em, or – opened the bilge-cock, precisely as I was told.

Grub that 'ud bind you crazy, and crews that 'ud turn you
      grey,
And a big fat lump of insurance to cover the risk on the way.
The others they dursn't do it; they said they valued their
      life
(They've served me since as skippers). *I* went, and I took
      my wife.
Over the world I drove 'em, married at twenty-three,
And your mother saving the money and making a man of me.
I was content to be master, but she said there was better
      behind;
She took the chances I wouldn't, and I followed your mother
      blind.
She egged me to borrow the money, an' she helped me to
      clear the loan,
When we bought half-shares in a cheap 'un and hoisted a flag
      of our own.
Patching and coaling on credit, and living the Lord knew
      how,
We started the Red Ox freighters – we've eight-and-thirty
      now.
And those were the days of clippers, and the freights were
      clipper-freights,
And we knew we were making our fortune, but she died in
      Macassar Straits –
By the Little Paternosters, as you come to the Union Bank –
And we dropped her in fourteen fathom: I pricked it off
      where she sank.
Owners we were, full owners, and the boat was christened for
      her,
And she died in the *Mary Gloster*. My heart, how young
      we were!
So I went on a spree round Java and well-nigh ran her ashore,
But your mother came and warned me and I wouldn't liquor
      no more:
Strict I stuck to my business, afraid to stop or I'd think,
Saving the money (she warned me), and letting the other men
      drink.
And I met M'Cullough in London (I'd saved five 'undred
      then),

And 'tween us we started the Foundry – three forges and
    twenty men.
Cheap repairs for the cheap 'uns. It paid, and the business
    grew;
For I bought me a steam-lathe patent, and that was a gold
    mine too.
'Cheaper to build 'em than buy em,' *I* said, but
    M'Cullough he shied,
And we wasted a year in talking before we moved to the
    Clyde.
And the Lines were all beginning, and we all of us started
    fair,
Building our engines like houses and staying the boilers
    square.
But M'Cullough 'e wanted cabins with marble and maple
    and all,
And Brussels an' Utrecht velvet, and baths and a Social Hall,
And pipes for closets all over, and cutting the frames too
    light,
But M'Cullough he died in the Sixties, and – Well, I'm
    dying to-night . . .
I knew – *I* knew what was coming, when we bid on the
    Byfleet's keel –
They piddled and piffled with iron. I'd given my orders for
    steel!
Steel and the first expansions. It paid, I tell you, it paid,
When we came with our nine-knot freighters and collared the
    long-run trade!
And they asked me how I did it, and I gave 'em the Scripture
    text,
'You keep your light so shining a little in front o' the
    next!'
They copied all they could follow, but they couldn't copy my
    mind,
And I left 'em sweating and stealing a year and a half behind.
Then came the armour-contracts, but that was M'Cullough's
    side;
He was always best in the Foundry, but better, perhaps, he
    died.
I went through his private papers; the notes was plainer
    than print;

And I'm no fool to finish if a man'll give me a hint.
(I remember his widow was angry.) So I saw what his drawings
    meant,
And I started the six-inch rollers, and it paid me sixty per
    cent.
Sixty per cent *with* failures, and more than twice we could
    do,
And a quarter-million to credit, and I saved it all for you!
I thought – it doesn't matter – you seemed to favour your ma,
But you're nearer forty than thirty, and I know the kind
    you are.
Harrer an' Trinity College! I ought to ha' sent you to
    sea –
But I stood you an education, an' what have you done for
    me?
The things I knew was proper you wouldn't thank me to
    give,
And the things I knew was rotten you said was the way to
    live.
For you muddled with books and pictures, an' china an'
    etchin's an' fans,
And your rooms at college was beastly – more like a whore's
    than a man's;
Till you married that thin-flanked woman, as white and as
    stale as a bone,
An' she gave you your social nonsense; but where's that kid
    o' your own?
I've seen your carriages blocking the half o' the Cromwell
    Road
But never the doctor's brougham to help the missus unload.
(So there isn't even a grandchild, an' the Gloster family's
    done.)
Not like your mother, she isn't. *She* carried her freight each
    run.
But they died, the pore little beggars! At sea she had 'em –
    they died.
Only you, an' you stood it. You haven't stood much beside.
Weak, a liar, and idle, and mean as a collier's whelp
Nosing for scraps in the galley. No help – my son was no
    help!

So he gets three 'undred thousand, in trust and the interest
   paid.
I wouldn't give it you, Dickie – you see, I made it in trade.
You're saved from soiling your fingers, and if you have no
   child,
It all comes back to the business. 'Gad, won't your wife be
   wild!
'Calls and calls in her carriage, her 'andkerchief up to 'er eye:
'Daddy! dear daddy's dyin'!' and doing her best to cry.
Grateful? Oh, yes, I'm grateful, but keep her away from
   here.
Your mother 'ud never ha' stood 'er, and, anyhow, women
   are queer . . .
There's women will say I've married a second time. Not
   quite!
But give pore Aggie a hundred, and tell her your lawyers'll
   fight.
She was the best o' the boiling – you'll meet her before it
   ends.
I'm in for a row with the mother – I'll leave you settle my
   friends.
For a man he must go with a woman, which women don't
   understand –
Or the sort that say they can see it they aren't the marrying
   brand.
But I wanted to speak o' your mother that's Lady Gloster
   still;
I'm going to up and see her, without its hurting the will.
Here! Take your hand off the bell-pull. Five thousand's
   waiting for you,
If you'll only listen a minute, and do as I bid you do.
They'll try to prove me crazy, and, if you bungle, they can;
And I've only you to trust to! (O God, why ain't it a man?)
There's some waste money on marbles, the same as
   M'Cullough tried –
Marbles and mausoleums – but I call that sinful pride.
There's some ship bodies for burial – we've carried 'em,
   soldered and packed;
Down in their wills they wrote it, and nobody called *them*
   cracked.

But me – I've too much money, and people might . . .
    All my fault:
It come o' hoping for grandsons and buying that Wokin'
    vault . . .
I'm sick o' the 'ole dam' business. I'm going back where I
    came.
Dick, you're the son o' my body, and you'll take charge o'
    the same!
I want to lie by your mother, ten thousand mile away,
And they'll want to send me to Woking; and that's where
    you'll earn your pay.
I've thought it out on the quiet, the same as it ought to be
    done –
Quiet, and decent, and proper – an' here's your orders, my
    son.
You know the Line? You don't, though. You write to the
    Board, and tell
Your father's death has upset you an' you're goin' to cruise
    for a spell,
An' you'd like the *Mary Gloster* – I've held her ready for
    this –
They'll put her in working order and you'll take her out as
    she is.
Yes, it was money idle when I patched her and laid her
    aside
(Thank God, I can pay for my fancies!) – the boat where
    your mother died,
By the Little Paternosters, as you come to the Union Bank,
We dropped her – I think I told you – and I pricked it off
    where she sank.
['Tiny she looked on the grating – that oily, treacly sea –]
Hundred and Eighteen East, remember, and South just
    Three.
Easy bearings to carry – Three South – Three to the dot;
But I gave McAndrew a copy in case of dying – or not.
And so you'll write to McAndrew, he's Chief of the Maori
    Line;
They'll give him leave, if you ask 'em and say it's business
    o' mine.
I built three boats for the Maoris, an' very well pleased they
    were,

An' I've known Mac since the Fifties, and Mac knew me —
    and her.
After the first stroke warned me I sent him the money to
    keep
Against the time you'd claim it, committin' your dad to the
    deep;
For you are the son o' my body, and Mac was my oldest
    friend,
I've never asked 'im to dinner but he'll see it out to the end.
Stiff-necked Glasgow beggar! I've heard he's prayed for
    my soul,
But he couldn't lie if you paid him, and he'd starve before he
    stole.
He'll take the *Mary* in ballast — you'll find her a lively ship;
And you'll take Sir Anthony Gloster, that goes on 'is wedding-trip,
Lashed in our old deck-cabin with all three port-holes wide,
The kick o' the screw beneath him and the round blue seas
    outside!
Sir Anthony Gloster's carriage — our 'ouse-flag flyin' free —
Ten thousand men on the pay-roll and forty freighters at
    sea!
He made himself and a million, but this world is a fleetin'
    show,
And he'll go to the wife of 'is bosom the same as he ought to
    go —
By the heel of the Paternosters — there isn't a chance to
    mistake —
And Mac'll pay you the money as soon as the bubbles break!
Five thousand for six weeks' cruising, the staunchest freighter
    afloat,
And Mac he'll give you your bonus the minute I'm out o' the
    boat!
He'll take you round to Macassar, and you'll come back
    alone;
He knows what I want o' the *Mary* . . . I'll do what I
    please with my own.
Your mother 'ud call it wasteful, but I've seven-and-thirty
    more;
I'll come in my private carriage and bid it wait at the
    door . . .

For my son 'e was never a credit; 'e muddled with books
    and art,
And 'e lived on Sir Anthony's money and 'e broke Sir
    Anthony's heart.
There isn't even a grandchild, and the Gloster family's
    done –
The only one you left me – O mother, the only one!
Harrer and Trinity College – me slavin' early an' late –
An' he thinks I'm dying crazy, and you're in Macassar
    Strait!
Flesh o' my flesh, my dearie, for ever an' ever amen,
That first stroke come for a warning. I ought to ha' gone to
    you then.
But – cheap repairs for a cheap 'un – the doctors said I'd do.
Mary, why didn't *you* warn me? I've allus heeded to you,
Excep' – I know – about women; but you are a spirit now;
An', wife, they w only women, and I was a man. That's
    how.
An' a man 'e must go with a woman, as you *could* not understand;
But I never talked 'em secrets. I paid 'em out o' hand.
Thank Gawd, I can pay for my fancies! Now what's five
    thousand to me,
For a berth off the Paternosters in the haven where I would
    be?
I believe in the Resurrection, if I read my Bible plain,
But I wouldn't trust 'em at Wokin'; we're safer at sea again.
For the heart it shall go with the treasure – go down to the
    sea in ships.
I'm sick of the hired women. I'll kiss my girl on her lips!
I'll be content with my fountain. I'll drink from my own
    well,
And the wife of my youth shall charm me – an' the rest can
    go to Hell!
(Dickie, *he* will, that's certain.) I'll lie in our standin'-bed,
An' Mac'll take her in ballast – an' she trims best by the
    head . . .
Down by the head an' sinkin', her fires are drawn and cold,
And the water's splashin' hollow on the skin of the empty
    hold –
Churning an' choking and chuckling, quiet and scummy and
    dark –

Full to her lower hatches and risin' steady. Hark!
That was the after-bulkhead . . . She's flooded from stem
    to stern . . .
'Never seen death yet, Dickie? . . . Well, now is your time
    to learn!

RUDYARD KIPLING

Cheltenham Waters

Here lie I and my four daughters,
Killed by drinking Cheltenham waters.
Had we but stuck to Epsom salts,
We wouldn't have been in these here vaults.

ANON.

Because I Liked You Better

Because I'd liked you better
    Than suits a man to say,
It irked you, and I promised
    To throw the thought away.

To put the world between us
    We parted, stiff and dry;
'Good-bye', said you, 'forget me.'
    'I will, no fear', said I.

If here, where clover whitens
    The dead man's knoll, you pass,
And no tall flower to meet you
    Starts in the trefoiled grass,

Halt by the headstone naming
    The heart no longer stirred,
And say the lad that loved you
    Was one that kept his word.

A. E. HOUSMAN

Indian Prayer (traditional)

When I am dead
Cry for me a little
Think of me sometimes
But not too much.
Think of me now and again
As I was in life
At some moments it's pleasant to recall
But not for long
Leave me in peace
And I shall leave you in peace
And while you live
Let your thoughts be with the living.

ANON.

Code Poem for the French Resistance

The life that I have is all that I have,
And the life that I have is yours.
The love that I have of the life that I have
Is yours and yours and yours.

A sleep I shall have
A rest I shall have,
Yet death will be but a pause,
For the peace of my years in the long green grass
Will be yours and yours and yours.

LEO MARKS

The Last Word

Creep into thy narrow bed,
Creep and let no more be said!
Vain thy onset! all stands fast.
Thou thyself must break at last.

Let the long contention cease!
Geese are swans, and swans are geese,
Let them have it how they will!
Thou art tired, best be still.

They out-talked thee, hissed thee, tore thee?
Better men fared thus before thee;
Fired their ringing shot and passed,
Hotly charged – and sank at last.

Charge once more, then, and be dumb!
Let the victors, when they come,
When the forts of folly fall,
Find thy body by the wall!

MATTHEW ARNOLD

Do Not Go Gentle into that Good Night

Do not go gentle into that good night,
Old age should burn and rave at close of day;
Rage, rage against the dying of the light.

Though wise men at their end know dark is right,
Because their words had forked no lightning they
Do not go gentle into that good night.

Good men, the last wave by, crying how bright
Their frail deeds might have danced in a green bay,
Rage, rage against the dying of the light.

Wild men who caught and sang the sun in flight,
And learn, too late, they grieved it on its way,
Do not go gentle into that good night.

Grave men, near death, who see with blinding sight
Blind eyes could blaze like meteors and be gay,
Rage, rage against the dying of the light.

And you, my father, there on the old height,
Curse, bless, me hold with your fierce tears, I pray.
Do not go gentle into that good night,
Rage, rage against the dying of the light.

DYLAN THOMAS

And Death Shall Have No Dominion

And death shall have no dominion.
Dead men naked they shall be one
With the man in the wind and the west moon;
When their bones are picked clean and the clean bones gone,
They shall have stars at elbow and foot;
Though they go mad they shall be sane,
Though they sink through the sea they shall rise again;
Though lovers be lost love shall not;
And death shall have no dominion.

And death shall have no dominion.
Under the windings of the sea
They lying long shall not die windily;
Twisting on racks when sinews give way,
Strapped to a wheel, yet they shall not break;

Faith in their hands shall snap in two,
And the unicorn evils run them through;
Split all ends up they shan't crack:
And death shall have no dominion.

And death shall have no dominion.
No more may gulls cry at their ears
Or waves break loud on the seashores;
Where blew a flower may a flower no more
Lift its head to the blows of the rain;
Though they be mad and dead as nails
Heads of the characters hammer through daisies;
Break in the sun till the sun breaks down,
And death shall have no dominion.

DYLAN THOMAS

Recessional

1897

GOD of our fathers, known of old,
   Lord of our far-flung battle-line,
Beneath whose awful Hand we hold
   Dominion over palm and pine –
Lord God of Hosts, be with us yet,
Lest we forget – lest we forget!

The tumult and the shouting dies;
   The Captains and the Kings depart;
Still stands Thine ancient sacrifice,
   An humble and a contrite heart.
Lord God of Hosts, be with us yet,
Lest we forget – lest we forget!

Far-called, our navies melt away;
   On dune and headland sinks the fire:
Lo, all our pomp of yesterday
   Is one with Nineveh and Tyre!
Judge of the Nations, spare us yet,
Lest we forget – lest we forget!

If, drunk with sight of power, we loose
   Wild tongues that have not Thee in awe,
Such boastings as the Gentiles use,
   Or lesser breeds without the Law –
Lord God of Hosts, be with us yet,
Lest we forget – lest we forget!

For heathen heart that puts her trust
   In reeking tube and iron shard,
All valiant dust that builds on dust,
   And guarding, calls not Thee to guard,
For frantic boast and foolish word –
Thy mercy on Thy People, Lord!

RUDYARD KIPLING

Evolution

Out of the dusk a shadow;
Then, a spark;
Out of the cloud a silence,
Then, a lark;
Out of the heart a rapture,
Then, a pain;
Out of the dead, cold ashes,
Life Again.

JOHN BANISTER TABB 1845–1909

On a Tired Housewife

Here lies a poor woman who was always tired,
She lived in a house where help wasn't hired:
Her last words on earth were: 'Dear friends, I am going
To where there's no cooking, or washing, or sewing,
For everything there is exact to my wishes,
For where they don't eat there's no washing of dishes.
I'll be where loud anthems will always be ringing,
But having no voice I'll be quit of the singing.
Don't mourn for me now, don't mourn for me never,
I am going to do nothing for ever and ever.'

ANON.

Old Men

People expect old men to die,
They do not really mourn old men.
Old men are different. People look
At them with eyes that wonder when . . .
People watch with unshocked eyes;
But the old men know when an old man dies.

OGDEN NASH

384

Invictus

Out of the night that covers me,
  Black as the Pit from pole to pole,
I thank whatever gods may be
  For my unconquerable soul.

In the fell clutch of circumstance
  I have not winced nor cried aloud.
Under the bludgeonings of chance
  My head is bloody, but unbowed.

Beyond this place of wrath and tears
  Looms but the horror of the shade,
And yet the menace of the years
  Finds, and shall find me, unafraid.

It matters not how strait the gate,
  How charged with punishments the scroll,
I am the master of my fate:
  I am the captain of my soul.

W. E. HENLEY 1849–1903

(This poem was written in Edinburgh Infirmary when, at the age of twenty-four,
Henley had gone to be treated by Lister, the famous surgeon. He had developed a
tubercular disease of the bone at the age of twelve and was crippled, with one leg already
amputated, only to be told that he needed an amputation of the other leg. Fortunately,
however, the leg was saved.)

Friends, Romans, Countrymen

from *Julius Caesar*, Act III, Scene ii

Friends, Romans, countrymen, lend me your ears;
I come to bury Caesar, not to praise him.
The evil that men do lives after them;
The good is oft interrèd with their bones;
So let it be with Caesar. The noble Brutus
Hath told you Caesar was ambitious.
If it were so, it was a grievous fault:
And grievously hath Caesar answered it.

Here, under leave of Brutus, and the rest,
For Brutus is an honourable man;
So are they all, all honourable men;
Come I to speak in Caesar's funeral.
He was my friend, faithful and just to me:
But Brutus says, he was ambitious;
And Brutus is an honourable man.
He hath brought many captives home to Rome,
Whose ransoms did the general coffers fill:
Did this in Caesar seem ambitious?
When that the poor have cried, Caesar hath wept.
Ambition should be made of sterner stuff:
Yet Brutus says, he was ambitious;
And Brutus is an honourable man.
You all did see that on the Lupercal
I thrice presented him a kingly crown,
Which he did thrice refuse. Was this ambition?
Yet Brutus says, he was ambitious;
And, sure, he is an honourable man.
I speak not to disprove what Brutus spoke,
But here I am to speak what I do know.
You all did love him once, not without cause;
What cause withholds you then to mourn for him?
O judgement, thou art fled to brutish beasts,
And men have lost their reason! Bear with me:
My heart is in the coffin there with Caesar,
And I must pause till it come back to me.

WILLIAM SHAKESPEARE

In Praise of Famous Men
from *The Apocrypha*

Let us now praise famous men, and our fathers that begat
us.

The Lord hath wrought great glory by them through his
great power from the beginning.

Such as did bear rule in their kingdoms, men renowned

for their power, giving counsel by their understanding, and declaring prophecies:

Leaders of the people by their counsels, and by their knowledge of learning meet for the people, wise and eloquent in their instructions.

Such as found out musical tunes, and recited verses in writing:

Rich men furnished with ability, living peaceably in their habitations:

All these were honoured in their generations and were the glory of their times.

There be of them that have left a name behind them, that their praises may be reported.

And some there be that have no memorial; who are perished as though they had never been; and are become as though they had never been born; and their children after them.

But these were merciful men, whose righteousness hath not been forgotten.

Their seed standeth fast, and their children for their sakes.

Their seed shall remain forever, and their glory shall not be blotted out.

Their bodies are buried in peace, but their name liveth forevermore.

ECCLESIASTICUS CHAPTER 44, VERSES I—IO; I2—I4

To George Washington

from *Ode Recited at the Harvard Commemoration*

I praise him not; it were too late;
And some innative weakness there must be
In him who condescends to victory
Such as the Present gives, and cannot wait,

Safe in himself as in a fate.
So always firmly he:
He knew to bide his time,
And can his fame abide,
Still patient in his simple faith sublime,
Till the wise years decide.
Great captains, with their guns and drums,
Disturb our judgement for the hour,
But at last silence comes;
These all are gone, and, standing like a tower,
Our children shall behold his fame,
The kindly-earnest, brave, foreseeing man,
Sagacious, patient, dreading praise, not blame,
New birth of our new soil, the first American.

JAMES RUSSELL LOWELL

Sonnet XVI

TO THE LORD GENERAL CROMWELL, MAY 1652,
ON THE PROPOSALS OF CERTAIN MINISTERS AT THE
COMMITTEE
FOR PROPAGATION OF THE GOSPEL

CROMWELL, our chief of men, who through a cloud
Not of war only, but detractions rude,
Guided by faith and matchless fortitude,
To peace and truth thy glorious way hast ploughed,
And on the neck of crowned Fortune proud
Hast reared God's trophies and his work pursued,
While Darwen stream, with blood of Scots imbrued,
And Dunbar field, resounds thy praises loud,
And Worcester's laureate wreath: yet much remains
To conquer still; Peace hath her victories
No less renowned than War; new foes arise,
Threatening to bind our souls with secular chains.
Help us to save free conscience from the paw
Of hireling wolves, whose Gospel is their maw.

JOHN MILTON 1608–74

388

Fame is a Food that Dead Men Eat

Fame is a food that dead men eat, –
I have no stomach for such meat.
In little light and narrow room,
They eat it in the silent tomb,
With no kind voice of Comrade near
To bid the feaster be of cheer.

But Friendship is a nobler thing, –
Of Friendship it is good to sing.
For truly, when a man shall end,
He lives in memory of his friend,
Who doth his better part recall
And of his fault make funeral.

AUSTIN DOBSON 1840–1921

For the Fallen
September 1914

With proud thanksgiving, a mother for her children,
England mourns for her dead across the sea.
Flesh of her flesh they were, spirit of her spirit,
Fallen in the cause of the free.

Solemn the drums thrill: Death august and royal
Sings sorrow up into immortal spheres.
There is music in the midst of desolation
And a glory that shines upon our tears.

They went with songs to the battle, they were young,
Straight of limb, true of eye, steady and aglow.
They were staunch to the end against odds uncounted,
They fell with their faces to the foe.

They shall grow not old, as we that are left grow old:
Age shall not weary them, nor the years condemn.

At the going down of the sun and in the morning
We will remember them.

They mingle not with their laughing comrades again,
They sit no more at familiar tables of home;
They have no lot in our labour of the day-time;
They sleep beyond England's foam.

But where our desires are and our hopes profound,
Felt as a well-spring that is hidden from sight,
To the innermost heart of their own land they are known
As the stars are known to the Night;

As the stars that shall be bright when we are dust,
Moving in marches upon the heavenly plain,
As the stars that are starry in the time of our darkness,
To the end, to the end, they remain.

LAURENCE BINYON 1869–1943

'Ostler Joe

I stood at eve, as the sun went down, by a grave where a
    woman lies,
Who lured men's souls to the shores of sin with the light of
    her wanton eyes;
Who sang the song that the siren sang on the treacherous
    Lorelei height;
Whose face was as fair as a summer day, and whose heart
    was as black as night.

Yet a blossom I fain would pluck to-day from the garden
    above her dust –
Not the languorous lily of soulless sin, nor the blood-red
    rose of lust,
But a sweet, white blossom of holy love that grew in the
    one green spot
In the arid desert of Phryne's life, where all else was parched
    and hot.

In the summer, when the meadows were aglow with blue
and red,
Joe, the 'ostler of 'The Magpie,' and fair Annie Smith
were wed;
Plump was Annie, plump and pretty, with a cheek as white
as snow;
He was anything but handsome, was 'The Magpie's'
'ostler, Joe.

But he won the winsome lassie; they'd a cottage and a cow,
And her matronhood sat lightly on the village beauty's brow.
Sped the months, and came a baby – such a blue-eyed baby
boy!
Joe was working in the stables when they told him of his joy.

He was rubbing down the horses, and he gave them, then
and there,
All a special feed of clover, just in honor of his heir.
It had been his great ambition, and he told the horses so,
That the Fates would send a baby who might bear the name
of Joe.

Little Joe the child was christened, and, like babies, grew
apace;
He'd his mother's eyes of azure, and his father's honest face.
Swift the happy years went over, years of blue and cloudless
sky;
Love was lord of that small cottage, and the tempest passed
them by.

Passed them by for years, then swiftly burst in fury o'er
their home.
Down the lane by Annie's cottage chanced a gentleman
to roam;
Thrice he came and saw her sitting by the window with her
child,
And he nodded to the baby, and the baby laughed and
smiled.

So at last it grew to know him (little Joe was nearly four);
He would call the 'pretty gemplum' as he passed the open
door;

And one day he ran and caught him, and in child's play
      pulled him in;
And the baby Joe had prayed for brought about the mother's
      sin.

'Twas the same old wretched story that for ages bards have
      sung;
'Twas a woman weak and wanton, and a villain's tempting
      tongue;
'Twas a picture deftly painted for a silly creature's eyes
Of the Babylonian wonders and the joy that in them lies.

Annie listened and was tempted; she was tempted and she
      fell,
As the angels fell from heaven to the blackest depths of hell;
She was promised wealth and splendor, and a life of gentle
      sloth,
Yellow gold for child and husband – and the woman left
      them both.

Home one eve came Joe, the 'ostler, with a cheery cry of
      'Wife!'
Finding that which blurred forever all the story of his life:
She had left a silly letter – through the cruel scrawl he spelt;
Then he sought the lonely bedroom, joined his horny hands
      and knelt.

'Now, O Lord, O God, forgive her, for she ain't to blame,'
      he cried;
'For I ought 'a' seen her trouble and 'a' gone away and died.
Why, a girl like her, God bless her! – 'twasn't likely as
      her'd rest
With her bonny head forever on a 'ostler's ragged vest.

'It was kind o' her to bear me all this long and happy time;
So, for my sake, please to bless her, though you count her
      deed a crime;
If so be I don't pray proper, Lord, forgive me, for you see
I can talk all right to 'osses, but I'm nervous like with Thee.'

Ne'er a line came to the cottage from the woman who had
    flown;
Joe, the baby, died that winter, and the man was left alone.
Ne'er a bitter word he uttered, but in silence kissed the rod,
Saving what he told his horses, saving what he told his God.

Far away in mighty London rose the wanton into fame,
For her beauty won men's homage, and she prospered in her
    shame;
Quick from lord to lord she flitted, higher still each prize
    she won,
And her rivals paled beside her as the stars beside the sun.

Next she trod the stage half-naked, and she dragged Art's
    temple down
To the level of a market for the women of the town,
And the kisses she had given to poor 'Ostler Joe for naught,
With their gold and priceless jewels rich and titled lovers
    bought.

Went the years with flying footsteps while her star was at
    its height;
Then the darkness came on swiftly, and the gloaming turned
    to night.
Shattered strength and faded beauty tore the laurels from
    her brow;
Of the thousands who had worshipped, never one came near
    her now.

Broken down in health and fortune, men forgot her very
    name,
Till the news that she was dying woke the echoes of her
    fame;
And the papers in their gossip mentioned how an 'actress'
    lay
Sick to death in humble lodgings, growing weaker every day.

One there was who read the story in a far-off country place,
And that night the dying woman woke and looked upon his
    face.

Once again the strong arms clasped her that had clasped her
    long ago,
And the weary head lay pillowed on the breast of 'Ostler Joe.

All the past had he forgiven, all the sorrow and the shame;
He had found her sick and lonely, and his wife he now could
    claim;
Since the grand folks who had known her one and all had
    slunk away,
He could clasp his long-lost darling, and no man could say
    him nay.

In his arms death found her lying; from his arms her spirit
    fled,
And his tears came down in torrents as he knelt beside his
    dead.
Never once his love had faltered through her sad, unhallowed
    life,
And the stone above her ashes bears the sacred name of wife.

That's the blossom I fain would pluck to-day from the
    garden above her dust;
Not the languorous lily of soulless sin, nor the blood-red rose
    of lust,
But a sweet, white blossom of holy love that grew in the one
    green spot
In the arid desert of Phryne's life, where all else was parched
    and hot.

GEORGE R. SIMS 1847–1922

On an Old Song

Little snatch of ancient song,
What has made thee live so long?
Flying on thy wings of rhyme
Lightly down the depths of time,
Telling nothing strange or rare,
Scarce a thought or image there,
Nothing but the old, old tale
Of a hapless lover's wail;

Offspring of an idle hour,
Whence has come thy lasting power?
By what turn of rhythm or phrase,
By what subtle careless grace,
Can thy music charm our ears
After full three hundred years?

Landmarks of the human mind
One by one are left behind,
And a subtle change is wrought
In the mould and cast of thought;
Modes of reasoning pass away,
Types of beauty lose their sway;
Creeds and causes that have made
Many noble lives must fade,
And the words that thrilled of old
Now seem hueless, dead, and cold;
Fancy's rainbow tints are flying,
Thoughts, like men, are slowly dying;
All things perish, and the strongest
Often do not last the longest;
The stately ship is seen no more,
The fragile skiff attains the shore;
And while the great and wise decay,
And all their trophies pass away,
Some sudden thought, some careless rhyme,
Still floats above the wrecks of Time.

WILLIAM EDWARD HARTPOLE LECKY 1838–1903

from *Adonais*

I

I weep for Adonais – he is dead!
O, weep for Adonais! though our tears
Thaw not the frost which binds so dear a head!
And thou, sad Hour, selected from all years
To mourn our loss, rouse thy obscure compeers,
And teach them thine own sorrow, say: 'With me

Died Adonais: till the Future dares
Forget the Past, his fate and fame shall be
An echo and a light unto eternity!'

VIII

He will awake no more, oh, never more! —
Within the twilight chamber spreads apace
The shadow of white Death, and at the door
Invisible Corruption waits to trace
His extreme way to her dim dwelling-place;
The eternal Hunger sits, but pity and awe
Soothe her pale rage, nor dares she to deface
So fair a prey, till darkness, and the law
Of change, shall o'er his sleep the mortal curtain draw.

XXI

Alas! that all we loved of him should be,
But for our grief, as if it had not been,
And grief itself be mortal! Woe is me!
Whence are we, and why are we? of what scene
The actors or spectators? Great and mean
Meet massed in death, who lends what life must borrow.
As long as skies are blue, and fields are green,
Evening must usher night, night urge the morrow,
Month follow month with woe, and year wake year to sorrow.

XXXVIII

Nor let us weep that our delight is fled
Far from these carrion kites that scream below;
He wakes or sleeps with the enduring dead;
Thou canst not soar where he is sitting now —
Dust to the dust! but the pure spirit shall flow
Back to the burning fountain whence it came,
A portion of the Eternal, which must glow
Through time and change, unquenchably the same,
Whilst thy cold embers choke the sordid hearth of shame.

XXXIX

Peace, peace! he is not dead, he doth not sleep —
He hath awakened from the dream of life —

'Tis we, who lost in stormy visions, keep
With phantoms an unprofitable strife,
And in mad trance, strike with our spirit's knife
Invulnerable nothings. — *We* decay
Like corpses in a charnel; fear and grief
Convulse us and consume us day by day,
And cold hopes swarm like worms within our living clay.

XL

He has outsoared the shadow of our night;
Envy and calumny and hate and pain,
And that unrest which men miscall delight,
Can touch him not and torture not again;
From the contagion of the world's slow stain
He is secure, and now can never mourn
A heart grown cold, a head grown gray in vain;
Nor, when the spirit's self has ceased to burn,
With sparkless ashes load an unlamented urn.

PERCY BYSSHE SHELLEY

A Hymn to God the Father

I

Wilt Thou forgive that sin where I begun,
    Which is my sin, though it were done before?
Wilt Thou forgive that sin, through which I run,
    And do run still: though still I do deplore?
        When Thou hast done, Thou hast not done,
        For, I have more.

II

Wilt Thou forgive that sin which I have won
    Others to sin? and, made my sin their door?
Wilt Thou forgive that sin which I did shun
    A year, or two: but wallowed in, a score?
        When Thou hast done, Thou hast not done,
        For I have more.

III

I have a sin of fear, that when I have spun
   My last thread, I shall perish on the shore;
Swear by Thyself, that at my death Thy son
   Shall shine as He shines now, and heretofore;
      And, having done that, Thou hast done,
         I fear no more.

JOHN DONNE

It is Time to be Old

It is time to be old,
To take in sail.
The god of bounds,
Who sets to seas a shore,
Came to me in his fatal rounds
And said: 'No more!
No farther shoot
Thy broad ambitious branches, and thy root.
Fancy departs: no more invent;
Contract thy firmament
To compass of a tent.'

RALPH WALDO EMERSON 1803–82

Final Apology

You think it horrible that Lust and Rage
Should dance attendance upon my old age;
They were not such a plague, when I was young.
What else have I to spur me into song?

W. B. YEATS

Requiem

Under the wide and starry sky,
Dig the grave and let me lie.
Glad did I live and gladly die,
    And I laid me down with a will.

This be the verse you grave for me:
Here he lies where he longed to be;
Home is the sailor, home from sea,
    And the hunter home from the hill.

ROBERT LOUIS STEVENSON

(Tablet on the grave of Robert Louis Stevenson in Samoa. He asked for these words of his 'Requiem' to be his epitaph.)

In Memory

In prime of life most suddenly sad tidings to relate
Here view my utter destiny and pity my sad fate
I by a Shot which rapid flew
Was instantly struck dead
Lord pardon the offender who
My Precious Blood did shed
        In memory of John Perry, Mariner, who was
        unfortunately killed by a Cannon ball by a person
        unknown In ye year 1779 Aged 24 yrs June ye 5

ANON.
(On a gravestone in Lansallos.)

Cherry Stones

Here lies the body of Mary Jones,
who died of eating cherry stones.
Her name was Smith it was not Jones,
but Jones was put to rhyme with stones.

ANON.

399

Felix Randal

Felix Randal the farrier, O is he dead then? my duty all
    ended,
Who have watched his mould of man, big-boned and hardy-
    handsome
Pining, pining, till time when reason rambled in it and some
Fatal four disorders, fleshed there, all contended?

Sickness broke him. Impatient, he cursed at first, but mended
Being anointed and all; though a heavenlier heart began some
Months earlier, since I had our sweet reprieve and ransom
Tendered to him. Ah well, God rest him all road ever he
    offended!

This seeing the sick endears them to us, us too it endears.
My tongue had taught thee comfort, touch had quenched thy
    tears,
Thy tears that touched my heart, child, Felix, poor Felix
    Randal;
How far from then forethought of, all thy more boisterous years,
When thou at the random grim forge, powerful amidst peers,
Didst fettle for the great grey drayhorse his bright and
    battering sandal!

GERARD MANLEY HOPKINS

(Felix Spencer, a thirty-one-year-old farrier, was a parishioner of Hopkins's in Liverpool
who died of pulmonary consumption on 21 April 1880.)

Sleeping at Last

Sleeping at last, the struggle and horror past,
Sleeping at last, the trouble and tumult over,
    Cold and white, out of sight of friend and of lover,
    Sleeping at last.

No more a tired heart downcast or overcast,
No more pangs that wring or shifting fears that hover,
 Sleeping at last in a dreamless sleep locked fast.

Fast asleep. Singing birds in their leafy cover
 Cannot wake her, nor shake her the gusty blast.
Under the purple thyme and the purple clover
     Sleeping at last.

CHRISTINA ROSSETTI
(Her last poem, written shortly before her death.)

Meanwhile

Meanwhile she comes back to me whenever I sleep, in my dream
And I say to her, welcome back, sit down in the meantime,
And she straightens the pillow, as always,
For it is unnatural for a mother not to straighten her son's pillow,
And for the son to be the one who straightens his mother's,
Wiping her cold sweat, lightly touching her hair,
Holding her cold hand, saying fear not
From the place you are going you shall not come back
Empty-handed, the way you came back so many times in the past
As the place you are going is a place of no hopes,
And no loss, remorse, sorrow, nor motherly pain,
The place you are going is short of nothing. It's a whole place.

NATAN ZACH
(Translated by Amos Oz.)

When You are Old

When you are old and grey and full of sleep,
And nodding by the fire, take down this book,
And slowly read, and dream of the soft look
Your eyes had once, and of their shadows deep;

How many loved your moments of glad grace,
And loved your beauty with love false or true,
But one man loved the pilgrim soul in you,
And loved the sorrows of your changing face;

And bending down beside the glowing bars,
Murmur, a little sadly, how Love fled
And paced upon the mountains overhead
And hid his face amid a crowd of stars.

W. B. YEATS

Fire and Ice

Some say the world will end in fire,
Some say in ice.
From what I've tasted of desire
I hold with those who favor fire.
But if it had to perish twice,
I think I know enough of hate
To say that for destruction ice
Is also great
And would suffice.

ROBERT FROST

Ghosts, Fire, Water
On the Hiroshima panels by Iri Maruki and Toshiko Akamatsu

These are the ghosts of the unwilling dead,
Grey ghosts of that imprinted flash of memory
Whose flaming and eternal instant haunts
The speechless dark with dread and anger.

Grey, out of pale nothingness their agony appears.
Like ash they are blown and blasted on the wind's
Vermilion breathlessness, like shapeless smoke
Their shapes are torn across the paper sky.

These scarred and ashen ghosts are quick
With pain's unutterable speech, their flame-cracked flesh
Writhes and is heavy as the worms, the bitter dirt;
Lonely as in death they bleed, naked as in birth.

They greet each other in a ghastly paradise,
These ghosts who cannot come with gifts and flowers.
Here they receive each other with disaster's common love,
Covering one another's pain with shrivelled hands.

They are not beautiful, yet beauty is in their truth.
There is no easy music in their silent screams,
No ordered dancing in their grief's distracted limbs.
Their shame is ours. We, too, are haunted by their fate.

In the shock of flame, their tears brand our flesh,
We twist in their furnace, and our scorching throats
Parch for the waters where the cool dead float.
We press our lips upon the river where they drink, and drown.

Their voices call to us, in pain and indignation:
'This is what you have done to us!'
– Their accusation is our final hope. Be comforted.
Yes, we have heard you, ghosts of our indifference,

We hear your cry, we understand your warnings.
We, too, shall refuse to accept our fate!
Haunt us with the truth of our betrayal
Until the earth's united voices shout refusal, sing your peace.

Forgive us, that we had to see your passion to remember
What we must never again deny: *Love one another*.

JAMES KIRKUP 1923–

The Hollow Men

A penny for the Old Guy

I

We are the hollow men
We are the stuffed men
Leaning together
Headpiece filled with straw. Alas!
Our dried voices, when
We whisper together
Are quiet and meaningless
As wind in dry grass
Or rats' feet over broken glass
In our dry cellar

Shape without form, shade without colour,
Paralysed force, gesture without motion;

Those who have crossed
With direct eyes, to death's other Kingdom
Remember us – if at all – not as lost
Violent souls, but only
As the hollow men
The stuffed men.

II

Eyes I dare not meet in dreams
In death's dream kingdom
These do not appear:
There, the eyes are
Sunlight on a broken column
There, is a tree swinging
And voices are
In the wind's singing
More distant and more solemn
Than a fading star.

Let me be no nearer
In death's dream kingdom

Let me also wear
Such deliberate disguises
Rat's coat, crowskin, crossed staves
In a field
Behaving as the wind behaves
No nearer –

Not that final meeting
In the twilight kingdom

III

This is the dead land
This is cactus land
Here the stone images
Are raised, here they receive
The supplication of a dead man's hand
Under the twinkle of a fading star.

Is it like this
In death's other kingdom
Waking alone
At the hour when we are
Trembling with tenderness
Lips that would kiss
Form prayers to broken stone.

IV

The eyes are not here
There are no eyes here
In this valley of dying stars
In this hollow valley
This broken jaw of our lost kingdoms

In this last of meeting places
We grope together
And avoid speech
Gathered on this beach of the tumid river

Sightless, unless
The eyes reappear
As the perpetual star
Multifoliate rose
Of death's twilight kingdom
The hope only
Of empty men.

V

Here we go round the prickly pear
Prickly pear prickly pear
Here we go round the prickly pear
At five o'clock in the morning.

Between the idea
And the reality
Between the motion
And the act
Falls the Shadow

For Thine is the Kingdom

Between the conception
And the creation
Between the emotion
And the response
Falls the Shadow

Life is very long

Between the desire
And the spasm
Between the potency
And the existence
Between the essence
And the descent
Falls the Shadow

For Thine is the Kingdom

For Thine is
Life is
For Thine is the

This is the way the world ends
This is the way the world ends
This is the way the world ends
Not with a bang but a whimper.

T. S. ELIOT

501. *This World is not Conclusion*

This World is not Conclusion.
A Species stands beyond –
Invisible, as Music –
But positive, as Sound –
It beckons, and it baffles –
Philosophy – don't know –
And through a Riddle, at the last –
Sagacity, must go –
To guess it, puzzles scholars –
To gain it, Men have borne
Contempt of Generations
And Crucifixion, shown –
Faith slips – and laughs, and rallies –
Blushes, if any see –
Plucks at a twig of Evidence –
And asks a Vane, the way –
Much Gesture, from the Pulpit –
Strong Hallelujahs roll –
Narcotics cannot still the Tooth
That nibbles at the soul –

EMILY DICKINSON

Death, Be Not Proud

Death, be not proud, though some have called thee
Mighty and dreadful, for thou are not so;
For those whom thou think'st thou dost overthrow
Die not, poor Death; nor yet canst thou kill me.
From rest and sleep, which but thy picture be,
Much pleasure; then from thee much more must flow;
And soonest our best men with thee do go –
Rest of their bones and souls' delivery!
Thou'rt slave to fate, chance, kings and desperate men,
And dost with poison, war, and sickness dwell;
And poppy or charms can make us sleep as well
And better than thy stroke. Why swell'st thou then?
One short sleep past, we wake eternally,
And Death shall be no more: Death, thou shalt die.

JOHN DONNE

Psalm 23

The Lord is my shepherd; I shall not want.
He maketh me to lie down in green pastures;
He leadeth me beside the still waters.
He restoreth my soul;
He leadeth me in the paths of righteousness for his name's sake.
Yea, though I walk through the valley of the shadow of death,
I will fear no evil: for thou art with me;
Thy rod and thy staff they comfort me.
Thou preparest a table before me in the presence of mine enemies:
Thou anointest my head with oil; my cup runneth over.
Surely goodness and mercy shall follow me all the days of my life,
And I will dwell in the house of the Lord forever.

THE BIBLE

Fear No More

from *Cymbeline*, Act IV, Scene ii

Fear no more the heat o' th' sun
Nor the furious winter's rages;
Thou thy worldly task hast done,
Home art gone, and ta'en thy wages.
Golden lads and girls all must,
As chimney sweepers, come to dust.

Fear no more the frown o' th' great;
Thou art past the tyrant's stroke.
Care no more to clothe and eat;
To thee the reed is as the oak.
The sceptre, learning physic, must
All follow this and come to dust.

Fear no more the lightning flash,
Nor th' all-dreaded thunder-stone;
Fear not slander, censure rash;
Thou hast finish'd joy and moan.
All lovers young, all lovers must
Consign to thee and come to dust.

No exorciser harm thee!
Nor no witchcraft charm thee!
Ghost unlaid forbear thee!
Quiet consummation have,
And renowned by thy grave!

WILLIAM SHAKESPEARE

Acknowledgements

The compiler and publishers would like to thank the following for permission to include copyright material in this anthology:

Anthony Sheil Associates Ltd for 'The Mountaineers' by Dannie Abse from *Poems 1951–56*; Bloodaxe Books Ltd for 'A Touch of Impatience' by Fleur Adcock from *The Virgin and the Nightingale* (1983); Oxford University Press Ltd for 'Smokers for Celibacy' by Fleur Adcock from *Time Zones* (1991); Bloodaxe Books Ltd for 'He Loved Three Things' and 'You Suck My Soul' by Anna Akhmatova from *Selected Poems* (1989), translated by Richard McKane; Hutchinson Ltd for 'A Book-shop Idyll' by Kingsley Amis; Bloodaxe Books Ltd for 'Snow Joke' by Simon Armitage from *Zoom* (1989); Faber & Faber Ltd for 'Too Dear, Too Vague', 'Twelve Songs, IX', 'When Statesmen Gravely Say "We Must be Realistic"' (Short), extract from 'In Memory of W. B. Yeats, III', 'Leap Before You Look', 'To the Man-in-the-Street, Who, I'm Sorry to Say' (Short), 'Night Mail', 'Lullaby (1937)', and 'If I Could Tell You' by W. H. Auden from *Collected Poems*; Peters Fraser & Dunlop Group Ltd for 'Jim', 'Tarantella' and 'Lines to a Don' by Hilaire Belloc; John Murray (Publishers) Ltd for 'Subaltern's Love Song', 'Late Flowering Lust', 'Upper Lambourne' and 'The City' by John Betjeman; *The Times* Ltd for 'For the Fallen' by Laurence Binyon from *The Times*, September 1914; Jon Silkin and David McDuff (translators) for 'The Kite' by Alexander Blok; Carcanet Press Ltd for 'Report on Experience' by Edmund Blunden from *Selected Poems*; Paul Berry (literary executor) for 'Perhaps' by Vera Brittain from *Verses of a V.A.D.* (Erskine Macdonald Ltd, 1918); Enitharmon Press Ltd for 'Turn the Key Deftly' by Edwin Brock; Anvil Press Poetry Ltd for 'Punishment Enough' by Norman Cameron from *Collected Poems*, edited by Warren Hope and Jonathan Barker (Anvil Press, 1990); Hogarth Press/Chatto & Windus Ltd and Harcourt Brace Jovanovich Inc. for 'Gray', 'Days of 1903', 'Candles' and 'Body Remember' by C. P. Cavafy from *The Complete Poems of Cavafy*, translated by Rae Dalven; HarperCollins Publishers for 'Afterwards' by Margaret Postgate Cole from *Poems*; Faber & Faber Ltd for 'I Think I am in Love'

411

Index of Authors

Abse, Dannie 327–8
Adcock, Fleur 101, 147–9
Akhmatova, Anna 106, 318
Allingham, William 11–12
American folk song 132–3
Amichai, Yehuda 247
Amis, Kingsley 274–5
Anon.
  Addendum to the Ten Commandments 243
  An old Cornish litany 22
  Burns grace at Kirkcudbright 325
  Busts and bosoms have I known 102
  Cheltenham waters 379
  Cherry Stones 399
  Frankie and Johnny 132–3
  Hymn and prayer for civil servants 340
  In memory 399
  Indian prayer 380
  Little Willie 17
  London bells 19
  Lovey-dovey 89
  Mary's lamb 322
  On a tired housewife 384
  On Prince Frederick 370–1
  Peas 324–5
  Polly Perkins 141
  Poor but honest 130–1
  Save the tot 223–4
  Solomon Grundy 23
  The bleed'n' sparrer 293–4
  The common cormorant 52
  The dying airman 227–8
  The foggy, foggy dew 118–19
  The vicar of Bray 300–1
  The wearing of the green 197–8
  We have known treasure 89–90
  Young men 322
  Your face 88
Armitage, Simon 345–6
Arnold, Matthew 230–1, 380–1
Attwell, Mabel Lucy 8
Auden, W. H.
  If I could tell you 112–13
  In Memory of W. B. Yeats 218–19
  Leap before you look 271
  Lullaby 86–7
  Night mail 331–3
  Note on intellectuals 334
  Twelve Songs, IX 152–3

  Too dear, too vague 119–20
  When statesmen gravely say 167

Barrington, Patrick 342–3
Beddoes, Thomas Lovell 80, 231, 264–6
Belloc, Hilaire 19–21, 67–8, 334–6
Betjeman, John 142–3, 317, 334, 344, 354–5
Bible, The 299, 408
Binyon, Laurence 389–90
Bishop, Morris 328
Blake, William 111, 258–61, 271–2, 338
Blok, Alexander 154–5, 214
Blunden, Edmund 347
Bourdillon, Francis William 117–18
Bridges, Robert 81–2
Brittain, Vera 207
Brock, Edwin 357
Brooke, Rupert 93–4, 135, 203, 310–11
Browning, Elizabeth Barrett 82, 124–5
Browning, Robert 55–9, 305–6, 307
Buller, Arthur 140
Bunyan, John 184
Burns, Robert 110, 178–9, 289–90, 349–50
Byron, Lord 161–2

Cameron, Norman 226
Cannan, May Wedderburn 209–10
Carroll, Lewis 26–8, 32
Causley, Charles 14–15, 145, 222–3
Cavafy, C. P. 93, 108, 356, 358
Cawser, Elsie 227
Chaucer, Geoffrey 244
Cheney, John Vance 295–6
Chesterton, G. K. 33, 165, 182, 233–5
Churchill, Winston 219, 220
Clough, Arthur Hugh 181
Cole, Margaret Postgate 218
Coleridge, Samuel Taylor 285–7
Cope, Wendy 96, 154
Cornford, Frances 204–5
Couzyn, Jeni 46–9
Cummings, E. E. 130

Davies, W. H. 294
Day Lewis, C. 66–7
De La Mare, Walter 263–4
Desprez, Frank 114–17

Dickinson, Emily, 6, 156, 263, 326, 407–8
Didsbury, Peter 338–9
Dobell, Eva 212
Dobson, Austin 389
Donne, John 235, 397–8, 408
Dowson, Ernest 88–9
Dyke, Henry van 242

Ecclesiastes 5, 73–4
Ecclesiasticus 386–7
Eliot, T. S. 68–9, 99–100, 158, 404–7
Emerson, Ralph Waldo 398
Ephelia 123

Fainlight, Ruth 227
Fitzgerald, Edward 363–4
Frost, Robert 184–5, 301–2, 402
Fuller, Roy 75, 229

Gilbert, W. S. 49–52, 53–5, 268–70
Gillilan, Pamela 366–7, 367–9
Gimson, A. C. S. 243–4
Goldsmith, Oliver 142
Graham, Harry 30, 228
Graham, James, Marquis of Montrose 301
Graves, Robert 108–9
Gray, Thomas 336–7
Gray, Victor 345
Grenfell, Julian 203
Gunn, Thom 5

Hammarskjöld, Dag 284
Hardy, Thomas 100, 197, 369–70
Hare, M. E. 340
Hawker, Robert S. 193–4
Heaney, Seamus 200–2
Henley, W. E. 385
Herbert, A. P. 319–22
Herbert, George 132
Herbert, Zbigniew 153–4
Herrick, Roderick 101
Hickson, William E. 30
Holmes, Oliver Wendell 106–7, 350–2
Holub, Miroslav 156
Hood, Thomas 10–11, 13–14, 118, 290–2
Hopkins, Gerard Manley 9, 400
Houseman, A. E. 95–6, 283–4, 379
Howitt, Mary 30–1
Hughes, Langston 190–3
Hughes, Ted 28, 28–9

Hunt, James Leigh 247

Jarmain, John 220, 221
Jeremiah 161
Job 239–40
Jonson, Ben 10, 44

Keats, John 117, 120–1, 129
Key, Francis Scott 185–6
Kipling, Rudyard
    A code of morals 149–50
    A dead statesman 167
    A smuggler's song 65–6
    A truthful song 287–9
    England 231
    Gehazi 341–2
    If – 72–3
    Recessional 383
    The Fabulists 215–16
    The female of the species 251–4
    The Mary Gloster 371–9
    The virginity 83
    The way through the woods 359
    Ulster 198–9
Kirkup, James 402–3
Kizer, Carolyn 358–9
Klemm, Wilhelm 212–13
Kumin, Maxine 139–40

Landor, W. S. 146
Lang, A. 158
Larkin, Philip
    Administration 138
    Annus mirabilis 98–9
    Marriage 158
    Plymouth 325
    Sad steps 318
    Talking in bed 319
    The view 315
    This be the verse 346
Lawrence, D. H. 136–7, 137
Lear, Edward 15–16, 18
Lecky, William Edward Hartpole 394–5
Lincoln, Abraham 187–8
Longfellow, Henry Wadsworth 60–3, 79, 254–7, 297–8, 352–4
Lorde, Audre 146–7
Lowell, James Russell 163–4, 387–9
Lowell, Robert 228–9

Macaulay, Thomas Babington 168–78
McCrea, John 205
McGinley, Phyllis 254

McHarrie, Dennis 166
MacNeice, Louis 144, 272–3
Malone, Walter 249–50
Marks, Leo 380
Marvell, Andrew 102–3
Masefield, John 293, 326
Melville, Herman 188–9
Mew, Charlotte 217
Meynell, Alice 94
Millay, Edna St Vincent 86, 161, 369
Miller, Alice Duer 231–2
Milne, A. A. 23–4, 24–5, 35
Milton, John 388
Mitchel, Adrian 134
Montrose, James Graham, Marquis of 301

Nash, Ogden
    England expects 309–10
    Old men 384
    Peekaboo, I almost see you 315–16
    Samson agonistes 319
    Song of the open road 257–8
    The guppy 8
    To my valentine 137–8
Neruda, Pablo 157
Newbolt, Sir Henry 183

O'Reilly, John Boyle 241–2
O'Shaughnessy, Arthur William Edgar
    284–5
Owen, Wilfred
    Anthem for doomed youth 210–11
    Dulce et decorum est 211
    Greater love 214–15
    Insensibility 207–9
    The dead-beat 203–4
Oz, Amos 401

Pagis, Dan 229–30
Parker, Dorothy 134, 140
Parkin, Philip 242–3
Pasternak, Boris 111, 333
Plath, Sylvia 323–4, 328–9
Plomer, William 224–6
Pope, Alexander 244–5
Porter, Cole 96–8
Previn, Dory 126–8, 128–9
Price, Jonathan 22
Prys–Jones, A. G. 167–8
Pushkin, Alexander 135

Raleigh, Walter 346
Ratushinskaya, Irina 112, 276–8, 278–9

Rochester, John Wilmot, Earl of 299,
    348–9
Rossetti, Christina 79–80, 90, 355, 355–
    6, 400–1
Rukeyser, Muriel 135–6
Rumens, Carol 147

St Paul 241, 245–6
Sandburg, Carl 215, 274
Sarton, May 113
Scott, Sir Walter 109–10
Seeger, Alan 164–5
Selkirk, Alexander 261–3
Shakespeare, William
    Before Agincourt 180–1
    Before Harfleur 179–80
    Fear No More 409
    Friends, Romans, countrymen 385–6
    Full fathom five 64
    Grief fills the room up 7
    Is this a dagger? 302
    Prologue, King Henry V 162–3
    Seven ages 1
    Sonnet 94 94–5
    Sonnet 116 91
    Sonnet 129 105
    Sonnet 138 86
    The quality of mercy 240–1
    This above all 74
    This England 306–7
    To be, or not to be 302–4
    Tomorrow 365
Sharples, Stanley J. 138–9
Shelley, Percy Bysshe
    Adonais 395–7
    Chorus of spirits 275–6
    Demogorgon 364–5
    Invocation 103–4
    The longest journey 84–5
    To – 92
Sidney, Sir Philip 90–1
Silverstein, Shel 21, 52–3
Sims, George R. 390–4
Skye, Augusta 71–2
Smith, Stevie 33–4, 337–38, 339, 344–5,
    357
Spender, Stephen 152
Spenser, Edmund 80, 82–3, 105
Stevenson, Anne 5
Stevenson, Robert Louis 17, 29, 39, 399
Swift, Jonathan 347–8

Tabb, John Banister 384

417

Tagore, Rabindranath 81, 92, 93, 123–4
Tennyson, Alfred, Lord 194–5, 329–31
Thackeray, William Makepeace 304
Thomas, Dylan 39–43, 365–6, 381–2, 382
Thompson, Francis 266–8
Tolkein, J. R. R. 360
Townsend, Sue 34
Traditional 8, 9, 45–6
Tsvetayeva, Marina 155

Waller, Edmund 85
Watkins, Vernon 43–4
Wesley, Charles 8
Whitman, Walt 186–7, 189–90, 242
Whitney, Helen Hay 297
Whittier, John Greenleaf 63–4
Whitworth, John 70–1
Wilberforce, Bishop Samuel 338
Wilcox, Ella Wheeler 122, 150–1, 270–1

Wilde, Oscar 64–5, 279–83
Wilmot, John, Earl of Rochester 299, 348–9
Wilson, T. P. Cameron 205–6
Woddis, Roger 232
Wolfe, Charles 195–6
Wolfe, Humbert 308–9
Wordsworth, William 257, 305, 343–4

Yeats, W. B.
    A drinking song 131
    A last confession 139
    An Irish airman foresees his death 166
    Final apology 398
    Never give all the heart 95
    On woman 250–1
    Politics 316
    The arrow 79
    The mermaid 153
    The old stone cross 308
    When you are old 401–2

Index of Titles

Abou Ben Adhem 247
Addendum to the Ten Commandments 243
Address at Gettysburg 187–8
Administration 138
Adonais 395–7
After love 139–40
Afterwards 218
Agnostic's creed, The 249–50
And death shall have no dominion 382
Angels and devils the following day 128–9
Annus mirabilis 98–9
Anthem for doomed youth 210–11
Arrow, The 79
Arrow and the song, The 79
At a war grave 220
Auguries of innocence 258–61

Baby Song 5
Bagpipe music 272–3
Ballad of Glyn Dwr's rising, A 167–8
Ballad of Reading Gaol, The 279–83
Ballad of the oysterman, The 106–7
Barefoot boy, The 63–4
Bargain, The 90–1
Bathroom Motto 8
Because I liked you better 379
Before Agincourt 180–1
Before Harfleur 179–80
Belle dame sans merci, La 120–1
Bill and Joe 350–2
Bleed'n' sparrer, The 293–4
Bloody men 154
Body, remember . . . 358
Bookshop idyll, A 274–5
Boring 70–1
Bridge, The 352–4
British journalist, The 308–9
Brook, The 329–31
Buckingham Palace 23–4
Burial of Sir John Moore after Corunna,
    The 195–6
Burns grace at Kirkcudbright 325
Busts and bosoms have I known 102

Candles 356
Cave man's prayer, The 247–8
Celia Celia 134
Cenotaph, The 217
Ceremony after a fire raid 365–6
Charge of the Light Brigade, The 194–5

Cheltenham waters 379
Cherry Stones 399
Chief petty officer 222–3
Chorus of Spirits 275–6
Christmas in Africa 46–9
City, The 344
Clearing station 212–13
Clod and the pebble, The 111
Code of morals, A 149–50
Code poem for the French resistance 380
Collier, The 43–4
Come away 366–7
Common cormorant, The 52
Considered reply to a child, A 22
Counting the beats 108–9
Crab 28–9

Daybreak 152
Days of 1903 356
Dead in Europe, The 228–9
Dead statesman, A 167
Dead-beat, The 203–4
Death, be not proud 408
Dedication to my wife, A 158
Delusions I did cherish 93
Demogorgon 364–5
Destruction of Sennacherib, The 161–2
Do not go gentle into that good night 381–2
Doctor Foster 9
Donkey, The 33, 33–4
Don't quite know 75
Dover Beach 230–1
Drake's drum 183
Dream-pedlary 264–6
Drink, Britannia 231
Drinking song, A 131
Drummer Hodge 197
Dulce et decorum est 211
Dying airman, The 227–8

Echo 90
18 June 1961 284
El Alamein 221
Elegy in a country churchyard 165
End, The 35
England 231
England, This 306–7
England expects 309–10
Englishman's home, The 228
Episode 153–4

419

Evolution 384
Exultation 326

Fabulists, The 215–16
Fairies, The 11–12
Fame is a food that dead men eat 389
Fancy 7
Farewell, A 113
Fear no more 409
Felix Randal 400
Female of the species, The 251–4
Figlia che piange, La 99–100
Final apology 398
Fire and ice 402
First day, The 79–80
First Lord's song, The 53–5
Flying bum: 1944, The 224–6
Foggy, foggy dew, The 118–19
For the fallen 389–90
Four things 242
Frankie and Johnny 132–3
Friends, Romans, countrymen 385–6
Full fathom five 64

Gehazi 341–2
Gentle Jesus, meek and mild 8
Ghosts, fire, water 402–3
Gift outright, The 184–5
Grand old Duke of York, The 8
Grass 215
Gray 108
Great Carbuncle, The 328–9
Greater love 214–5
Greatest of these, The 245–6
Green 137
Grief fills the room up 7
Guppy, The 8

Handbag 227
He loved three things 318
Hill, The 135
Hollow men, The 404–7
Home-thoughts, from abroad 307
Horatius 168–78
Hound of heaven, The 266–8
House, The 154–5
Hug o'war 21
Hymn and prayer for civil servants 340
Hymn to God the father, A 397–8

I had a duck-billed platypus 342–3
i like my body when it is with your 130
I loved you 135

I remember 357
I remember, I remember 10–11
I saw a jolly hunter 14–15
I think I am in love 96
If – 72–3
If I could tell you 112–13
Impromptu on Charles II 299
In death divided 369–70
In Flanders fields 205
In memory 399
In Memory of W. B. Yeats 218–19
In praise of cocoa, Cupid's nightcap 138–9
In praise of famous men 386–7
Indian prayer 380
Insensibility 207–9
Into Battle 203
Invictus 385
Invocation 103–4
Irish airman foresees his death, An 166
Is this a dagger? 302
It is time to be old 398
It's the first of January 276–8

Jazz fantasia 274
Jellyfish 28
Jim 19–21
John Anderson, my jo 349–50

King of Brentford, The 304
Kite, The 214
Kubla Khan 285–7

Lamplight 209–10
Landlord's tale, The 60–3
Lasca 114–17
Last confession, A 139
Last word, The 380–1
Late-flowering lust 317
Leap before you look 271
Leaves of grass 242
Leisure 294
Lemon haired ladies 126–8
Lepanto 182
Let America be America again 190–3
Let's do it, let's fall in love 96–8
Limerick 340
Lines from Endymion 129
Lines to a don 334–6
Listeners, The 263–4
Little Willie 17
Lochinvar 109–10
London, 1802 305
London bells 19

Long, dark months 220
Longest journey, The 84–5
Looking at each other 135–6
Lord is full of mercy, The 247
Lost leader, The 305–6
Love 156
Loved you Wednesday 86
Lover's quarrel, A 150–1
Lovey-dovey 89
Luck 166
Lullaby 86–7
Lust 93–4

Macavity: the mystery cat 68–9
Magpies in Picardy 205–6
Make bright the arrows 161
Man that looks on glass, A 132
Man with the hoe, The 295–6
Man's a man for a' that, A 289–90
Man's requirements, A 124–5
March in the ranks hard-prest, and the road
   unknown, A 186–7
Marriage 158
Martyr, The 188–9
Mary Gloster, The 371–9
Mary's lamb 322
Meanwhile 401
Mermaid, The 153
Monarch of all I survey 261–3
Mothers who don't understand 71–2
Mountaineers, The 327–8
My delight and thy delight 81–2
My heart leaps up 257
My love is like a red, red rose 110
My love is like to ice 105
My shadow 17
My young man's a Cornishman 145
Mystery 338

Naked 157
Never give all the heart 95
New eyes each year 242–3
New year's eve 136–7
Night has a thousand eyes, The 117–18
Night mail 331–3
Nightmare, The 268–70
No, I'm not afraid 278–9
No man is an iland 235
Non sum qualis eram bonae sub regno
   Cynarae 88–9
Not waving but drowning 345
Note on intellectuals 334
Now that I am forever with child 146–7

O captain! my captain! 189–90
Ode [we are the music makers] 284–5
Oedipus 344
Of all the souls that stand create 263
Oh who is that young sinner 283–4
Old Cornish litany, An 22
Old men 384
Old stone cross, The 308
Old Vicarage, Grantchester, The 310–11
Old woman, The 9
On a tired housewife 384
On an old song 394–5
On my first daughter 10
On my son 44
On Prince Frederick 370–1
On women 250–1
Once I was young 243–4
Once to every man and nation 163–4
One day I wrote 82–3
One perfect rose 134
'Ostler Joe 390–4
Owl and the Pussy Cat, The 18

Parental ode to my son, aged three years and
   five months, A 13–14
Peas 324–5
Peekaboo, I almost see you 315–16
Perhaps 207
Pied piper of Hamelin, The 55–9
Pluck 212
Plymouth 325
Poem 111
Poem for Blok 155
Politics 316
Polly Perkins 141
Poor but honest 130–1
Pre-existence 204–5
Price of wisdom, The 239–40
Priest in the sabbath dawn addresses his
   somnolent mistress, A 338–9
Prologue, King Henry V 162–3
Psalm 23 408
Psalm 146 299
Pseudo-hymn 338
Punishment enough 226

Quality of mercy, The 240–1
Quangle Wangle's hat, The 15–16

Recessional 383
Reflection, A 118
Remember now thy creator 73–4
Rendezvous 164–5

Renouncement 94
Report on experience 347
Requiem 399
Resolutions when I come to be old 347–8
Return 93
Road not taken, The 301–2
Roads go ever ever on 360
Rosa mystica 64–5
Rose Aylmer 146
Royal naval air station 229
Rubá'iyat of Omar Khayyám, The 363–4

Sad steps 318
Saddest lines, The 157
Safe period 147
Salvage song (or: the housewife's dream) 227
Samson agonistes 319
Satire upon the heads; or, never a barrel the better herring 336–7
Save the tot 223–4
Say not the struggle naught availeth 181
Scots, wha hae 178–9
Song of Torrismond, The 80
Sea-fever 326
Secret people, The 233–5
Seven ages 1
Sick 52–3
Sleeping at last 400–1
Smokers for celibacy 147–9
Smuggler's song, A 65–6
Sneezles 24–5
Snow joke 345–6
So let us love 80
Social note 134
Soldier, The 203
Solitude 244–5, 270–1
Solomon Grundy 23
Song 297, 355–6
Song by the subconscious self 158
Song of a young lady to her ancient lover, A 348–9
Song of Hiawatha, The 254–7
Song of the open road 257–8
Song of the shirt, The 290–2
Song of the western men, The 193–4
Sonnet 18 94–5
Sonnet 43 82
Sonnet 116 91
Sonnet 129 105
Sonnet 138 86
Sonnet XVI 388
Speech of silence, The 122

Spider and the fly, The 30–1
Spring and fall 9
Star-spangled banner, The 185–6
Stern parent, The 30
Student, A 244
Subaltern's love-song, A 142–3
Sunday morning, King's Cambridge 334
Suburban classes, The 339
Surgeons 6

Talking in bed 319
Tarantella 67–8
Tender-heartedness 30
Their finest hour 219
There was a young lady 140
They who are near to me 81
Thin people, The 323–4
Think of Europe 232
This above all 74
This be the verse 346
This world is not conclusion 407
Thou shalt dwell in silence 123–4
Thunderstorm in town, A 100
Time 369
Time for everything, A 5
To – 92
To any reader 39
To be, or not to be 302–4
To George Washington 387–9
To his coy mistress 102–3
To my valentine 137–8
To one that asked me why I loved J. G. 123
To Phyllis 85
To the French people 220
To the Man-in-the-Street, Who, I'm Sorry to Say 336
Tomorrow 365
Too dear, too vague 119–20
Touch, The 301
Touch of impatience, A 100–1
Tree house 21
Trial and error 254
Trilogy for X 144
Truthful song, A 287–9
Turn the key deftly 357
'Twas at the pictures, child, we met 319–22
Twelve Songs, IX 152–3
Tyger, The 271–2

Ulster 198–9
Under Milk Wood 39–43
Unfortunate coincidence 140

422

Unto a broken heart, 1704 156
Uphill 355
Upon the nipples of Julia's breast 101
Upon Westminster Bridge 343–4
Upper Lambourne 354–5
Urals for the first time, The 333

Vagabond 293
Valiant-for-truth's song 184
Vicar of Bray, The 300–1
Vicar of Wakefield, The 142
Victory, The 5
View, The 315
Village blacksmith, The 297–8
Virginity, The 83

Walking away 66–7
Walking song 30
Walrus and the carpenter, The 26–8
Warning to cat owners, A 34
Way through the woods, The 359
We have been here before 328
We have known treasure 89–90
We two lay sunk 92

Wearing of the Green, The 197–8
What is good 241–2
What the bones know 358–9
Whatever you say, say nothing 200–2
Whatsoever things are true 241
When I was one-and-twenty 95–6
When statesmen gravely say 167
When you are old 401–2
When you died 367–9
Where are you, my prince? 112
Where be you going, you Devon maid?
   117
Where go the boats? 29
White cliffs, The 231–2
Why are the clergy . . . ? 337–38
Widdicombe Fair 45–6
Wishes of an elderly man 346
Written with a pencil in a sealed wagon
   229–30

Yarn of the Nancy Bell, The 49–52
'You are old, father William' 32
You suck my soul 106
Young men 322
Your face 88

Index of First Lines

A box of teak, a box of sandalwood 325
A good sword and trusty hand! 193–4
A handsome young airman lay dying 227–8
A lady is smarter than a gentleman, maybe 254
A man that looks on glass 132
A March in the ranks hard-prest, and the road unknown 186–7
A mermaid found a swimming lad 153
A single flow'r he sent me, since we met 134
A statesman is an easy man 308
A Student came from Oxford town also 244
A thing of beauty is a joy for ever 129
A Tree house, a free house 21
Abou Ben Adhem (may his tribe increase!) 247
Above the field drowses the kite 214
After the planes unloaded, we fell down 228–9
Afterwards, the compromise 139–40
Ah, my Beloved, fill the Cup that clears 363–4
Ah, what avails the sceptred race! 146
All the world's a stage 1
Ancient person, for whom I 348–9
And death shall have no dominion 382
And these few precepts in thy memory 74
And why you come complaining 86
As from the house your mother sees 39
At dawn she lay with her profile at that angle 152
At last I ceased repining, at last I accept my fate 249–50

Because I liked you better 379
Bent double, like old beggars under sacks 211
Between the GARDENING and the COOKERY 274–5
Billy, in one of his nice new sashes 30
Bloody men are like bloody buses 154
Body, remember not only how much you were loved 358
Breathless, we flung us on the windy hill 135
Business men with awkward hips 344

Busts and bosoms have I known 102
By the time you swear you're his 140

Cats don't have a Highway Code 34
Christopher Robin 24–5
Come, dear old comrade, you and I 350–2
Come to me in the silence of the night 90
Creep into thy narrow bed 380–1
Crippled for life at seventeen 212
Cromwell, our chief of men, who through a cloud 388

Dark brown is the river 29
Day by day your estimation clocks up 138
Death, be not proud, though some have called thee 408
Delusions I did cherish 93
Despite the drums we were ready to go 327–8
Do not go gentle into that good night 381–2
Do you remember an Inn 67–8
Doctor Foster went to Glo'ster 9
Does the road wind uphill all the way? 355
Drake he's in his hammock an' a thousand mile away 183
Drink, Britannia, Britannia, drink your Tea 231
Drum on your drums, batter on your banjoes 274
Dunno a heap about the what an' why 293

Earth has not anything to show more fair 343–4
Every morning there is war again 212–13
Exultation is the going 326

Fame is a food that dead men eat 389
Far better never to have loved 154–5
Farewell, thou child of my right hand, and joy 44
Father heard his children scream 30
Fear no more the heat o' th' sun 409
Felix Randal the farrier, O is he dead then? my duty all ended 400

File into yellow candle light, fair choristers of King's 334

For a while I shall still be leaving 113

Four things a man must learn to do 242

Fourscore and seven years ago our fathers brought 187–8

Frankie and Johnny were lovers, O Lordy, how they could love! 132–3

Friends, Romans, countrymen, lend me your ears 385–6

From Ghoulies and Ghosties 22

From the private ease of Mother's womb 5

Full fathom five thy father lies 64

Gentle Jesus, meek and mild 8

God bless our good and gracious King 299

GOD of our fathers, known of old 383

Good Friday was the day 188–9

Good night then: sleep to gather strength for the morning 220

Grief fills the room up of my absent child 7

Groping back to bed after a piss 318

Had we but world enough, and time 102–3

Half a league, half a league 194–5

Half past nine – high time for supper 138–9

Hamelin Town's in Brunswick 55–9

Happy are men who yet before they are killed 207–9

Happy the man, whose wish and care 244–5

Have ye beheld (with much delight) 101

He dropped, – more sullenly than wearily 203–4

He either fears his fate too much 301

He is older than the naval side of British history 222–3

He loved three things in this world 318

He will come out 284

He will unlock the four-hooked gate of her bra 147

Heard the one about the guy from Heaton Mersey? 345–6

Here, in this transport 229–30

Here is the test of wisdom 242

Here lie I and my four daughters 379

Here lies a poor woman who was always tired 384

Here lies Fred 370–1

Here lies the body of Mary Jones 399

Here lies to each her parents' ruth 10

His name 366–7

How can I, that girl standing there 316

How do I love thee? Let me count the ways 82

How many times do I love thee, dear? 80

How should I know? The enormous wheels of will 93–4

How the days went 146–7

I always eat peas with honey 324–5

I am a broken-hearted milkman, in grief I'm arrayed 141

I am Monarch of all I survey 261–3

'I cannot go to school today,' 52–3

I come from haunts of coot and hern 329–31

I could not dig: I dared not rob 167

I expect that the battle of Britain is about to begin 219

I fled Him, down the nights and down the days 266–8

I had a duck-billed platypus when I was up at Trinity 342–3

I have a little shadow that goes in and out with me 17

I have a rendezvous with Death 164–5

I have been young, and now am not too old 347

I have loved England, dearly and deeply 231–2

I know not what my secret is 158

I know that I shall meet my fate 166

I laid me down upon the shore 204–5

i like my body when it is with your 130

'I love you,' you said between two mouthfuls of pudding 22

I loved you; even now I may confess 135

I must down to the seas again, to the lonely sea and the sky 326

I must not think of thee; and, tired yet strong 94

I never found them again – those things so speedily lost . . . 356

I never saw a man who looked 279–83

I never was attached to that great sect 84–5

I praise him not; it were too late 387–9

I remember, I remember 10–11

425

I saw a jolly hunter 14–15
I shall rot here, with those whom in
their day 369–70
I shot an arrow into the air 79
I stood at eve, as the sun went down, by
a grave where a woman lies 390–4
I stood on the bridge at midnight 352–4
I suppose they'll say his last thoughts
were of simple things 166
I tell this tale, which is strictly true 287–
9
I test my bath before I sit 319
I think I am in 96
I think I remember this moorland 328
I think that I shall never see 257–8
I thought of your beauty, and this arrow
79
I thought you were my victory 5
I was patient at the start 100–1
I was playing golf the day 228
I weep for Adonais – he is dead 395–7
I will not play at tug o'war 21
I wish I could remember the first day
79–80
I wish I loved the Human Race 346
If England were what England seems
231
If I should die, think only this of me
203
If I were a Cassowary 338
If there were dreams to sell 264–6
If you can keep your head when all
about you 72–3
If you wake at midnight, and hear a
horse's feet 65–6
I'm dead bored 70–1
I'm writing just after an encounter 200–
2
In Flanders fields the poppies blow 205
In good King Charles's golden days 300–1
In Grantchester, in Grantchester! – 310–
11
In prime of life most suddenly sad
tidings to relate 399
In the low tide pools 28–9
In the Navy of the seventies 223–4
In the nightmare of the dark 218–19
In the vegetarian guest-house 224–6
In Xanadu did Kubla Khan a stately
pleasure-dome decree 285–7
Into the organpipes and steeples 365–6
'Is there anybody there?' said the
Traveller 263–4

Is there, for honest poverty 289–90
Is this a dagger which I see before me
302
It is eighteen years ago, almost to the
day 66–7
It is time to be old 398
It was a tall young oysterman lived by
the river-side 106–7
It was my bridal night I remember 357
It was such a pretty little donkey 33–4
It's all very well to write reviews 114–
17
It's no go the merrygoround, it's no go
the rickshaw 272–3
It's the first of January 276–8
I've paid for your sickest fancies; I've
humoured your crackedest whim
371–9

John Anderson, my jo, John 349–50
Just for a handful of silver he left us
305–6

Lady, lady, should you meet 134
Lars Porsena of Clusium 168–78
Last night, ah, yesternight, betwixt her
lips and mine 88–9
Laugh, and the world laughs with you
270–1
Lay your sleeping head, my love 86–7
Let America be America again 190–3
Let me not to the marriage of true minds
91
Let us now praise famous men, and our
fathers that begat us 386–7
Let us pause to consider the English
309–10
Listen my children, and you shall hear
60–3
Little snatch of ancient song 394–5
Little Willie from his mirror 17
Long, dark months of trials and
tribulations lie before us 220
Looking at a half-gray opal 108
Love by ambition 119–20
Love is for some a heavy cross 111
Love me Sweet, with all thou art 124–5
'Love seeketh not Itself to please' 111
loved i two men 128–9

Macavity's a Mystery Cat: he's called
the Hidden Paw 68–9
Make bright the arrows 161

Make bright the arrows; gather the 161
Márgarét, áre you grieving 9
Mary had a little lamb 322
May God be praised for woman 250–1
Meanwhile she comes back to me
    whenever I sleep, in my dream 401
Middle-aged life is merry, and I love to
    lead it 315–16
Milton! thou should'st be living at this
    hour 305
Miss J. Hunter Dunn, Miss J. Hunter
    Dunn 142–3
More than a catbird hates a cat 137–8
My delight and thy delight 81–2
My head is bald, my breath is bad 317
My heart leaps up when I behold 257
My love is like to ice, and I to fire 105
My mother's old leather handbag 227
My saucepans have all been surrendered
    227
My son, the mist is clearing and the
    moon will soon be high 167–8
My true love hath my heart, and I have
    his 90–1
'My wife and I – we're *pals*. Marriage is
    fun.' 158
My young man's a Cornishman 145

Naked, you are simple as a hand 157
Nature reads not our labels, 'great' and
    'small'; 295–6
Never give all the heart, for love 95
New eyes each year 242–3
No grave is rich, the dust that herein
    lies 220
No, I'm not afraid: after a year 278–9
No man is an Iland, intire of it selfe;
    every man is a peece of the 235
Nobody heard him, the dead man 345
Not a drum was heard, not a funeral
    note 195–6
Not to marry a young Woman 347–8
Not yet will those measureless fields be
    green again 217
Now Jones had left his new-wed bride
    to keep his house in order 149–50

O Cambridge, attend 336–7
O captain! my captain our fearful trip is
    done 189–90
O for a Muse of fire, that would ascend
    162–3
O, my luve's like a red, red rose 110

O say, can you see, by the dawn's early
    light 185–6
O, the grand old Duke of York 8
O Thou who seest all things below 340
O, what can ail thee, knight at arms
    120–1
O, Young Lochinvar is come out of the
    west 109–10
Oedipus said to the Sphinx 344
Of all the souls that stand create 263
Oh for boyhood's painless play 63–4
Oh, my beloved, shall you and I 218
Oh Paddy dear, and did you hear the
    news that's going round? 197–8
Oh, to be in England 307
Oh who is that young sinner with the
    handcuffs on his wrists? 283–4
On the top of the Crumpetty Tree 15–
    16
Once I was young 243–4
Once more unto the breach, dear friends,
    once more 179–80
Once to every man and nation 163–4
Once, when Britain's power was
    massive 232
One autumn afternoon when I was nine
    46–9
One day I wrote her name upon the
    strand 82–3
One word is too often profaned 92
Out of the dusk a shadow 384
Out of the night that covers me 385

People expect old men to die 384
Perhaps some day the sun will shine
    again 207
Phyllis! why should we delay 85
Pile the bodies high at Austerlitz and
    Waterloo 215
Please remember – don't forget 8
Put not your trust in princes 299

Rarely, rarely, comest thou 103–4
Red lips are not so red 214–15
Remember now thy Creator in the days
    of thy youth 73–4
Remembering the past 358–9
Remote and ineffectual Don 334–6
Return often and take me 93
Roads go ever ever on 360

Say not the struggle naught availeth 181
Scots, wha hae wi' Wallace bled 178–9

Sexual intercourse began 98–9
Shall I compare thee to a summer's day? 94–5
She was poor, but she was honest 130–1
She wore a new 'terr-cotta' dress 100
Should you ask me, whence these stories? 254–7
Sleeping at last, the struggle and horror past 400–1
Smile at us, pay us, pass us; but do not quite forget 233–5
So let us love, dear love, like we ought 80
Solomon Grundy 23
Some have meat and cannot eat 325
Some of us are a little tired of hearing that cigarettes kill 147–9
Some say the world will end in fire 402
Stand on the highest pavement of the stair 99–100
Stop all the clocks, cut off the telephone 152–3
Surely there is a vein for the silver 239–40
Surgeons must be very careful 6

Talking in bed ought to be easiest 319
Tell me where is Fancy bred 7
The Assyrian came down like the wolf on the fold 161–2
The common cormorant or shag 52
The dark eleventh hour 198–9
The dawn was apple-green 137
The days of our future stand before us 356
The dove is a symbol of love pure and true 89
The land was ours before we were the land's 184–5
The life that I have is all that I have 380
The Lord is full of mercy 247
The Lord is my shepherd; I shall not want 408
The magpies in Picardy 205–6
The men that worked for England 165
The night has a thousand eyes 117–18
The Owl and the Pussy-Cat went to sea 18
The piano, hollow and sentimental, plays 229
The quality of mercy is not strain'd 240–1
The sea is calm to-night 230–1

The sense of danger must not disappear 271
The solemn Sea of Silence lies between us 122
The sun was shining on the sea 26–8
The thundering line of the battle stands 203
The view is fine from fifty 315
There are flowers now, they say, at Alamein 221
There are only two things now 136–7
There is far too much of the surburban classes 341
There once was a man who said, 'Damn! 340
There was a Boy whose name was Jim 19–21
There was a King in Brentford – of whom no legends tell 304
There was a young lady named Bright 140
There was an old woman 9
These are the ghosts of the unwilling dead 402–3
Th'expense of Spirit in a waste of shame 105
They are always with us, the thin people 323–4
They fuck you up, your mum and dad 346
They said this mystery shall never cease 338
They say that women, in a bombing raid 226
They shut the road through the woods 359
They throw in Drummer Hodge, to rest 197
They who are near to me do not know that 81
They're changing guard at Buckingham Palace 23–4
This day is called the feast of Crispian 180–1
This is the Night Mail crossing the border 331–3
This is the prayer the cave-man prayed 247–8
This royal throne of kings this sceptered isle 306–7
This World is not Conclusion 407
Thou happy, happy elf! 13–14
Thou shalt dwell in silence in my heart like the 123–4

428

Thou shalt not covet thy neighbour's
    wife 243
Though I speak with the tongues of men
    and of angels 245–6
Time does not bring relief, you have all
    lied 369
Time will say nothing but I told you so
    112–13
To be, or not to be – that is the question
    302–4
To begin at the beginning 39–43
To everything there is a season 5
To see a World in a Grain of Sand 258–
    61
To suffer the woes which Hope thinks
    infinite 364–5
To the man-in-the-street, who, I'm
    sorry to say 334
To whom I owe the leaping delight 158
'Tom Pearse, Tom Pearse, lend me your
    gray mare' 45–6
Tomorrow, and tomorrow, and
    tomorrow 365
Tonight I can write the saddest lines
    157
Tread lightly, she is near 64–5
Try as he will, no man breaks wholly
    loose 83
'Twas at the pictures, child, we met
    319–22
'Twas on the shores that round our coast
    49–52
Two roads diverged in a yellow wood
    301–2
Two sticks and an apple 19
Two thousand cigarettes 156
Tyger, Tyger, burning bright 271–2

Under a spreading chestnut-tree 297–8
Under the wide and starry sky 399
Unto a broken heart 156
Up the airy mountain 11–12
Up the ash tree climbs the ivy 354–5

Wake up, my heart, get out of bed 338–9
We 'ad a bleed'n' sparrer wot 293–4
We are the hollow men 404–7
We are the music-makers 284–5
We came over the moor-top 328–9
We come from the mind 275–6
We have known treasure fairer than a
    dream 89–90
We only ask for sunshine 297

We planned to shake the world together,
    you and I 209–10
We turn out the light to undress by 357
We two lay sunk in the dusk of dreams
    92
We two were lovers, the Sea and I 150–
    1
We waited for an omnibus 30
We walk by the sea-shore 153–4
Whales have calves 8
'What is the real good?' 241–2
What is this life if, full of care 294
What lively lad most pleasured me 139
What passing-bells for these who die as
    cattle? 210–11
whatever you give me 126–8
Whatsoever things are true 241
When all the world would keep a matter
    hid 215–16
When clerks and navvies fondle 144
When Eve upon the first of Men 118
When fishes flew and forests walked 33
When I am dead 380
When I am dead, my dearest 355–6
When I am sad and weary 134
When I was a bachelor, I lived by myself
    118–19
When I was a lad I served a term 53–5
When I was born on Amman hill 43–4
When I was One 35
When I was one-and-twenty 95–6
When lovely woman stoops to folly 142
When my chandelier 28
When my love swears that she is made
    of truth 86
When statesmen gravely say – 'We must
    be realistic –' 167
When the Himalayan peasant meets the
    he-bear in his pride 251–4
When the little Bluebird 96–8
When you are old and grey and full of
    sleep 401–2
When you died 367–9
When you're lying awake with a dismal
    headache, and repose is taboo'd by
    anxiety 268–70
Whence comest thou, Gehazi 341–2
Where are you, my prince? 112
Where be you going, you Devon maid?
    117
White founts falling in the courts of the
    sun 182
Who would true Valour see 184

Why are the clergy of the Church of England 337–38

'Why can't you tidy your room?' they cry 71–2

Why do I feel excited 75

Why do I love? go ask the glorious sun 123

'Will you walk into my parlour?' said the Spider to the Fly 30–1

Wilt Thou forgive that sin where I begun 397–8

Wine comes in at the mouth 131

With fingers weary and worn 290–2

With proud thanksgiving, a mother for her children 389–90

Without an accoucheuse, in darkness, pushing her 333

Yes, we were looking at each other 135–6

'You are old, Father William,' the young man said 32

You cannot hope 308–9

You, love, and I 108–9

You suck my soul through a straw 106

You think it horrible that Lust and Rage 398

Young men who frequent picture palaces 322

Your face 88

Your name is a bird on my hand 155